D0871916

DS
126.5
Z8

—REGULATIONS—

FINES ARE CHARGED FOR OVERDUE AND/OR
LOST LIBRARY MATERIALS; AND, IN ACCOR-
DANCE WITH BOARD POLICY 8741, "GRADES
TRANSCRIPTS, DEGREES, AND REGISTRATION
PRIVILEGES SHALL BE WITHHELD UNTIL ALL
LIBRARY BOOKS OR OTHER LIBRARY MATERIALS
ARE RETURNED (TO THE LIBRARY CIRCULATION
DESK)."

Contra Costa College Library
2600 Mission Bell Drive
San Pablo, California 94806

Israel: the sword and the harp

By the same author

Israel: the sword and the harp

the mystique of violence
and
the mystique of redemption

Controversial Themes in Israeli Society

Ferdynand Zweig

CONTRA COSTA COLLEGE
LIBRARY
SAN PABLO, CALIFORNIA

Rutherford • Madison • Teaneck
Fairleigh Dickinson University Press

ISRAEL: THE SWORD AND THE HARP. © Ferdynand
Zweig 1969. First American edition published 1969
by Associated University Presses, Inc., Cranbury, New
Jersey 08512.

APR 1 5 1971

DS
126.5
Z8

Library of Congress Catalogue Card No.: 74-86291

SBN 8386 7534 4

Printed in the United States of America

Contents

Introduction

THE BOOK is the outcome of an experience, the experience of working and living in Israel over a period of years. First I spent three academic years, 1953–6, as Visiting Professor of Sociology and Labour Relations at the Hebrew University in Jerusalem, and later on two more academic years, 1964–6 as Visiting Professor at Tel-Aviv University. During my stay in Jerusalem I conducted a large-scale research project, the outcome of which was my book *The Israeli Worker* (Herzl and Sharon Press, New York, 1959) and on which I draw to some extent also in this book. During my stay in Tel-Aviv I carried out a great deal of observation and study for my lectures, and I also had the opportunity to compare my own findings with the results of the fieldwork of my students of sociology and labour relations conducted under my supervision. I also followed closely publications and literature concerning Israel not only in European languages but also in Hebrew, which is a great asset, as the self-awareness, self-analysis and self-criticism of the Israeli society is developed to a very high pitch.

Working and living in Israel is a great privilege and experience for any student of sociology interested in swift social change in the world of non-conformity, conflicts and creativity. The process of the birth of a new nation or rebirth of an old presents a drama of great intensity which could easily have been spread over centuries, but which was here compressed into a few years. It is an intensive life lived in vehemence, turmoil and boisterousness. We are faced with a volcanic eruption of Jewish creative energy, which for centuries has been dammed up and which has suddenly found release. The Jews descended on the ancient land of Israel like an avalanche, and the same impetus is used in building up the new nation. They represent a highly dynamic force which develops by leaps and bounds, and, taking unexpected twists and turns, defies all expectations and predictions. Who would have dared to forecast twenty years ago that a 'remnant' of Jewry swept by the storms of history would turn into a dominant power in the Middle East? Who also would have dared to prognosticate a generation ago a forty[1] years' Arab-Jewish war?

The strange transformation which the Jewish people are undergoing in their new land is inexplicable to Israelis themselves, in spite of their constant search for meaning. They feel that they are caught in a whirlwind of mighty currents of history stretching from ancient times up to more recent upheavals in Europe, enacting a drama far transcending their own existence. In fact they are caught between two powerful mystiques: the mystique of violence and the mystique of redemption. Both of them have always flourished in the Holy Land, the land of innumerable holy and unholy wars. Both mystiques now wrestle tenaciously for the soul of Israel.

Which mystique is going to win in the end? Does the answer depend on the peace settlement with the Arabs, or does a peace settlement depend on the answer?

The contest between the mystique of violence and the mystique of redemption is the most fateful and crucial conflict on which the future of the Israeli society depends. It is the contest between two conceptions of society, two visions, in fact two Israels. In a way it expresses also the discord between Israel and the Diaspora.

The new Israeli, who styles himself as a robust and sturdy native, buoyant and self-confident, is in spite of all his transformations, still a Jew who did not escape the fate of his ancestry. The anti-Jewish hatred, from which he wanted to escape, is still around him, among the Arabs in his midst and the Arabs who surround him. The double loyalty of the Diaspora Jew, which he meant to reject, is still his destiny, the loyalty to Israel and the loyalty to the Diaspora, with which he is linked by many emotional and practical bonds. The heavy load of the past, including the anguish of the Holocaust, from which Israel emerged directly as its heir and successor, weighs heavily on him. The supreme ethico-religious vocation of his ancestry is still his inheritance and his responsibility of which he cannot divest himself. True he is a warrior now, but not a warrior with a Fieldmarshal's baton

[1] One can say that Jewish-Arab hostilities started from the 1929 Wailing Wall outbreak of Arab violence.

in his knapsack, but rather one with the staff of a prophet in his hand.

Is he really re-creating the conditions suitable for the new Israel, the direct inheritor of the ancient Israel, as he claims to be? This is the most important and the most exciting question asked, not only by the Diaspora but by the world at large. The Jewish existence has never been merely marginal to man's quest for values, and in this century less so than in previous centuries. The Jewish people, small in number, forms, as has been said, a 'world historical entity of its own', and Israel is but a part of this entity.

This book treats Israel as part of the Jewish world at large in regard to dialogues, conflicts and encounters with other nations and forces. It is a work of a participant observer who presents processed observations and experiences rather than the work of an inquisitive interviewer offering his field data. It is a work treating with the most controversial subjects of Israeli society, and is therefore basically critical, asking questions rather than answering them. I have also tried to present the lesson which can be drawn from the Israeli experience for the understanding of the human condition at large, and that is no mean lesson.

London, March 1968   F. ZWEIG

To my wife, Doris Ruth
for
her most generous assistance and
unfailing interest.

Part I

identity and self-image

1.

The Sabra Figure

UNDERSTANDING the Israel-born Jew, the Sabra, so called from the soft fruit of the prickly pear, is the clue to understanding Israeli society, because what the Sabra is today Israeli society will be tomorrow. Already 40 per cent of Israeli Jews are Sabras, and, with the slowing down of immigration, the ratio is rapidly increasing.

The Sabra figure is an *ideal typus* in Max Weber's sense, that is a model of attitudes and behaviour, and not an average type in a statistical sense. It is a mental construct based on the Sabra image as seen by others and by himself. It is based on a system of values or a set of bearings, primarily of West European origin. There are many sub-groups of natives who fit this model only partially or not at all.

This applies, for instance, to the Orthodox native. Reared in the Synagogue and the Yeshiva, dressed in long black coats derived from the Ghetto and defying the *chamsin*, aggressively religious, often rejecting the values of Israeli society, still speaking mostly Yiddish, very much under parental authority and the authority of the elders, he stands out as a typical non-conformist. However, he shares some of the features of the Sabra model, his aggressiveness, his self-confidence, his buoyancy. The stoning of cars driven on the Sabbath is an act which would be unimaginable among Orthodox Jews in the Diaspora.

The Oriental native, the offspring of families of Afro-Asian origin, does not entirely fit the model of the Sabra either. He would often in fact call himself *Yelid Haaretz* (a native), not a Sabra. He is part of an extended patrilineal family with considerable subordination to parental authority and a sense of belonging focussed to a large extent on his family. He will have a considerable degree of belief in magic and superstition, probably enjoyed less formal schooling, and was more engrossed in the street corner gang. His childhood training was different from that of his

European counterpart and he often belongs to a low status protest group. He often reflects the socio-cultural position of the lower status group, a group with special problems, but all the same he is exposed to many of the same environmental and educational factors as is the Western Sabra. He looks up to the Sabra model and tries to style himself on this, absorbing the same myths and values. The contrast between him and the Western Sabra is not as great as the contrast between their respective parents.

Now let us look more closely at the model of the Sabra. It can be described in short as that of a buoyant, extrovert type with a heightened sense of living and purpose, centred around the new nation and the New State, and in complete antithesis to the model of the Ghetto Jew. The contrast between different generations is perhaps nowhere more profound than in Israel. The Israeli-born youth and his immigrant parents are worlds apart. They are practically different races. A Jew transformed into an Israeli is a sturdy, robust and lusty fellow, non-emotional, with rough edges and no complexes, and with eyes in which wide open places are reflected. He is taller and broader, more erect than his father, a sporty type, more spirited, who can stand up to any challenge. Contrast him with his father and his stoop, his anxious eyes, his emotionalism, his softness, his perpetual defensiveness. The father looks at the son and can scarcely recognize himself in him. The father of Amos Lev, who fell in the Sinai Campaign in November 1956 at the age of twenty-seven, writes:[1]

> Yes, here was one of the miracles of the history of our people: the father—a man from the Diaspora, and his son—one of the conquerers of Sinai, the spiritual birthplace of the eternal people.

The Jewish father has two minds about his son's metamorphosis. On the one hand he regrets the disappearance of his own image and that of his forefathers. On the other hand he is proud, and this pride is his overwhelming sentiment. There is little doubt that the Jewish race has been re-cast in Israel, as though contact with the land had produced a new phoenix.

Now let us review some of the factors which contribute to the shaping of the Sabra figure. First, let us consider the effect of the environmental factors, the climate and the scenery around him.

---

[1] Amos Lev, *With Ploughshare and Sword. Life in the Army of Israel*, p. 344. Herzl Press and Thomas Yoseloff. New York 1961.

Since early childhood he has spent most of his time in the open, in the hills or on the beach, in the fields or in the desert. The desert has a great fascination for him. It renews the ancient call in him as *a Hebrew,* a man of the desert. The desert with its mysterious blue haze calls for both meditation and perigrination. His eyes are often lost in the vastness of the desert, which first revealed to him the small voice. In contrast to his parents he is a child of nature—even if he lives in a town—in harmony with nature, listening to it, lovingly trying to understand its needs and requirements and doing everything possible to replenish it and to dress it in ancient glory. From early childhood he has played and worked with his mates. The Sabra is so deeply involved in his peer group that it is difficult to know one until one knows the whole group. He is immersed completely in his peer group, he becomes a constituting particle of the group consciousness.

The compulsory education of all children between the ages of five and fourteen—actually most children join a nursery school at the age of two or three—contributes greatly to the moulding of the Sabra. At school he imbibes the myths of the nation, the official ideology of co-operation and pioneering, the love of the land and the love of the Bible, the values of farming and manual labour.[1]

The Bible becomes a living thing, which he studies with reverence and an extreme and avid interest. The Bible comes to life and its heroes become living figures on which he tries to mould himself. What happened 2,000 years ago is of greater interest to him than the immediate past. At school he acquires a sense of history and historic responsibility.

He styles himself on a peasant's mentality, although he is not a peasant and far from simple. But he rejects complexity and intellectuality, and he likes to think of himself as a simple straightforward man without far-fetched ideas and claims.

[1] The State Education Law, 1953, defines the aims of Israeli education in paragraph 2 as follows: 'The object of State education is to base elementary education in the State on the value of Jewish culture and the achievements of Science, on love of the homeland and loyalty to the State and the Jewish people, on training in agriculture and manual labour, on pioneering, and on striving for a society built on freedom, equality, tolerance, mutual help and love of mankind'. The Law established a unified system of State education, providing for the standardization of 75 per cent of the curricula of all schools.

Youth movements are another factor forming his character and his behaviour. Practically all teenagers belong to one of the many youth movements such as Zofim (Scouts), Hashomer Hatzair (Young Guards), Hanoar Haoved (Working youth), Bnai Akiba (Sons of Akiba), etc. Very early he joins a para-military organization or one of the frontier settlements which are integrated in the regional defence schemes.

Obligatory service in the army for both sexes,[1] thirty months for men and twenty for women, with reserve service up to the age of forty-nine—although service in the active units is only up to thirty-nine—is another important factor in the mental make-up of the Sabra. There he is taught qualities of discipline combined with those of initiative and leadership. The army is a school of patriotism with very high standards of performance, and with an emphasis on quality and idealism, 'inspired by a sense of history and sense of destiny'.[2]

Surrounded by the constant threat of annihilation, in the midst of the never ending war for survival he developed the qualities of hardness, matter-of-factness, resolution, vigour, self-reliance and supreme faith in his ability to defend his rights. There is no bargaining over his rights, and he feels that his land can be wrested from him only with his life. He ripens to maturity very early, and soon reasserts his own views and his own personality in an aggressive way. He rejects emotionality, softness, familism, possessiveness and the bourgeois mentality. He rejects the advice and experience of his foreign-born parents as meaningless and invalid for Israel. Opportunity for identification with his parents is small, and, when he considers his parents, it is only to reassert his differences. He is free from the sense of inferiority and anxiety which often characterizes the Jews in the Diaspora. He has no 'nobody likes me' complex. He does not care whether others like him or what they think about him. He is what he is and has a right to be what he is on his land. The land is his and he has been born on the land, the land nourished him and brought him into existence.

[1] At the end of 1967 Israel increased the period of compulsory military service for new conscripts to 3 years to cope with the requirements arising from the occupation of new territories.

[2] *Ben Gurion Looks Back in Talks With Moshe Pearlmann*, p. 197. Weidenfeld and Nicholson. London 1965.

His taciturnity may be partly explained by the requirements of national security; ' The less you talk the less you are likely to get into trouble' a Sabra would say. He hates verbosity, and long-winded phrases, he has little time for big talk, for juggling with words and abstractions. He hates 'This is so, but on the other hand . . .' He sees everything more clearly in black and white terms than his father did. He is more decisive, more resolved and more determined. He has more staying power, more stamina. He does not believe in arguments, the world will not be saved by arguments; power and force have the last word, not good arguments. He is inclined to be sceptical of dogmas, philosophies and systems, about most of the '-isms' which moved his father. He was lectured a great deal about Zionism, the creed of his fathers, but even this no longer moves him, he calls it *Zionut*, the Zionist claptrap.

This is the background for the astonishingly wide popularity of Westerners in Israel, as they seem to embody the image of a new country at its birth, a pioneer vigour and a fighting spirit. They seem to express nationalism incarnate at a heroic level, combining freedom, power and love of the country. The Sabra is the frontierman *par excellence*.

The Sabra is regarded by the Diaspora Jews as *Goyish*. This reminds me of what I heard from Poles residing in Britain after the war, when I made a study of Polish workers in England. Many times they said to me, 'We Poles have become very much like the Jews in Poland.' The meaning of this was that the Poles in Britain had acquired a minority complex, the status of the marginal man. In reverse, the Sabras became *Goyish* in a similar sense, meaning that they acquired the status of a majority man in the centre of things. In brief we can describe him as a new type of Jewish Gentile. When abroad a Sabra student is often more drawn to Gentile than Jewish students.

A very small but articulate group of Sabras call themselves Canaanites, meaning sons of the Land of Canaan, separate from the Diaspora, wishing to cut the links between Israel and the Diaspora as much as possible. They are natives of the region and want to be regarded as such.

The Sabras are in general areligious, if by religion is meant the old Judaic creed professed by their parents, going to the syna-gogue, fasting and praying and keeping all the injunctions of the

Rabbinical Law. But they are not without a religion of their own; they accept the Bible as a sacred book but they treat it rather as a hallowed national history. They accept the Land as a holy Land, promised to their forefathers. For the eighteenth-century rationalists Nature was God, for the Sabras the Deity seems to be Nature as crystallized and revealed in the Land of Israel. They accept also the traditions and customs of Israel and its festivals.

It is a secularized form of ancient Judaism, a new, intense national religion, organically entwined with nationhood, a spiritual flavour of nationality—you may call it religionality, as religion is fused with nationality. All the religious festivals are being secularized, or are in the process of secularization. *Bar Mitzva* is the initiation rite, devoid of its religious flavour and open to both sexes. *Pesach* is the festival of the Exodus, not only of the first Exodus from Egypt, but also of the second from Babylonia, the third from Spain, the fourth from Germany and even more so of the last exodus which led to the emergence of the State of Israel. *Purim* becomes the season of carnival, celebrating the renewal of life, the victory of the Jewish people not only over Haman in the old Persian Empire but over all anti-semitic persecutions, including Hitler and Eichmann. Did not Eichmann share the fate of Haman?

Chanukkah, the festival of lights, is a celebration not only of the Maccabean uprising, but also of Bar Kochba, of Massada, Jerusalem and the uprising of the Warsaw Ghetto. *Sukkot* is not only the festival of the wanderings in the Sinai Desert of old, but also of the wandering Jew in all the deserts of the world, including the wanderings in the Sinai Desert of recent decades. *Rosh Hashana*, New Year, is the festival of the new rains in Israel, the new season and the new promise. *Yom Kippur,* the Day of Atonement is the day of national consolation and stocktaking. And *Tisha be Ab* is the remembrance of the destruction of Jerusalem with the promise of restoration and resolution that this will not happen again.

How the thoroughly secularized Jewish soldiers, most of them atheists or agnostics, wept, danced and sang ancient songs, including the psalm: 'If I forget thee Jerusalem', when they kissed the old 'Wailing Wall' of the ancient Temple of Solomon!

One can say, therefore, that the Sabras are in the main religious men in a new secularized version of the Jewish religion. They have no time for dietary laws, *Kosher abd Treife*, for ritual absolution in *Mikvas*, for *Chalitza* etc. They turn also against Messianism, supernatural claims for Judaism, the idea of a specific mission for Jewry or of its uniqueness. They want to be a 'normal' nation like any other nation with all the limitations of a normal nation, including violence and criminality, but also with all the rights of a normal nation, especially the right to be master of their own home.

The Sabra model described here is, as I said, only an ideal type, or some would say stereotype, as current in Israel. But in this stereotype there are a number of characteristics which have been tested in real life and proved to be the genuine article. All the qualities which go into the making of a frontierman, a first-class member of a defence force, or a good soldier and officer, qualities springing from the Sabra's love for the country for which he is willing to give his life, have been tested in three wars, especially in the last war, in which the Sabras played a leading part. The effect of the Hebraization of the common educational system, of the nationalization of culture, and of all the various homogenizing factors are not stereotypes but facts which cannot be disputed.

As may be expected, the Sabra model will have a number of sub-models with deviations. Two of them, the Orthodox and the Oriental Sabras have already been mentioned. Still others would be: the first generation Sabra, and the Sabra rooted in the country for more than one generation; the Sabra of veteran parentage, and one whose parents were more recent immigrants; the Sabra completely home grown and the Sabra with a touch of foreign education; the product of the Kibbutz and the Moshav, and the town Sabra. However, all of them would bear the stamp of the homogenizing factors mentioned above to a high degree.

From what has been said it can be gathered that the Sabra is a most interesting figure who gives the anthropologist, sociologist and psychologist much food for thought. The Sabra figure may be adduced in support of many theories of a very divergent nature.

First, he may be adduced in support of theories which stress the deep influence of environmental factors on personalities. He is shaped by the climate, by the land, by the flora and fauna, by the landscape, by the air, winds and sea around him. However, these environmental factors may be taken as part of a larger situation, and so the Sabra figure may be adduced in support also of the situational approach to human society and personality. This approach stresses the impact of a situation as a whole, where all the strategic factors which make up a situation have a moulding effect on the pattern of society and of leading personality types. The Sabra figure has been moulded by the requirements of the total situation. The new Israeli has had to be not only a settler but also a watchman (*Shomer*), a guardsman, a fighter. Since 1929, and more so since 1936 the year of the Arab Rebellion, and then the three wars of 1948–9, 1956 and 1967, the constant wrestling with his enemies has shaped his character more than anything else. Living under conditions of siege, he developed qualities which serve him in good stead in times of emergency.

Second, the Sabra figure may be named in support of the dialectical conception of history, as he forms the complete anti-thesis to the Diaspora Jews, his foreign-born parents. The conflict between generations is nowadays very pronounced everywhere and more so in immigrant countries, but in Israel the conflict reaches the model of complete antithesis. Practically all along the line the values of the preceding generations are discarded in an open breach. The Diaspora Jewry is treated with disparagement if not outright contempt. Also the mental traits, talents and abilities, characteristic of the Diaspora Jewry are at a discount, while new traits, talents and abilities previously absent are displayed, and valued.

Third, the Sabra figure may be named in support of the theory which stresses the enormous plasticity of human material, which can be moulded and shaped in various directions. In one genera-tion for instance the characteristic model of the same race can be a merchant type, docile and meek, verbose and intellectual, while the next generation may produce a fighting man, bent on action, not on words, disparaging arguments and theories. The Jewish soldier who, in Eastern Europe, was often the laughing stock of the professional soldier, has proved himself, in Israel, beyond all doubt, to be a model fighter in modern warfare, and his exploits are studied by the general staff of the most progressive armies in the world. If such a transformation can take place in one or two generations, it is very difficult to uphold a theory of the innate characteristics of any race or of any nation. But of course the plasticity, adaptability and wide range of traits of the Jewish stock is proverbial and this has to be taken into account.

Fourth, the Sabra figure may be named in support of theories which stress the impact of social structure and culture patterns on personality. Every social system produces its own model or range of models of personality and every personality structure has to be viewed in the context of the social system which has created and nourished it. The educational system, the kindergarten, the schools, the youth movements, the army, the radio and public relations, the myths and values of society, all these factors have made the Sabras what they are. The Sabra is the product of an intense process of education and the concentrated cultural and ideological work of pioneers, teachers, writers, journalists and educationalists of various kinds and descriptions, which have combined forces to produce a model, according to certain preconceived lines, suitable for the task ahead of him.

Fifth, the Sabra figure may be named in support of holistic theories of man as a psycho-somatic unity, in which new mental traits produce also a new somatic frame. The Sabra strikes an observer as also somatically different from the parents. He looks a different racial type from his parents, who often cannot recognize themselves in their children. It supports the idea that man is a unity and that the bodily frame responds to changes in the mental make-up.

Sixth, the Sabra figure could be used in support of an idealistic interpretation of history, which stresses the power of ideology in the historical process. Man makes himself. Man is what he thinks he is. The Jew became a new man, because he wanted to be a new man. He remodelled himself anew. This is an instance of the rebirth of an old nation. But as always, rebirth means also death. *Hic natus Israelus, hic mortus Judaeus.* The Jews became a new society because they adopted new values, new standards, new ideology. The Israeli society is a voluntaristic creation if there ever was one; it has been conceived, planned and carried out according to a preconceived scheme.

The moral evaluation of the Sabra figure depends of course on the set of values and standards adopted as the criterion. Of course courage, uprightness, simplicity, self-reliance are qualities which are appreciated almost universally. But toughness may degenerate into hardness, self-confidence into pride and conceit; aggressiveness and militance have a quality of nationalistic flavour and ardent patriotism which, if not counterbalanced by humanity, tolerance and passion for human solidarity can easily degenerate into jingoism and exclusiveness.

In the last decades, in the interlude of affluence and relatively peaceful co-existence with the Arab States, i.e., between the Suez Campaign in 1956 and the Six Day War in 1967, the Sabra figure has considerably mellowed down and become more inclined towards the older values of Judaism. The new shock of the experiences of 1967 strongly enhanced his values of aggressive defence, and it is possible that under these renewed siege conditions the Sabra may again slip into his previous unadulterated model of toughness. The crux, as in everything else in Israel, hinges on the question of peace. Peace is the key to the further development of the Sabra figure and of his new identity.

2.

Common Features of the Ingathering Tribes

The Mino-Majority

THE FOREIGN-BORN Israeli Jews present a much more complex figure than the Sabras, coming from many ethnical, biological and cultural strains. The first general observation about them would be that they have very little in common, apart from a shared religious matrix. But more studious observation leads one to revise the above impression. Most of them, having come from East European *Shtetls* (small Jewish town), or Hitler's oppression or Moslem rule, formed a harassed and discriminated against minority. They had been affected by a minority complex and by a syndrome of marginality. And now they find themselves in the position of a dominant majority in their new country. They had their roots in the Diaspora, and now they are expanding in an atmosphere of freedom and independence, as well as being dominant as a group.

The model of the social psychology of foreign-born Jews can well be constructed as an elliptic figure, with their characteristics plotted along the two axes of an ellipse (the principal axis and the minor axis perpendicular to it). Along the principal axis we could group characteristics derived from the Diaspora; along the minor axis characteristics developed in Israel.

As in an ellipse the principal axis has two foci: one formed by the minority complex, i.e., a syndrome of inferiority, anxiety and insecurity due to ethnical or religious discrimination, and the other formed by excessive individualism, non-conformity and the highly developed egocentricism which is primarily due to the syndrome of marginality.

By a syndrome of marginality I mean not only the 'cultural hybridization' of men who share the tradition of two distinct peoples or societies,[1] but also exclusion from participation in the affairs of a country due to restrictions and discrimination,[2] and at the same time voluntary non-participation in the affairs of the dominant group. The Jew in the Diaspora often became a marginal man, partly because he was 'on the margin of two cultures, which never completely interpenetrated and fused', 'the cosmopolitan and the citizen of the world' (Park). And partly because he was ostracized and excluded from the decision making of the majority (Stonequist). But he also became so because often he did not want to participate in this decision-making anyway, feeling that it did not primarily concern him. This voluntary marginalism was not infrequent in Jewish self-segregation, and is a form of self-estrangement typical of a non-conformist and individualist. Some Jews in the Diaspora were in the limbo of both Jewish and non-Jewish worlds, opting out of both, or discriminated against by both, for opposite reasons. A Jew can be a marginal man in both Jewish and non-Jewish milieus.

Both foci, the minority complex and excessive individualism, are derived from the Diaspora, but are still operative to a considerable degree in Israel, assuming new forms, new combinations and new adaptations to the challenge of the new social and physical environment. Both foci appear among the various tribes with different emphasis. The strength of the minority complex of each tribe will be related to the historical experience of the tribe, and the degree of discrimination, anxiety, inferiority and insecurity experienced in their country of origin. The strength will vary also in each social stratum of the tribe and in each individual according to their own class or personal experience. The other focus of excess of individualism will also relate to the actual experience of marginality in respect of the three senses previously described, hybridization, exclusion, and voluntary non-participation. This marginality can be cultural, social, political, economic or integral. It can be what Max Weber called *pariah* existence, not excluding social parasitism. The degree of marginality could have been mild or severe, permanent or temporary,

---

[1] In Robert Ezra Park's sense. 'Human Migration and the Marginal Man" *American Journal of Sociology*, p. 33 (1926–8).

[2] E. V. Stonequist, 'The Marginal Man: A Study in Personality and Culture Conflict'. In *Contributions to Urban Sociology*, Ed. E. W. Burgess *et al*. Chicago Press 1964.

varying in the different phases of the life cycle of the individual.

The characteristics of the second axis, the minor axis of the ellipse, form a dialectical antithesis to the characteristics of the principal axis. Each focus of the principal axis produces its own opposite and negation, in an endeavour to overcome the Diaspora mentality regarded as a psychological disability in the new State. The strength of the dialectical antithesis of each focus will be related to the strength of the focus itself, the strength of reaction to the strength of action. This will hold true both for the ingathering tribes as a whole, and also for each separate tribe, social class or individual within a tribe.

The minority complex is overcome by the majority psychology of the dominant group in the new State. Some tribes or some segments or individuals may develop the attitude: 'Now we are in the position of a dominant majority, let others know how it feels to be a minority, and discriminated against'. Others may develop a painstakingly tolerant attitude. Still others an attitude which is a cross between those two. Those attitudes will be related to the historical and personal experience of Jews in the Diaspora. The majority psychology of a Syrian or Iraqi Jew, who was deprived of his citizenship and his property in his country of origin, may be entirely different from the attitude of an American or British Jew who always enjoyed full rights of citizenship. By and large the mentality of the ingathering tribes will be a combination of a minority complex with a majority psychology in various patterns of interpenetration and interaction.

The second focus of excessive individualism, has generated also its dialectical antithesis in the ideology of socialism and co-operativism on the one hand and that of nationalism on the other. The individualistic Jew did not form ideal material for building a new society and a new State. The capitalist, the merchant, the agent, the financier, were not the proper elements for pioneering. In any society he would not have been suitable material for building a new State, and this was especially true in the conditions of Palestine. The deserts and the swamps, unsanitary, unfriendly, hostile, unprofitable, requiring immense capital investments in infra-structure and in the re-training of manpower, could not have been brought to fruitful life by individualistic and capitalistic Jews. This is the background of the incipient Israeli socialism, co-operativism and solidaristic pioneering.

The other, even stronger and more persistent, more widely spread and deeper adjustment to the new conditions of a nation building its new home and embattled on all sides by hostile neighbours is a strong feeling of national solidarity, national pride and aggrandizement. Nationalism provides an obvious check on excessive individualism.

On each axis are grouped a number of different characteristics related to the focal points mentioned. The characteristics grouped alongside each axis form however in each instance a coherent and self-supporting chain. Both axes penetrate and interact with each other producing unique tensions and movements. Their contradiction has often produced unease and anxiety. The minority complex of a now dominant majority may produce feelings not only of unease but also of guilt and anguish. The excessive individualism of a socialistic or nationalistic leader, often breaking out into anarchic behaviour, may be harrowing.

Now, let us describe in more detail the characteristics of the principal axis, which can be presented as follows:

   (i) Familism
  (ii) Economism
 (iii) Careerism
 (iv) The Quest for Independence
  (v) Lack of Team Spirit
 (vi) Lack of Discipline
 (vii) A tendency towards Excessive Criticism
(viii) Factionalism
 (ix) Status Seeking
  (x) A craving for Self-Expression

(i) Familism

Familism, defined as an excessive psychical investment in the family, especially in the upbringing and education of children, and as an almost compulsive concern about being a good father, is a common feature in Israel. Strong family feeling and strong kinship ties are a well-known phenomenon among Diaspora Jews, but in Israel they reach new heights. In the Diaspora, they were a natural response to the challenge of the general insecurity of the Jew, his alienation from society and his sense of inferiority. The family was a refuge of Jewishness, where he could relax and be completely himself and feel a master, 'a king'. The family was a sort of substitute for the community at large. In Israel the family becomes a refuge and haven for all the values the immigrant stood for before he came to Israel; it is a symbol of his pre-Israel community, harbouring all those treasures which he rescued from his own home. It is the place where he can express his feelings in his own language. If members of other tribes do not approve of him, it does not matter so much as long as he is sure of his family's support. If he suffers from frustrations and disappointments, his children, who are his hope for the future, will make up for it, and it was mostly for them and for their future happiness that he came to Israel. They will be the fulfilment of his achievement and accomplishment. Actually by coming to Israel, which probably set him back in class and status, he showed his feeling for the family in trying to give his children a better life for the future, a better life often denied to himself by his shortcomings as an immigrant.

(ii) *Economism*

The strong individualism of the Jew expresses itself in economism, which accords well with familism. Family and property reinforce each other in more than one sense. *Mishpacha* (family) and *Parnassa* (livelihood) are often mentioned together. A strong acquisitive drive, a high degree of rationality in economic life, a great reliance on economic calculus, are attitudes which are not only the outcome of the strong individualism and familism of the Jew, but are also the product of his experience in the Diaspora, where his only security was based on money. They were also a result of the predominance of commercial and financial occupations among the Diaspora Jews. In Israel not only the business man approaches the model of a *homo economicus*, but also the industrial worker who follows closely business trends, the level of prices and profits. As one foreman said to me jokingly during my investigations, 'During the midday break the worker, instead of relaxing and enjoying himself, goes to the lavatory and tries to reckon out how much his employer has made from him'.

Economism produces an atmosphere of strong competitiveness. Many English business men wanting to settle in Israel complain that they find the commercial life in Israel excessively competitive and are often unable to stand its strains. This atmosphere of strong competition is also felt in the professions, and often produces an atmosphere of tension.

(iii) *Careerism*

The outcome of individualism linked with familism and econom-ism is careerism, that is the cultivation, advancement and venera-tion of professional achievements. The most frequent Hebrew terms for this drive are *hishtalmut*, the bettering or improving of one's skill and learning, and *hitkadmut*, meaning going ahead and making progress. When two Israelis meet after a certain time, the question they are bound to ask each other is, 'what progress have you made?' (*hitkadamta*). Everyone wants to learn, to acquire a profession, to improve his standing in a profession, and to perfect himself in the profession as much as possible. Of course this attitude has a very long tradition in the Jewish life of the Diaspora. The trend was interrupted in the period of pioneering, but, since the inception of the State of Israel, it has reasserted itself and has gone ahead with great strides. A mass drive to universities, polytechnics, research institutes, and seminaries is out of pro-portion to the resources of the country. The total number of university students in 1965 was over 16,000, or 60 per 10,000 population, almost twice the ratio in Great Britain (31). The emphasis is on the 'know-how', on mastery over things. There is a strong technological trend discernible in the whole society.

(iv) *The Quest for Independence*

The quest for positions of economic independence is a strong impetus, discernible in nearly all sections of the population, especially among wage and salary earners. It is linked with individualism (to endow a business with one's own personality), with familism (a man wants to leave his shop or office to his children), with economism (if a man is independent he can make full use of his talents and capacity for hard work), with careerism (he wants to be 'somebody', to achieve importance). When Israelis were unable to achieve a status of economic independence, they often banded together to form strong co-operative move-ments. The Kibbutznik or the Moshavnik are not wage and salary earners but independent men, self-employed.

Among wage and salary earners the achievement of indepen-dence is one of the main aspirations both of youth and age, both among European and Oriental immigrants. To quote a few cases from my investigations:

A youngster of eighteen, a painter's apprentice, was explaining to me his motives behind his own quest for independence. 'Isn't it natural that every man wants to be master of his own fate? Wasn't it natural for the Jews in the Diaspora to want to achieve independence? Isn't the independence of a nation a precious thing and isn't the same true of an individual? I don't want to take orders from others.'

A Jewish worker from Persia told me: 'A job, even a government job which is the best sort, is a livelihood (*parnassa*) depending on other peoples' favour. First you have to ask and beg them to give you a job, and then to keep you in the job. But an independent business is *parnassa* from Heaven; it comes directly from the Lord, you can lose it only through your own faults or as punishment from heaven.'

An Orthodox Jew explained to me that for him an independent business is *sine qua non* for his piety, as in a job it is not easy to keep all the commandments and to go twice a day to the synagogue. 'Only when you are your own boss, can you serve God as it is written in the *Torah*.'

This quest for independence has both positive and negative effects in industry and commerce. On the positive side, the worker is eager to know more and to learn everything he can about the trade. He watches the manager or the foreman to acquire all his tricks and all the secrets of the trade, so that he can apply them in his own workshop. The worker or the foreman often becomes a pioneer opening a new business of his own.

On the negative side this tendency leads to excessive competition in and atomization of business. Instead of one prospering business with expanding facilities, two or more businesses lead a shadowy existence. It results also in excessive secrecy in technical matters, as the owner-manager, especially in small workshops, is reluctant to train his own men beyond a certain point. He is afraid to take his best men into his confidence and to show them all the tricks of the trade.

(v) *Lack of Team Spirit*

This is the outcome of the individualistic spirit of the Jew. He is very good in an emergency, in meeting new and unexpected situations. He uses his judgement, takes responsibility and acts on the spur of the moment. He is a born improvisor, but he is not so good when he is part of a team.

'The trouble is', I often heard people say during my investigations, 'that everyone wants to be a "prima donna", he does well as a solo player, but not as part of a team. He is not concerned about his effect on others, he thinks primarily of himself, while industrial work is teamwork, it stands and falls with team spirit. There is too much of the "I" among our staff, even more so among the clerical and technical staff than among the manual workers.'

The difficulty of forming teams is in Israel especially great in view of cross cultural differences, of divergencies in the assessment of the rhythm of work, of standards of performance and of differences in work morale. Team spirit is easier to achieve when the group sets itself negative or prohibitive or restrictive objectives, than when it seeks positive achievements.

(vi) *Lack of Discipline*
Lack of discipline expresses itself in many ways. Its manifestations can be seen on the road, in schools and factories, in Trade Union activities, in political and social life generally. Lack of discipline is mainly responsible for the fact that most social controls in Israel are operating less effectively than in other firmly established societies. The physical controls enforced by the police, such as road regulations and traffic controls, are not very well kept. Institutional controls, such as for instance Trade Union discipline, are not very effective. The considerable majority of all strikes are unofficial, held against the advice of the Histadrut, and they here occur also in the Histadrut's own establishment. A great many unofficial Work Committees are operating in industry against the advice of the Histadrut. Also the economic controls imposed by management are not very effective, as shown by the high rate of absenteeism, by slack time keeping, by unofficial breaks and by a high accident rate. The opprobrium controls (the mechanisms of disapproval, ridicule, ostracism, etc.) are also lacking in effectiveness, as general standards and values are not very firmly established, and society lacks cohesiveness, being divided into so many ethnical cultural entities. As the saying in Israel goes, everyone does what he wants, and as he sees fit.

(vii) *A tendency towards Excessive Criticism*

Everyone holds an opinion of his own and is strongly tempted to criticize everyone else. The teacher is criticized and corrected by his students, the employer by his employees, the foreman by his workers. The man on the job not only attends to his work, but also thinks and reasons about it all the time. In the workshops one constantly hears: 'Why?', 'Why is this?', and 'Why is that?' The Jewish worker does not take anything for granted; he wants to know. The foreman and manager often feel annoyed; hearing this frequent 'Why?' 'Don't ask questions but get on with it', they may answer irritably, when they have no time and the job is pressing. On my investigations the foreman often told me that, when they give an order to do a job in a certain way, they may very often get a piece of work done better and sometimes worse, but rarely in the way prescribed in the order. The salesman in the shop frequently knows better than the customer what the customer wants. From my own experience as a university teacher I can say that the professor may dictate the text of the questions for examination papers, but he will invariably be corrected by the secretary or typist who will have a better way of putting it; and sometimes it really is better. Also as a university lecturer, I had the unique experience of being told by the students that I was wrong, but I must say they had the grace to apologize when the point was made clear to them. Such criticism is offered with great self-confidence, and in a very assured manner. It is clear that no offence is intended, and students are surprised when they find that the teacher is offended. There is no authority however highly established that does not come under the hammer of criticism. Nowhere else could an acting Prime Minister be called 'a deliberate liar' publicly by a university student, as Mr Eshkol was called at a public meeting attended by one thousand persons (16 March 1967) by the chairman of the Hebrew University Students Union, who called out, interrupting his speech, 'You are lying deliberately'.[1]

(viii) *Factionalism*

Winston Churchill, in the fifth volume of his *History of the Second World War*, refers to Jewish factionalism, writing:

[1] *Jerusalem Post*, 18 March 1967.

The Greeks rival the Jews in being the most politically minded race in the world. No matter how forlorn their circumstances or how grave the peril to their country, they are always divided into many parties, with many leaders who fight among themselves with desperate vigour. It has been well said that wherever there are three Jews it will be found that there are two Prime Ministers and one Leader of the Opposition.

This factionalism still goes on with undiminished vigour. It expresses itself not only in the number of political parties, but also in the constant threats of division arising from fine points of argument. Nice distinctions are elevated to the level of principles and what is called *Prinzipienreiterëi* is pursued earnestly to the very limit. The original Labour Party *Mapai* split into three parts, the others called *Mapam* and *Ahdud Avoda*, and 1965 witnessed another split of the *Mapai* itself, producing the new *Rafi*. The great leader Ben Gurion did not hesitate to split the party which he himself founded about fine points of principles. The Liberal Party is split into two, and even the Communist Party, authoritarian in most other countries, is not exempt from this tendency towards splintering.

Factionalism is largely a heritage of the Diaspora. Jews, devoid of independence or political responsibility, did not have to redeem their political pledges and principles in practice. People who know that they cannot hope to influence events, develop and passionately defend views which suit their feelings and rationalize their wishes, however unrealistic they may be. In such circumstances there is no forum for the development of a united and stable movement, as the movement has no practical functions. Its views are merely a projection of feelings into the realm of politics. They are a mixture of will, thought and feeling, with a predominance of feeling. According to the depth of the feeling, the political position is also deeply felt. A deep emotionalism characterized Jewish politics in the Diaspora, and still continues to do so in Israel.

Political opinions are held and expressed very strongly. They are strictly adhered to, and are often interpreted in a dogmatic way. 'Here I stand, I cannot do otherwise'—Luther's stand—is often re-enacted by simple Jews in Israel. The passion which in another society is spent on sport is, in Israel, devoted to politics. Ideas become mixed with passion and are pursued to their logical conclusion, whatever it may be, even if it is a cul-de-sac or an absurdity. The proximity of the sublime to the ridiculous is nowhere as real and potent as in Israel. The convergence of opposite extremes often assumes grotesque proportions. Ideas and ideals take on a larger than life aspect.

This strong impulse towards idealism and principalism may be contrasted with the equally strong impulses towards materialism and a bargaining between factions which often resembles horse-trading methods. Factionalism in Israel is also tinged with what might be called privatization of politics. Positions in the party are a sort of private possession. This privatization comes to the fore in a tendency to form large economic estates and dependencies around the parties so as to secure a more extensive following by offering benefits, positions and jobs, and a share in the contributions from abroad.

(ix) *Status Seeking*

Status seeking, frowned upon in pioneering days, has become a very strong tendency, gaining momentum since the inception of the State. It expresses itself primarily in an eagerness for promotion, and a constant multiplication of grades in professional and clerical work as well as among manual workers. The background to status seeking is the dignity consciousness and the dignity concern of the Jew, inherited from the Diaspora. The Jew has always been concerned with honourable treatment (*Kavod*). During my investigations I often heard that both in factories and offices this results in conflicts and squabbles about real, assumed or suspected infringement of what the individual regards as his due in respect and dignity.

Status seeking in Israel expresses itself primarily in a drive to climb higher and higher on the ladder of promotion, and when the top rung is reached to continue to climb by extending the ladder. Government employees have fifteen grades of salary, and since 1962 another grade has been added to grade two, called *two plus*. Engineers, architects, chemists, economists had eight grades from A to H, but later on another grade was added called *A plus*, and since 1954 a still higher grade called *A plus plus*. Doctors and veterinary surgeons had eight grades, and in 1954 *A plus* was added. Lawyers had six grades, and in 1960 three more grades were added.[1]

[1] *Statistical Abstract of Israel*, 1965.

In manual work, every job, skilled, semi-skilled and unskilled, is graded with far more detail than in Britain or the U.S.A. Where in Britain there are one or two grades, we may find four or five in Israel. To quote some examples: in the British building industry, there is only one grade for craftsmen (skilled men). In the Israeli building industry there are five grades of craftsmen, known as Classes C, B, A, AA, and Superior Class. Carpenters are divided into eight classes known as Classes E, D, C, B, AB, A, AA, and Superior Class. Machine operators in Israeli agriculture and transport drivers have four grades. In foundries there are seven grades of skilled men and four grades of unskilled men. In the woodworking industry, manual workers are divided into eight grades, the last two called AA and Superior Class.

The wage differential between one grade and the next is often very small indeed. In the building industry, there were for a long time two grades with identical wage rates. All the same the distinction seemed to be appreciated. This craving for status may be also a remnant of middle-class psychology.

Another line of status distinction is that based on the differentiation between daily and monthly workers. The vast majority of manual workers in industry are daily workers, paid only for the hours they actually work. But some old hands and very skilled men have achieved the status of monthly workers, and share the privileges of clerical workers, especially in regard to sick pay, holidays, etc. Monthly workers are covered by a separate collective agreement and have greater stability of employment. Yet another line of distinction is that between permanent and temporary workers. This is the basic and most important status distinction among Israeli workers. The first question you ask a worker is 'Are you on the permanent staff? (*Kawua*)'. A permanent worker gets full social benefits and seniority rights. He is in full possession of his job. He cannot be dismissed except for specific reasons. A temporary worker is an underprivileged worker with many handicaps.

(x) *A craving for Self-Expression*
The individualism and strong personality consciousness of the Jew is shown also in an almost automatic craving for self-expression. This is a very popular topic of conversation in Israel.

Painting, sculpture, modelling, pottery, marquetry, singing and music,[1] drama and acting, ballet and opera, writing, film making, artistic photography, jewellery, work with gold and silver, in fact all the arts and crafts flourish. The number of art galleries in Tel-Aviv is probably greater than in London, and even the smallest town such as Ramat Hasharon has an art gallery. Art flourishes not only in the towns but also in the villages, in the Kibbutzim and the Moshavim. There are two extensive art colonies, one in Safad and the other in Ein Hod, and several others are about to be born.

The Israeli Jew discovers in art a new potential of joy, freedom and fulness, of self-assertion and self-identification. Art in Israel is an outlet and has an enormous functional value. A great deal of passion is spent in this way. It enables immigrants alienated from society to 'Lie still and keep quiet'. It is for many a substitute for life itself, a sort of escapism. It transports man from reality into the dreamland. Before, the 'dreamers of the ghetto' were spinning their ideas, now the dreamers of Israel weave their dreams into works of art. It is also a substitute for religion for many.

This mass self-expression in art produces pop art at its best. The proliferation of art gives life and joy. It makes life in Israel so much more interesting. On the other hand the vulgarization of art has its anti-art aspects. The abundance, if not super-abundance, of art for all, strips art of its magical powers, it disrobes and dethrones it. The phrase 'self-expression' is on everybody's lips and sometimes becomes a subject for jokes.

All these characteristics described under the previous sub-headings ((i)–(x)) form what we termed the principal axis of the ellipse, which presents the mentality of the ingathering tribes. They came to Israel with most of those characteristics, bringing them as their heritage from the Diaspora. They may be regarded as the warp of the texture of society into which the woof, derived from the new situation and from the new necessities and requirements of the Jewish State, is woven.

[1] There are 25 musical conservatoirs with some 9,000 students. The Israel Philharmonic Orchestra has 27,000 regular subscribers. Three million theatre tickets are sold per year, a world record per head of the population.

The immigrants were individualists, but these individualists have been suddenly thrust into a strong social framework often with emergency conditions to bind them together. They were marginal men squeezed out of their countries of origin and suddenly transported into the centre of affairs with full responsibility for their own state. They formed previously a community of protest, protest against a hostile environment, but this community has had to develop into a community of affirmation and positivity. It was basically a middle-class community with middle-class habits and tastes, which has now had to develop a full social structure, primarily based on working-class standards.

And so we come to the second, the minor axis of our ellipse. Along this axis we will find a whole chain of characteristics which are the exact opposites of the qualities described under the previous sub-headings. They form a dialectical antithesis in the Hegelian sense, an expression of the tendency to overcome characteristics incompatible with the new situation and new requirements. And so along the second axis we find patriotism counteracting the limitations of familism; and the Kibbutz philosophy keeping economism in check. We find an antithesis to careerism in the psychology of pioneering, the antithesis to the quest for independence in the working-class ethos, the antithesis to the lack of the team spirit in the ethos of fellowship and co-operation, the antithesis to lack of discipline in the discipline of an army camp. Excessive criticism is counteracted by the ethos of leadership, factionalism by a trend towards political integration, status seeking by the trend towards egalitarianism, the drive towards self-expression by an ideology of collective and communal action. Let us review these trends.

Patriotism

The joys of independence are widely and genuinely felt and deeply experienced. It is a treasure which must be defended at all costs and made the fullest use of. It is not only a treasure but a biological necessity. There is no possiblity of retreat from the land, this is the first and the last bastion to be defended. The Roman motto, *Dulce et decorum est pro patria mori*, becomes not only a slogan but a reality which has been proved by tens of thousands of Israelis in raids and skirmishes and in the three wars, including the Six Day War, in which valiant acts of heroism were performed not only by Sabras but also by foreign-born Jews. Their patriotism has been tested, and has proved to be no less tangible a reality than that of the Sabras.

A whole secular religion is being evolved around the love and veneration for the land as a sanctum. The land becomes for the ingathering tribes holy in a literal sense, that is a sacred trust to be defended, developed and beautified. This veneration of the land and the resultant patriotism form a check on familism and careerism.

The Kibbutz Philosophy

The Kibbutz philosophy which far transcends the boundaries of the Kibbutz itself stands in contrast to economism and commercialism. It proclaims the value of land, of labour and social service, of production instead of distribution, of making things instead of money. It treats the economic calculus as a secondary consideration. The policy of the State, to a large extent in the hands of Kibbutz members, often follows lines suggested by the Kibbutz philosophy, flouting the economic calculus and engaging in projects with visionary quality.

Another antithesis to economism and careerism which should be mentioned in this connection is the ideology of charity which has strong roots in the Diaspora. In many countries large masses of the Jewish population lived in abject poverty and had to be supported by charity. Whole Jewish communities had to rely on contributions from Jews from abroad. The State of Israel at present also depends to a large extent on contributions from abroad and whole sections of the community and a number of enterprises, institutions, universities and colleges draw a large part of their income from contributions from abroad. This attitude of a charitable tolerance of uneconomic enterprises with inherent weaknesses, is found also in the economic policy of the State, with its almost indiscriminate support of all and sundry. Why should the State refuse its support to those claimants who cannot support themselves, if the whole of Israel is dependent on benefactions? This is what I call charity socialism, which I will expound in another context. It deflects the operation of the so-called economic laws and it counteracts the pull of the *homo economicus*. The other side of the Jew as *homo economicus* is found in the Jew as *homo caritatis*.

Pioneering

The spirit of pioneering has been, since the inception of the State, somewhat on the decline but after the June War it has revived and is again on the ascendant. It has a long tradition in Jewish avant-guardism, in Jews acting as begetters of movements and champions of causes, breaking new ground. Many young Israelis are still following the path of the pioneers in voluntary social service, in peace corps service abroad, in frontier work at home, and new Kibbutzim are still being formed. After the June war settlements of the Kibbutz Haneuchad on Golan Heights and in Northern Sinai have been established and a religious Kibbutz re-established its settlement in the Etzion Block on the Western Bank.

A great deal of teaching is done on a voluntary basis. Actually the whole of Israel is one great school as everyone is teaching everyone else something. So Israeli idealism complements Israeli careerism.

The Working Class Ethos

The quest for independence is kept in check by economic realities on the one hand and the working class ethos on the other. The economic realities express themselves in a constant rise of the ratio of employees to the general manpower available (in the period 1955–63 from 63·9 per cent to 69·9 per cent among the Jewish population) and in a constant fall of the ratio of employers, self-employed people and members of co-operatives (from 22·1 per cent to 18·7 per cent in the same period).[1] Whatever aspirations the Israelis may have for independence, economic necessities squeeze them into wage and salary employment. The ratio of employees, if added to the members of the Kibbutzim, is very high, and not very different from that to be found in Western industrial countries.

The working-class ethos, although somewhat weakened in the last decade, is still in vogue in Israel. The 1st of May is a recognized holiday not only in factories and offices but also in schools and universities. The Trade Union membership is the highest in the Western world. The Histadrut has a somewhat socialist flavour, stating in the first paragraph of its by-laws, 'the general federation of Jewish labour in Israel unites and brings together

[1] *Statistical Abstract of Israel*, 1965.

workers who live by the sweat of their brow without exploiting other peoples' work, in order to arrange satisfactorily all agricultural, economic and cultural matters of the working class in Israel and for the sake of building a Jewish workers' society in Israel'.

How this working-class society should be built, and on what principles, the Histadrut does not proclaim, as it includes in its membership several working-class political parties with divergent views. However, one principle of this desired society is stated explicitly, as expressed in the paragraph above, that everyone should work without living on other peoples' earnings. Thus the new society is to be a society of wage and salary earners without room for those who do not work. This ideology may be considered as the express negation of the quest for independence.

Fellowship and Co-operation

The lack of team spirit described above is counterbalanced by the ethos of good fellowship (*chaveirut*) on the one hand, and the widespread growth of associations and organizations on the other. The ethos of fellowship has its backing in a traditional and popular motto: *Kol Israel chaveirim* ('all Jews are comrades and brothers'). This ethos has been somewhat weakened in recent years by growing affluence but it is still very much in evidence.

We have to note here an impressive network of co-operatives not only in agriculture but in every economic field. We have also to take into account the spread of clubs, associations of all kinds, institutes and cultural ventures. The Israeli society is in fact highly organized; one might even call it over-organized to a very large extent. Everybody is organized, even painters, sculptors, actors. Whoever keeps apart does so at his own risk. An unorganized man has little chance of success in Israel. It is strange that one of the most individualistic of people has developed such a strong network of all kinds of organizations. There is no group, even the smallest, which has not discovered the need, and the urge to be organized. Organizations are based on all kinds of principles. Not only a work-place is organized but also a house, a neighbourhood, a synagogue, students in a school or in a university.

Training for Discipline

The lack of discipline in private life, partly due to the permissiveness of parents and schools, is counterbalanced by the training for discipline which goes on in many of the institutions, which were lacking in the Diaspora, such as the army, police, merchant navy, civil aviation and the para-military organizations and youth movements. Service in the armed forces is a lifetime affair which starts very early in schools, and lasts up to the age of forty-nine, the age up to which the reservists are liable to be called up. The whole Israeli society is one army camp with Nahal[1] settlements and Kibbutzim at strategic points.

The quality of the training has been tested in various campaigns including the Six Day War. The turn-out of the soldiers is regarded as individualistic and their relationship to the superior officers as easygoing but that does not detract from the effectiveness of the discipline as far as performance is concerned. Also physical training and sports clubs, such as the Wingate Institute for physical education, the Government Seminary for physical training instructors, and the schools for sports instructors run by the Sports Authority make their contribution to training for discipline.

The Ethos of Charismatic Leadership

The tendency to excessive criticism finds its dialectical counterpart in the ethos of charismatic leadership. This ethos is not without a tradition in Judaism. Moses was the prototype of the charismatic leader and Jewish religious history abounds in charismatic leaders, prophets, priests and heroes, *zaddikim* (wonder-working Rabbis), etc. Messianic and millenial hopes are linked with the charismatic leader of the Davidic Kingdom. The Oriental population, especially the Yemenites, saw in Ben Gurion a modern version of the leader of the Davidic Kingdom. Actually Ben Gurion, from the inception of the State until 1963, enjoyed the position of a charismatic leader, and when he eventually decided to retire from the Premiership, he chose his successor, to whom he gave his blessing, although later on he turned savagely against him, accusing him of lying and incompetence. Hero worship, the worship of the memory of past leaders, men of

[1] *Nahal* is a unique combination of soldiering and farming, of sword and ploughshare.

letters or science or great benefactors, is a very pronounced feature of the Israeli scene. Dogmatism, fanaticism and funda- mentalism are the other side of the Israeli character.

A Tendency towards Political Integration

Factionalism finds its counterpart in the tendency towards political integration. The earlier split in the Mapai was made good in the merger of three splinter parties, Mapai, Achdut Avoda and Rafi in January 1968. Two other parties, Herut and a major part of the Liberal Party have also undergone a process of unification. Since the June War all parties, except two Communist Parties, have joined in a coalition government, a truly national govern- ment, which is still in existence at the time of writing. The Israeli society is well aware of the paramount necessity of unity and of greater political and social integration. After all, the national emergency which started almost forty years ago has not yet finished. Since the June War, Israel is heading towards the formation of three main political parties: the United Labour Party, the Gahal (Liberal Herut) bloc, and the Religious Front.

Egalitarian Tendencies

Status seeking clashes violently with another tendency, until recently very strong, that of egalitarianism. This has weakened in the last few years but is still operative. Israeli society *aspires* to a measure of 'socialism' with full social welfare services and full social security. In the pioneering days wage and salary differentials were practically non-existent.[1] Later on, they were introduced in a small way and in recent years have visibly increased. The co- efficient of inequality of income (for 1957) according to Mr M. Sandberg's calculations published in the *Economic Quarterly* (Nos 25/26 and 39) is not very much smaller than in Britain or in Sweden (4·98 against 5·46 for Britain and 5·21 for Sweden).

However, the ethos of egalitarianism is still in operation and exerts its influence on the way of life and on the pattern of relationships. The Israeli worker is indistinguishable from the middle-class man in the way he is clothed, fed and sheltered. He sends his children to the same schools, he goes to the same places

[1] Up to 1952, salary differentials in the Civil Service were 2:1, the lowest in any society. In industry the principle of equity largely determined wage differentials.

amusement, he has the same cultural needs and he also owns
his house or apartment.

The worker lives with his employer on easy terms of comradeship, he turns to him on all occasions, very often addressing him
by his first name. This is practically always true in small-scale
establishments but even in larger firms the relationship is free,
easy going and informal. The worker often treats his employer
or manager as an equal. 'Yitzhak', the worker will say to his
employer, 'I would like you to explain to me this or that.' On
my investigations, I often heard the workers asking, 'Have I not
the same needs and wants as my employer? Don't I go to concerts
and theatres, don't I buy books, don't I let my children study in
the same way as my employer does?' Men in the army also often
address their officers by their first names, and the salute is a
greeting rather than anything else.

The Ideology of Collective Action

Collective action is the counterpart to the drive for self-expression.
Committee meetings and their long deliberations are a very
popular pastime in Israel, both in government service and public
institutions and also in private associations, clubs and businesses.
They consume a great deal of time, energy and money. What is
called 'meeting weariness' or 'meeting sickness' (*Mahala Yeshivot*)
is an accepted phenomenon of Israeli industry. The Histadrut
enterprises are especially conference ridden. The manager hardly
has time to carry out his managerial functions as he is all the time
engaged in committee deliberations, going from one committee
to another trying to bring them into line. A manager was described
to me as *chevra man* (a Liaison Officer). Actually the *chevra man*,
the activist in the party or association and business, the begetter of
organizations and movements, is a very well-known figure in
Israeli society at large. This is also a phenomenon of self-expression
but of a different kind as it involves collective action. Mobilization
for collective action has often a purely economic background. The
Israelis have discovered that individual interests can by clubbing
together be easily converted into public interests and public pressure
groups. Individuals A, B and C may each have individual interests,
but the interests of A plus B plus C, when organized, are promoted
to the rank of social interests. In fact they are converted into a
public interest with an ideology behind it. Israel abounds in a net-

work of pressure groups of various kinds and sizes. Each pressure group, often very small, such as a neighbourhood, is an organization of its own.

The two axes, described under previous headings as the principal and minor axes of the ellipse-mentality of the Ingathering Tribes, are, as we saw, closely related to each other, the one being the counterpart of, or the reaction to, the other: and both interacting in a specific way. These axes do not have equal force in the community. Most of the traits of the first axis, having a longer tradition behind them, seem to be stronger than the traits of the second axis. The dynamism of the traits on both axes is unequal. In the pioneering stage the dynamism of the minor axis was very great; in the interlude between the Suez Campaign and the Six Day War, a period of relative affluence and security, its dynamism was much weaker, and the traits of the principal axis were once more gaining ground. After the Six Day War, the spirit of pioneering is expected to be renewed in the face of great, new and urgent challenges. But it is too early to forecast whether and for how long the impact of the war will last.

The traits of both axes are not equally distributed among the population. Some sections of the population display rather the traits of the first axis than those of the second, or vice versa. The two axes have different validities in the veteran towns and in the new towns, in Tel-Aviv and Jerusalem, in the Kibbutzim and Moshavim and the new settlements. However, there is little doubt that in the long run the minor axis has a good chance of prevailing.

I do not know whether what has been said previously about the psychology of the Ingathering Tribes is particularly Jewish or Israeli, or whether it could have been said *mutatis mutandis* about immigrants of any minority people immigrating to a new country, especially those who are thereby turning into a dominant pioneering group. While pondering over the common features of the mental make-up of the Ingathering Tribes, I coined a new term: mino-majority. The social psychology of the foreign-born Israelis is basically the psychology of a harassed minority suddenly turned into a dominant majority. It is a complete reversal of social roles, a complete *Umwertung der Werte*. Consequently many of the virtues of yesterday became the sins of today and vice versa.

But one should add here that both roles find common ground in a situation of continuous hostility. Both the previous Jewish minorities and the present majority are embattled groups facing hostility, the first the hostility of dominant groups, the second the hostility of a minority (but a minority supported by most of the neighbouring states, and so forming a majority in the whole region). This continuance of hostility makes the reversal of the roles even more poignant and accentuated. It introduces an element of tension and violence, and strengthens the element of dominance in the 'majority psychology'. In a way it reduces the therapeutic value, the 'normalcy effect' of the general character transformation.

This reversal of role for the ingathering Tribes implied at the same time a reversal of role for the Arab population, which, from its majority status, suddenly turned into a minority. In this way the mino-majority faced a newly formed and hostile majo-minority, i.e., a population which has not accepted a new status as second-class citizens in the Jewish State, but has retained a great deal of its previous 'majority psychology'. This produces a specific atmosphere which, in many ways, gives a peculiar twist to all the characteristics of the social psychology of foreign-born Israelis which we placed on the two axes. The members of the mino-majority understand very well the emotions, idiosyncrasies and sensibilities of the new minority, and are therefore subject to very mixed feelings, ranging from rancour to a sense of anxiety, insecurity and guilt. They would like to see their new position acknowledged, reasserted and reaffirmed officially as well as in everyday life, and they need acts of self-confidence and self-approbation to bolster their newly acquired status.

All this is expressed, not only in the dialectical opposition of the two axes as presented, but also in the great polarity of those axes, in the wide difference between the opposed characteristics, the great tension between them and the great unrelieved dynamism of each position and anti-position. One could say that the specific characteristic of the foreign-born Israeli is a very high degree of polarity in his mental make-up accompanied by his great unrelieved tensions.

Israeli society can be compared to a mass of high energy particles, compressed into a small space and interacting intensely upon each other. To use a simile of physics, just as high energy particles compressed into a very small space may produce what the physicists call implosion, so high energy particles in society, compressed into a small space and interacting intensely upon one another, can equally produce a violent discharge of social and cultural energy. This is, I think, the background to the violent discharge of social energy witnessed in recent Israeli history.

3.

Jewish Races, Jewish Cultures, and the Search for Jewishness

ONE COULD say that present-day Israel presents an ideal setting for the search for what one may call Jewishness. Is there such a thing as Jewishness, and if so what is it? Many of the myths about the essence of Jewishness are exploded by the realities of Israel. One of them is the conception of a single Jewish race. Instead one may speak about Jewish races, i.e., physical types impregnated with some Jewish characteristics. These may, however, have a common racial origin, which makes for a common racial thread or entity with a great deal of variety within it.

Assuming that there was once a common racial stock in biological terms, this stock will have undergone a thorough transformation in each separate country, being remoulded by climate and culture, and also through the infusion of blood by marriage, conversion or illicit relations, and even through the psychological influence of the models and ideal types which pregnant women have in their mind's eye. We do not know yet how these ideal types, which parents have in mind, and to which they subconsciously aspire, may influence the formation of the foetus in the mother's womb, but such a belief goes back to ancient times, and may be found in the Bible. A law of protective or autosuggestive mimicry operates throughout nature. Can it be that the 'biblical blue' of the Israeli horizon with its translucent aquamarine and turquoise tints has found its reflection in the blue eyes of the many Sabra children born to dark-eyed parents, this being a puzzling and intriguing phenomenon of Israel.

It is a common experience to see in Israel the tall figures and oblong blond faces of Scandinavian Jews, or red-haired Jews from the Ukraine, or Arabian-looking Jews from the Arab countries, or Hindu types from India, or the Spanish-looking Sephardis. One can often hear American tourists saying to their guides of Arab-looking Jews from North Africa: 'If you say those men are Jews, I have to believe you: but it is difficult for me to see them as such, as they clash so much with the Jewish type I know'.

Actually it is not entirely true that a Jew from the Arab countries looks like an Arab, or a Jew from Scandinavian countries like a Scandinavian. An Arab or a Scandinavian would at once sense the difference. When, in Jerusalem, I once remarked to a Jewish lady from Sweden, 'You look completely Scandinavian', she answered, 'Only to you: in Sweden no one would take me for Swedish; I have only a touch of the Scandinavian in my Jewish looks'. The same holds true for most members of the Tribes. There seems to be a specific strain in the Jewish stock of every country, which makes it different from the Jews of other countries but not identical with the race of the host country. This fact made Jews easy prey for discrimination and persecution, but equally it was an element in the survival of the Jews. One could say that every country formed its own race of Jews. The Polish Jews were different from the Jews of other countries, but they also differed considerably from Poles themselves. The Jews of a given country were partly a product of that country's making. But this was true to a certain extent only, as the Jews who came into a country were not a *tabula rasa*, they came with certain characteristics of their own. In the process of time, however, they were moulded and shaped by the impact of their new environment and culture.

The other important myth exploded by the realities of Israel is the myth of a unitary Jewish culture. There is no such thing as a single Jewish culture, but rather a whole gamut of Jewish cultures which became intermarried with the culture patterns of the countries and civilizations of their origin. There is an enormous cultural range within the Jewish people. One can ascribe to them all kinds of traits and characteristics, but valid only in the context of a given civilization. Even within a single civilization and culture, there has often been a considerable atomization of cultural patterns among the Jews. Some integrated their culture with the ethnical majority, others with a minority, some with the upper class, others with the lower classes.

This is the reason why the Jew is the despair of the sociologist, or of anyone who wants to classify him neatly. The concept of

Jewish culture exists only as a huge and loose range of Jewish cultures with a large variability of traits and value orientations. It is enough to point out the contrast between the culture patterns of Russian, German, American and Yemenite or Moroccan Jews. Their value orientations, beliefs and expressive symbols, their receptiveness and response, their basic images of reality, their capacity for leadership, their economic, technical and cultural abilities, their community orientation will differ fundamentally. The personality structure produced by each of those cultures will differ from country to country or from civilization to civilization.

So the same situation exists with regard to Jewish culture as was found with regard to the idea of a Jewish race. Each distinct Jewish culture differs from the culture of its host country or civilization, but a Jewish culture developed in one civilization differs from a Jewish culture developed in another. They have something in common, of course, as do many other cultures which are in touch with each other. They are linked with the religious or ethnical-religious value orientations and traditions which preceded their separation. They have been in touch with each other and shared some of their values. We can speak about a chain of Jewish cultures, by which we mean that they are in contact with each other, giving and taking, but this does not make them into one cultural unity. The contacts between some Jewish cultures may have been very close, such as for instance those between German and Polish, or between English and American Jewish cultures. Others may have been practically non-existent, as for instance those between the American and North African Jewish cultures.

If we call the original Jewish characteristic J (Jewish) and the characteristics of the host nation G (Gentile) we can describe the Jews in a given country as a product of the interaction between J and G. We can hardly call it a mixture, as the new compound has a very complex nature, resembling not so much a mechanical action as a bio-chemical reaction. The impact of environment with its human and cultural elements on the Jewish Tribes often became even more complex as many Jews passed from one country to another. It is an exciting question as to which cultural and environmental values tended to form the most desirable combination of J and G, and to give rise to the most creative and productive type of Jew. The answer would probably be different for different phases of historical experience in a single country, and different again for different social and class conditions. When the Jews were given full freedom and a full chance of development, high cultures produced a highly cultured Jew with a rich cultural heritage. From the vantage point of Israel one can see that backward countries often produce a backward type of Jew, highly cultured countries a highly cultured Jew, technically minded countries a technically minded Jew, and so on.

The impact of Christian culture on the European Jew is discernible in his way of thinking and feeling, and equally the impact of Islamic culture on the Jew coming from the Arab countries, even with regard to religious rites. If one enters a synagogue of the Yemenite Jews, one can sense at once the impact on them of Islamic culture, hearing the nasal chant reminiscent of the Muzzein's call to prayer, and seeing the barefoot worshippers, the ornamental symbols and the paraphernalia of the East.

So one can well study in Israel the specific characteristics of many Gentile nations as reflected in their Jewish communities. One sees clearly that the ideal model of behaviour as a man and a citizen as held by the Jews has been derived to a large extent from their non-Jewish environment.

So an English Jew tries to behave like an English gentleman. He will speak with a minimum of gestures, in a low voice, with understatement, and he will emphasize the rules of fair play, sportsmanship, tolerance and compromise. The public school educated gentleman is his archtype on which he wants to model himself.

The German Jew is notable for his strict and upright deportment. He is disciplined and behaves in an orderly way. Very rationalistic and materialistic, an organizer, a planner, a good manager and technician. No nonsense about him. The German *shikunim* (settlements) can be recognized even from a distance.

The Polish Jew is romantic and adventurous, loathing order, discipline, planning, organization, acting on the spur of the moment, always asking 'why' and 'why not'.

The Russian Jew is a reformer, thinking always in terms of a nation or a society, always using big words, and attempting to save the whole world by his rhetoric.

The American Jew is an ideal business man, combining idealism with dollar supremacy, trying to do business and to initiate philanthropy on a big scale, an organization man with his emphasis on publicity, with drive and power, energy and enthusiasm, who looks around to see whether other people have noticed what he has done, a man with his heart in his pocket and his pocket in his heart.

The Austrian Jew is light hearted, artistic, cheerful, hearty, vivacious and does not take life too seriously, being inclined to introduce a lively and joking tone to society.

The Hungarian Jew is a sporting, solid type, proud and independent with great staying power and resilience, always very smartly dressed.

The Rumanian Jew is the type of a commercial agent, very sensitive, always on the defensive, and on the look out for a *bakshish* (tip) to give or to take.

The Yugoslavian Jew is highly cultured, straight, sociable, eager to serve, resembling the Hungarian or Austrian type.

The Italian Jew is of an aristocratic type, well educated, highly artistic, concentrating in the liberal professions.

The Asian and African Jews, coming from the Moslem cultures, present altogether different types of personality, some of them going back in time for hundreds of years.

The Yemenite Jew is of an almost Biblical type, with silky curls and sidelocks and soft big eyes, patriarchal, very dignity conscious and proud, small, delicate, sensitive, devoted to his family and to his religion, readily responding to the call of the Land.

The Kurdi Jew is strong and muscular, with great staying power, given to hard work in building or agriculture, the best manual worker in the country, but also prone to blood feuds.

The Persian Jew is a commercial type who presents a complete contrast to the Kurdi although he is a close neighbour.

The Egyptian Jew is a typical Levantine type, strongly influenced by French culture, always claiming benefits and lodging complaints.

The Moroccan Jew is very impulsive, prone to fighting and quarrels and regarded as the most troublesome group among the immigrants, but with great energy and drive. When properly handled he will work very hard and give his best.

Of course I am conscious of having indulged in oversimplified generalizations. Every tribe has a large range of qualities derived from individual differences, family traditions, educational back-grounds, and professional, social and economic situations. Some countries provide in themselves a great range of ethnical and geographical differences. For instance in Poland the type of the 'West Galicianer' differs from that of the 'East Galicianer', or from the Congress Poland Jew or from the Litwak, or from the 'Poznaner' Jew. But, by and large we can find, in daily contact with the tribes in Israel, that some of general characteristics ascribed to them in the stereotypes above, and arising from differences of culture, geographical environment and historical experience, hold true to a considerable degree. The American Jew or the Hungarian Jew or the Polish Jew or the Yemenite or the Kurd is easily recognizable, not only when they speak Hebrew, each with his own national accent, but also from attitudes and modes of behaviour, and frequently from physical appearance.

Miscegenation in biological terms as well as the miscegenation of attitudes, behaviour patterns and ideas have produced the Jew as we know him today in his numerous types and varieties. There are many questions which arise in this connection. Has the Jew selected the best from the host cultures and then combined this with the best from his own? Which cultures were compatible with his own and which incompatible? Was the selection of cultural elements by the Jew based on their intrinsic values, or rather on their commercial, social and any other utilitarian value? In most cases the Jew acquired characteristics of the surrounding culture under a pressure to conformity, rather than because of its superior intrinsic value. But in countries with other consider-able ethnical minorities, such as Sudeten Germany, Transylvania, Austrian Galicia, or Polish Lithuania, the Jew often had a very difficult choice as to with whom to assimilate, with the ruling majority of the country, with the other ethnic minority, or with a local minority. The minorities often accused Jews of assimilation with the ruling majority and the ruling class as well, which caused additional friction and animosities.

The blending of the factors 'J' (Jewish characteristics) with the factors 'G' (Gentile characteristics) was often deep and har-monious, producing a genuine new article, a well integrated and balanced personality structure. The Jew absorbed much culturally exogeneous material, and blended it with a mixture of ancestral memories and exotic oriental imagery, derived mainly from the

Bible. A Jew with a harmonious blending of 'J' and 'G' could identify himself with the native culture and at the same time maintain a dedication to his past and to the deepest values of his ancestry. The most extreme cases are entirely assimilated Jews.

In many other cases, the blending of 'J' and 'G' was superficial and disharmonious, producing an unbalanced and disintegrated personality, a sort of imitation or artificial article, as when a man tries desperately to identify himself with everything around him, or when an outsider wants to be an insider and aspires to be taken for 'one of us'. One such extreme case is what one may call the imitation Jew, another the Jew with only a smattering of Gentile culture, still another a cultural *Marrano*, a double faced Jew with double values and a double behaviour pattern, one for his Jewish connections and one for the Gentiles. This is the most strained, the most awkward and the most disturbing personality structure of the Jew. And when the Israelis invite Diaspora Jews to settle in Israel, contending that the Jew can nowhere be entirely himself except in Israel, they have primarily in mind such extreme cases.

The outcome of blending 'J' with 'G', whether successful or not, was conditioned not only by the general characteristics of 'J' and 'G' in a given cultural setting, but also by specific social and class characteristics, and of course also to a very large extent by the characteristics of the individual involved. This blending may for instance be very successful in one social class, for instance in the middle class, while equally unsuccessful and disharmonious in classes below or above this level. There are educational levels conducive to a successful blending and others which exclude them. The same then applies to individual personality structure and characteristics, depth, width, resilience, adaptability, convertability and so on.

From the examples considered we can see that the blending of 'J' with 'G' will produce a whole gamut of personality types among Diaspora Jews. We could envisage a whole series of studies to investigate the impact of 'G' on 'J' and the kind of blending which results in each separate cultural setting, class and social structure, and profession and personality structure. But the main difficulty of such studies would be to ascertain the nature and the essence of the 'J'. As the Jews are an extremely mobile race and endowed with a high degree of absorbability, it is very difficult to ascertain in any cultural context what is Jewish and what is not. Let us consider the cases of the Spanish Jews moving to England or Holland, or of the German Jews moving to Poland in the fifteenth and sixteenth centuries. What had begun as 'G' in Spain became after settling in England and Holland 'J'. The cultural traits absorbed in Spain became in due course to all intents and purposes Jewish. They were so thoroughly digested and mixed with 'J', and became so surrounded with the halo of tradition, that they were regarded by the Jews as Jewish. In this way 'G' was after a certain time transformed into 'J', which in turn became exposed in a new country to a new 'G', a hybridization of a second degree. And so the process of hybridization goes on all the time, each time from a new vantage point.

A Jew immigrating to a new country often therefore has in his cultural make-up a whole range of alien cultural material which we may call 'G.1', 'G.2', 'G.3' and so on. 'G.1' is already hallowed by tradition and became 'J', part of the Jewish heritage. 'G.2' is only partly and loosely amalgamated with 'J' and will be strongly exposed to the winds of change. 'G.3' may be regarded as completely foreign to 'J' and will be rejected outright. So the process of adding and rejecting, amalgamating and absorbing, reordering and reabsorbing on an ever higher level, goes on all the time, and when we are confronted with the problem as to what is genuinely Jewish in Jewish culture, or in Jewish personality, we find ourselves in a dilemma.

One answer would be to go back to ancient Israel and regard its cultural values as truly Jewish. But the ancient Israelis were already intermingled with and under the strong influence of the Egyptians, Canaanites, Assyrians, Phoenicians, Babylonians, Persians, Hittites, Greeks, and Romans, to mention only a few principal influences. And some of these influences are already reflected in the most 'Jewish' sources of the Jewish heritage, the Bible and the Talmud. Aramaic, the language of the Talmud, the *lingua franca* of the Second Jewish Commonwealth was not the Jewish language but the language of the whole Middle Eastern region.

A similar answer would be to regard only religious values as Jewish, and all other cultural values as non-Jewish. Needless to say, the consequence of accepting both these answers would be the self-mutilation and self-impoverishment of Jewish culture. It would amount to passing a death sentence on most Jewish culture as developed during the last two thousand years.

The only rational solution would be to regard as truly Jewish everything which was produced, absorbed, amalgamated and fused by Jewish communities in their long historical trek. In this way we get a variety of Jewish cultures, not one, a chain of dynamic and living Jewish cultures, moving and restructuring themselves in various settings, adjusting and readjusting themselves to the cultural currents of the world. We have to admit that the first essential trait of Jewish cultures consists of their high degree of absorbability, the spongelike capacity to absorb and to reconstruct alien material in their own meaningful way, producing from it a new, highly original and significant pattern of their own.

The difference between Israel and the Diaspora, as regards the blending of 'J' with 'G', is that, while in the Diaspora countries the blend usually consists of single 'J' with a single 'G' or a series of 'G's', in Israel the blend is formed from various strains of 'J' with a residual influence of various strains of 'G'. The fresh impact of 'G' is very restricted, practically confined to foreign contacts. We can expect, therefore, that this melting pot of all strains of 'J' will produce a new variety, which we may call J. Omega, a variety of Jewishness to the highest degree. The product which we can expect from this blending will follow certain laws of bio-chemical or rather bio-social and bio-cultural synthesis. In new surroundings, in a new situation under a new élite, some cultural values taken over from various ethnical strains will prove stronger, more adaptable and more fitting than others. Diminutions and suppressions of some cultural values will follow the expansion and functional growth of others with accretions and additions of their own. The new product, J. Omega will be partly an active adaptation, partly a synthesis and partly a creation of its own.

The agents of transformation will come from three main sources. The first will contain the external forces, all the situational factors impinging upon national character in the new situation. The second source is the process of synthesis as such. The melting pot has its own laws. Some national strains have a higher social status and prestige, and a greater power of resistance and attraction than others. The homogenization, the acculturation, the assimilation, equalization and nivelation will form a selective process of very high complexity. The third source is the directive agent, the deliberate policy of the Hebraization of a whole nation which means not only the revival of the Hebrew language but also the revival and renewal of the whole Hebrew culture with an emphasis on ancient traditions. So the law of bio-chemical synthesis in the Israeli melting pot will follow the refraction induced by the impact of two other agents, the external and the directive.

The external agents may be described as Middle Eastern, as the main situational forces convergent on the geographical location where the new home is built. We may call this process the Easternization of the Jews.

The internal agent in the melting pot can be described as Judaic, as the constant appearing of the numerous varieties of 'J', which is likely to strengthen the Jewish element. We may call this process the Judaization of the Jews.

The directive agents are very complex but follow in the main a dualistic course, one pointing in the direction of the archaic, the other in the direction of modernity. One is a tendency to link up the new Israeli culture with the threads of an ancient culture interrupted two thousand years ago. This aspect may be called the process of Archaization of Israeli society. The other tendency is expressed in the aspiration of the vast majority of the Israelis to build a modern, highly technological, scientific and affluent society, approaching a socialist model of economy. This aspect may be called the process of Modernization.

The full description of the new brand of society which is likely to follow the operation of the three agents described above could read: an archaic-modern, potently Judaic, Middle Eastern society. We see how complex are the forces operating as the agents of the evolution of the Jewish people in Modern Israel. Reality and dreams are here intermingled. And so are the forces of creation and the forces of adaptation. The weight of history is counterbalanced by the weight of modern technology, the contracting forces in Judaism by the expanding forces, the strong intellectual forces by equally strong emotional forces. A living balance between those forces cannot be achieved in a decade or two only.

The question arises: should the Israeli melting pot act as a pressure cooker or as a process of slow combustion? Should all the ingredients find their proper place or only those with the highest prestige value imparted by the élite? Can homogeneity be achieved by growth from inside or by enforcement from outside?

Only a fair, equitable balance between various strains, based on organic growth, could give Israel a fair chance to develop a rich and enriching culture, as human and warm as those developed by the old communities in the productive centres of the Diaspora. Such a balance, however, would need a constructive, broad creed, far transcending anything so far produced in Israel.

4.

The Impact of Hebraization and Multi-Lingualism

THE HEBRAIZATION of Jewish society has meant primarily its nationalization. In the trinity of Zionist aspirations, land, language, and sovereignty, that of language played a vital part as the soul of a nascent nation. Hebraization meant the recapturing of the old soul of the Hebrews, going back, not to the times of Bar Kochba, when Aramaic was mostly spoken, but to the more ancient times of the Maccabeans. It was a long journey back in time not without many pitfalls, for it meant a cultural break with the English-speaking Diaspora, and a danger of cultural archaization and parochialism. But Hebraization was the most important factor not only of nationalization but also of homogenization, adding to self-esteem, self-approbation, national solemnity and pride, and providing a most important focus for national loyalty, second only to the possession of the land.

The process itself was most ambitious, arduous and enervating, but its achievements can be classed as a most remarkable success story, probably one of the greatest miracles of the twentieth century, even greater than the emergence of the State of Israel. The revival of an ancient and purely literary and liturgical language has no parallel in history (the attempt to revive the Gaelic language in Ireland or the attempt to spread the Hindi language throughout India largely failed). Almost in a single generation the Hebrew language jumped out of the worn pages of the Tanakh (the Hebrew Bible), left dusty shelves, and became a living thing, part of the living community in Israel.

As Mr Ben Gurion related in his memoirs, the early pioneers who arrived in Palestine at the beginning of this century found that only very few people understood them when they spoke Hebrew. In 1961 the index of Hebrew speaking among

Israeli Jews was 67·8,[1] and the percentage is increasing every year.

The index of Hebrew speaking goes primarily by country of birth (Sabras and foreign-born Jews), and also by age, sex, date of immigration, education, residence, and wealth.

The index of Hebrew speaking is highest among Sabras, for whom in 1961 it was 90·4, while for foreign-born Jews it was only 55·8. It declines with age. For the elderly immigrants Hebrew is a very difficult language. They often feel like morons or children who have not yet learnt to express themselves, their thoughts weighing heavily on their awkward lips. For the newly arrived immigrants, the use of Hebrew can be a torture and the loss of their previous language, of a cultured and subtle way of expression, is often compared to the loss of the soul. The index among Jews who immigrated between the ages of 2 and 14 is 71·6, among the age group 45 to 59, 20·6, and in the 60-plus age group only 9·3. Even among Sabras (with a general index of 90·4), Hebrew speaking declines with age to 56·7 for the 65-plus group.

The date of immigration is an obvious factor. The index is 72·8 for veterans (immigrated before 1947), 56·7 for established immigrants (1948–54), but only 38·2 for new immigrants (since 1955).

The sex differential is considerable, especially for Oriental women whose index is low, 43·6 in 1961. The index for foreign-born males is 60·1, but for females only 51·4.

Education is of course an important factor in Hebraization. While foreign-born Jews without any schooling have an index of only 34, those with between one and four years of schooling have 39·9, and those with eleven or more years of schooling 64·9.

The highest index of Hebrew speaking is recorded for Jerusalem 73·6, compared with an index of 67·8 for the country as a whole. Tel-Aviv-Jaffo is a little above the average with 69·9, and Haifa a little below average with 67·6. New towns with 60·3, and new villages with 49·3, fall considerably behind.

Wealth, as measured by housing density, is a very interesting and rather surprising factor. Wealthy men, those with less than

[1] The Index is a weighted average built on such criteria as 'only language' (100), 'first language' (75), 'additional language' (25). See: *Languages, literary and education attainment. Part II Census 1961.* Central Bureaux of Statistics. Jerusalem 1966.

0·99 persons per room, have an index of 62·0, while the middle class, with 1·00 to 1·99 persons per room, have 68·3. Where the economic pressure to conform and learn Hebrew is not so great, people do not bother too much to acquire the language.

Immigrants are subject to intensive schooling by volunteer teachers, and also in 74 Ulpanim (boarding language schools) providing for 8,000 adults, and are also served by special Hebrew newspapers which carry language lessons, radio courses, etc.

The language situation in Israel is a highly complex phenomenon and it presents a fine opportunity to sociologists of language. It is characterized by the interaction of linguistic, ethnical, religious and social conditions at large. One can well study linguistic cross currents as they combine with social status and class, with culture, education and ritual. We can observe the processes of fusion and syncretization, the pidginization, the creolization and the dialectization of language, and at the same time also the congruence between language and status. Every language has a status of its own.

Multi-lingualism

Israel is not the only country with problems of multi-lingualism. India, the U.S.S.R., Switzerland, Canada and many other countries also have this problem. The uniqueness of Israel consists in its greater multiplicity of languages, in a greater interaction of various languages intermingled in a very confined space, and in a certain artificiality of the dominant language, deprived of a separate living ethnic basis. The various languages in Israel are deprived of a natural habitat, of their own geographical location, comparable to that of French in French Canada, or of Ukrainian in the U.S.S.R.

There are about 70 languages now used in Israel and each one finds itself in a meleè, unique in the complexity of its ingredients and in its inter-penetration. The average number of languages in daily life, according to the survey of 1961, was 1·8: that for foreign-born Jews 2·1, and for Israel-born Jews 1·3. Among European-American-born Jews, the average rises to 2·2, and among their males the proportion is even higher.

Switching from one language to another in a single conversation is a common experience. Even in a family circle more than one language may be spoken. One may start with Hebrew, switch

over to Yiddish, then use the language of the country of origin,
or of several countries through which the family has passed.
Actually this is not a new situation peculiar to Israel; it was
always so among immigrant families in the Diaspora, but it is
more pronounced in Israel than anywhere else. The Jew, by
virtue of his wanderings, has acquired a smattering of many
languages which he uses as the opportunity arises.

Jewish and Non-Jewish Languages

In considering the position of these various languages a distinction must be made between Jewish languages developed and
cultivated in the Diaspora, to which a certain attachment is felt
as a traditional family language—and other languages. There are
two main Jewish languages, the Yiddish of the Ashkenazim,
spoken by 23 per cent of the Jews whose first language was not
Hebrew, and the Ladino, the Spanish jargon of the Sephardic
population (5·3 per cent). In fact there is also an Arabic jargon
for the former inhabitants of Arab countries, but it is not highly
developed and is not recognized as a Jewish language. Due to
the seclusion of ghetto life, Jews in the Diaspora have shown a
general tendency to develop jargons, moulding both phonetically
and grammatically the language of the countries of their adoption
enriching them with the ingredients of Hebrew terms taken from
the Tanakh and the sing-song taken from readings of the Torah
and Prayer Book.

The force of attachment to such a language is astonishing.
Jews from Turkey or Greece, whose forefathers left Spain four
centuries ago, are still speaking Ladino, just as Jews who came
to Poland from Germany in the fourteenth century still speak
Yiddish. Yiddish has its own adherence in Israel and is still used
for expressing the more cordial, more intimate and deeper tones
and feelings, it is more *heimish*. As Bialik once said, 'One speaks
Hebrew, but Yiddish is just spoken, it flows from itself'. Two
men speaking perfect Hebrew may from time to time insert a
word in Yiddish which, with its undertone of familiarity, will
bring them nearer, relaxing the social atmosphere. A speaker
who wants to come nearer to his audience often uses a phrase in
Yiddish saying, 'In Yiddish, one would say this or that', so the
audience knows he is 'one of us'. I found this very valuable in
my Hebrew lectures at the University, and, whenever I used a

Yiddish term for illustration, there was always an amused stir. Yiddish is still the *lingua franca* among the older generation of Ashkenazim. The older population can forgive a newcomer to Israel for not knowing a word of Hebrew but looks with suspicion on anyone who does not know Yiddish. Such a man is asked with resentment 'What Jew are you that you do not know Yiddish'. Every Jew knows *mame lushon*, the mother tongue.

At one time Yiddish was officially supressed in Israel, and the Yiddish speaker looked on with open disapproval as a *Bundist* or *Yiddishist*. Now, as the battle of the languages has been largely won by Hebrew, Yiddish is much more tolerated, and there is even a certain revival of this language in a restricted field. It should be mentioned that, for ultra-orthodox Jews, Yiddish is the true Jewish language, and they often oppose the use of Hebrew for every day. Hebrew for them is the sacred language of the Tanakh and the Prayer Book and should be used only as a language for communication with the Divine. The extreme opposite is true of the Sabras, who regard Yiddish as the lingo of the Diaspora, as a surviving trace of ghetto life.

One can see in Israel that nearly all languages are 'jargonized' by Jews in a certain sense because of their ghetto-like mentality. Indeed in Israel one can see that the ghettos of the Diaspora were partly also of the Jews' own making. The Jews like to herd together, and to maintain the close community ties necessary for the practice of their religion, as well as for cultural and social activities. The settlements of immigrant Jews in Israel, especially those of the Oriental Jews, go mostly by communities, a village being for Moroccan, or Iraqui or Kurdi Jews, for Yemenites or Algerians, etc. This pattern has a powerful influence on the structure and the phonetics of the language, because a closely knit group shows a tendency to modify a language in its own way, the more so the less it is open to outside influences.

There is also a tendency to jargonize the Hebrew language, especially in the more closely knit groups from the Orient. One can see clearly in Israel that language closely follows the patterns of social intercourse and of social integration. In the new towns and villages, where whole communities of Oriental immigrants are settled, a certain danger of the jargonization of Hebrew exists.

The Social Status of Languages

The highest social status is accorded to English, firstly because of its high standing in international relations, in science, culture and education at large, secondly because of the high social standing of the Americans and British, and thirdly as a means of communication with the free Diaspora, of which English-speaking people form an overwhelming majority. English as a mother tongue is spoken by only 4·1 per cent of those Jews whose first language is not Hebrew, but it is in fact unofficially the second language in Israel, and a working knowledge of English is not only a condition for entry to institutions of higher education, but also to all positions of authority. Everybody wants to speak and read English, and an English-speaking immigrant is handicapped in his learning of Hebrew because everyone wants to practise his English on him. An intellectual or scientific circle will invariably speak English or switch on to English sooner or later.

Next in prestige comes Hebrew as the first official language of Israel. It is revered as a symbol of national independence and as the sacred language of the Bible, but, as a vernacular, it is treated as a local language with a restricted radius of application and usefulness. Hebrew is the language of the ruling élite, and is obligatory for all formal occasions and for all public gatherings. Even a lecture in a foreign language will start with a Hebrew introduction from the chairman. Acquiring some Hebrew is essential for practically all jobs, and also for participation in the political and cultural life of the country. The new immigrant is largely judged by his willingness and ability to acquire a working knowledge of Hebrew, which is a symbol of his attachment to common values.

The third language, so far as social status is concerned, is German. It is the most common subsidiary language of the Jews from Europe, and a main language of commerce and industry. One can strike a better bargain in German, while English is avoided in bargaining, as an English-speaking customer is often taken for a tourist or capitalist. German confers a certain distinction, as a measure of educational attainment, but not so strongly as does English. Although the prestige of the German language has declined with the aftermath of Hitler, it is still cultivated by way of press, periodicals and books; in fact it has recovered slightly in the wake of German reparations.

The prestige of French, once very high in the Middle East, has dropped considerably with the mass immigration of North African Jews, most of whom speak French but not of a high standard.

The prestige of the Slav languages, such as Polish, Czech, Russian, Serbo Croat and Bulgarian is less than that of any of the languages previously mentioned. The same applies to Greek, Italian, Hungarian, Turkish, Persian and other languages.

The Arabic language has a prestige of its own as the language of the region at large and of a substantial and fast-growing minority in Israel. It has also a very large following among Jews from Arab countries who form half of the Jewish population in Israel and who often live in closely knit communities. 30·4 per cent of these Jews, whose first language is not Hebrew, speak Arabic. It is the second official language of the country. Since the June War its status has risen considerably in what is a *de facto* bi-national State.

The difference between high prestige and low prestige amongst languages is expressed primarily in the survival value of the language into the next generation, and in the degree of its cultivation. The high prestige language is cultivated, regarded as a valuable asset and imparted to the next generation. The younger generation born to English- or German-speaking parents still know these languages pretty well, while the younger generation of Poles, Czechs or Bulgarians hardly know these languages at all. From amongst the Slav languages, Russian may form an exception because of the high political status of Russia in world affairs. Amongst other languages, French and Italian survive the best.

Fusion and Syncretization of Languages

All languages in Israel are exposed to linguistic cross currents, to fusion and syncretization because of the constant simultaneous use of so many languages. The languages most affected are Hebrew, English, German and Yiddish. Yiddish is more and more impregnated with Hebrew, and is becoming a new language differing considerably from that of the Diaspora. Hebrew is becoming impregnated to a certain extent with English, and to a smaller extent with Slavonic languages, as shown in such words as *nudnik* (bore) or *protekcja* (favouritism). Some international words like *Koalicja* or *dynamika* or *botanika* or *kartelizacja* are pronounced the same way, and have exactly the same ending, as in Polish.

A large number of Hebrew terms are used in every language, especially institutional, organizational and every-day terms, greetings and courtesy terms, as for instance *shalom* or *bavakasha* (please), *todah* (thank you), *slicha* (sorry), *oleh* (immigrant), *vatik* (established resident), *tor* (queue), *tahana* (station), *shikun* (apartment block), *qwish* (road), *shuk* (market) and so on.

The syncretization of languages is found to such an extent in Israel, that one understands perfectly why the inventor of Esperanto was a Jew. The Jews are most interested in an easy international language as a practical means of communication between their own kith and kin. Actually, all languages are spoken with a high admixture of elements of other languages, out of convenience, tradition or necessity, or because to switch over from one language to another in a split second can be mentally exhausting. Israel, if it were allowed to, could easily produce a natural Esperanto of its own, and I should not be surprised if this did actually happen.

The Pidginization and Creolization of Languages

The use of so many languages which are divorced from their natural and original habitat leads to the pidginization and creolization of languages. This is a very serious cultural phenomenon, leading to pidginization of thought, malformation and malexpression and slip-shod circumlocution. The most widely spread is Pinglish (Palestine English or pidgin English). It is strongly established and gathers strength with every year. The smallness of the country, the difficulty experienced by non-Jews and non-Israeli Jews in learning Hebrew, the necessity of keeping close contact with English-speaking Jews, the economic dependence of Israel on the outside world, the poverty of written literature and textbooks in Hebrew, makes English speaking desirable both for the individual and for the community. Just as the dollar is the second currency of Israel, so Pinglish is a second language, strongly impregnated with Hebrew, and spoken in a Hebrew way, especially by Sabras.

Amongst older people Hebrew itself is subject to pidginization.

Dialectization of Hebrew

The tendency towards a ghetto community structure, and the presence in Israel of so many Tribes coming from so many different countries leads to a dialectization of Hebrew. It leads also to phonetic variations as the Hebrew language is written without vowels. Each Tribe develops its own Hebrew accent which is clearly and easily recognized. You can recognize a *Yekke* (German) from his accent and inflexion, as equally a Russian, a Pole, an Englishman, a Frenchman, a Yemenite or a North African Jew. A very interesting question is often raised: which of those accents should be regarded as truly representative of the language, from the points of view of the past and of the future. From the point of view of the past, the Yemenite is often regarded as the nearest to the ancient accent. From the point of view of the future, the Polish-Russian accent comes nearest to the accent of the Sabra with his strong guttural and throaty sounds.

The Effects of Multi-lingualism

Multilingualism is a major cultural factor, opening a window on the world at large, and opening Israel to cultural influences and cross currents. Books, periodicals, magazines and films from all parts of the world are available in great profusion in Israel, and even dramatic productions are in different languages. (Out of 25 daily papers, 9 are in foreign languages.) Of course this multilingualism has its own drawbacks and disadvantages. The need to use so many languages in daily life produces a certain wastage of intellectual effort and a certain jumpiness in thought. In Israel it is easy to realize what an important medium of thought, and what a basic instrument of cultural and inner development is a language thoroughly and fully mastered. A man compelled to use many languages during the day cannot develop intellectually and culturally so easily as a man who thinks in perfect and firmly established groves of thought. We think in linguistic terms and, when those terms become jumpy and variable, the thought process meets impediments which can be overcome only with considerable effort. Solecism can have a deep psychological effect, as an offence against grammar is easily transferred into an offence against logic. For the time being, Israel is a country of broken languages and these broken languages produce a general feeling of cultural inferiority. Anyway, the language situation in Israel is far removed from the conception of the word as Logos, the idea accepted on the same plot of land by those worshippers of the perfect, heavenly shaped and divinely inspired Word. But of course the time is yet short for a new Logos in Israel, as the melting pot is still hot.

The Impact of Hebrew on the Israeli Mentality

The impact of the Hebrew language on the mentality of the Israeli Jews is a subconscious process of considerable potency which cannot be easily discerned but only intuitively grasped. Hebrew was a liturgical language which still has a strong religious content, full of theological flavour, and of solemn and hallowed phrases. This language has now been turned into a vernacular, and colloquialism is the order of the day. In spite of this, the language is still full of echoes from the Tanakh, Talmud and Prayer Book, and it is certainly full of religious images and symbols. The most ordinary everyday words such as *Abba* (father), *Adoni* (sir), *Shem* (name), *Shma* (hear), *slicha* (sorry), *Mode Ani* (I thank you), *Havdala* (difference), *Zechut* (merit), *Kavanah* (tendency), *Tikun* (repair)—all of these have a religious connotation and evoke religious images and symbols. Archaic but graceful forms of expression such as, 'This finds favour in my eyes' which means, 'I like it', or, 'In a good hour', or, 'Without the evil eye' which simply means 'good luck', or 'his hope was not rained upon' for 'not fulfilled' (*lo nitgashma*), give a poetic tinge to everyday phraseology and express trends of thought and feeling belonging to a different age. Many such graceful and archaic turns of phrase adorn the new language, influencing unconsciously but deeply Jewish thought and feeling. The 'tutoyant' form of Hebrew in which everyone is addressed as Thou has a deep effect on the feeling of comradeship. The shortness of phrases in Hebrew, where often a whole sentence can be expressed in one word, also affects the mental make-up. The habit of writing from right to left, and the complete divergence of Hebrew from European languages in syntax and phonetics, makes for considerable insularity of the Sabra and his difficulty in learning other languages.

The strongly sex-conscious grammar of Hebrew is an expression of the principle of the separation of sexes in ancient Israel, and may have a subconscious influence on the mentality of its modern speakers. The same applies to patronymic forms such as 'father nature' instead of 'mother nature', or 'father of inventions' instead of 'mother of inventions', as in European languages, this being an expression of the patriarchial society of ancient Israel.

The ethical connotation of many terms, as for example the use of 'I did not merit' for 'I failed' or the root link between happiness and straightforwardness, is the expression of the strong ethical-religious character of a language in search and praise of the living God.

The Hebrew language, having been almost frozen for more than 2,000 years (already in Roman Palestine Aramaic was spoken more than Hebrew), retains something of the pristine naiveté of the ancient Tribes, of the poetry of the childhood of the race and of its folklore. This poetry and freshness of vision, and this yearning for the living God, are all expressed in the structure of the language.

While writing my lectures in Hebrew I could sense clearly that certain modes of interpretation and classification were suggested by specific terms of phraseology which differ from those of Indo-European languages. The thought itself, its organization and formulation, was affected by the character of the language.

It is interesting to note also the characteristic vocalization of the language. Many a stranger has noticed the disturbing sound of the many gutturals in Hebrew. The strongly guttural accentuation of the language as spoken by the Sabras expresses the stubbornness and tenacity of the native on his own soil. Hebrew has contributed to the moulding of the Sabra figure and vice versa. Hebrew speaking entails also a very decisive use of the voice, more so than, for instance, in speaking Yiddish in a soft undertone. One often hears, 'A hard language for hard people in a hard country.'

Further Prospects

This linguistic profusion, or shall we say confusion, as it exists at present in Israel, is a considerable handicap to the development of a genuine and deep culture. A nation of Hebrew stutterers, and we have to remember that the large majority of Israeli Jews are still first-generation immigrants, does not easily evolve a genuine cultural style. An enormous amount of mental energy is spent on struggling with the Hebrew language. A great deal of emotional energy is expended in fighting the sense of failure, frustration and inferiority felt by those who are unable to master the language. They get used to a crude mode of expression, stiff, forced and clumsy. They are cross with themselves, and feel that they are dropping below the level of former times. The danger of the corruption of words cannot be denied.

The Israelis are fighting very hard not to be provincial, not to be colonial in a cultural sense. Israeli youth is very eager to absorb international culture by cultivating foreign languages, primarily English. With the rise of educational standards, English is increasingly cultivated and Pinglish is increasingly used. If this trend continues, the country may move into a permanent system of a full quatro-lingualism with Hebrew, Yiddish, Arabic and English. Those four languages are strongly entrenched with no danger of losing ground, and are increasingly impinging on each other. Yiddish is the language of a large part of the Diaspora, both in the West and in the East, and its survival amongst the orthodox section of Israeli population seems certain. If Israel continues as a *de facto* bi-national State with its newly conquered territories, we can easily envisage a situation in which Arabic will be the language of the working class, Yiddish the language of the lower middle class, Hebrew the language of the middle-middle and upper-middle class, and English the language of the upper class.

So, viewing the foreseeable future, one can envisage both this quatro-lingualism, and also the continuation of multi-lingualism in one form or another. The Jewish people will not easily shed the languages they have acquired in their historical trek.

5.

The Journey in Time

LIVING in Israel is like moving in an animated museum of historical ethnology. The paradox of Israel is that, in its modern society, there are many fossilized remnants of arrested or moribund civilizations. There are various layers of civilization and culture referring to different parts of history, beginning with the Yemenite, the Kurdi, the Iraqui, the Syrian, the Persian and the Moroccan Jews, and then proceeding to more recent layers of the Diaspora. One can meet figures reminiscent of a patriarch riding on an ass, and also scenes as if re-enacted from medieval times. In a small gathering one can easily see all the historical layers presented here, so to speak, in living form. One sees how enormous is the conservative force of Judaism to have preserved, almost intact, so many living records of history.

In Israel one can see very clearly how misleading is the general scale of time. Different tribes and their sections (as, for instance, the Chassidim of the Mea Shearim in Jerusalem), live in different categories of time. Some tribes still live in the magical phase of historical development, others in the theological or metaphysical, and still others in the technological and scientific phase.

Time scales in Israeli society are subject to many operations and transformations, both for single Tribes and for the community as a whole.

First, there is the movement forward, the journey in time which many of the Tribes have to undertake suddenly in order to catch up with the twentieth century. The Yemenite Jews thought that the Messiah had brought them suddenly to the Promised Land and landed them overnight in the twentieth century. So they had to leap into this century completely unprepared. This leaping in time is a painful operation. To combine magic with modern technology, the primitive with the scientific, the dream with reality, produces a certain mélange not without confusion, schizophrenia, anxiety and guilt. The taking over or imitation of the values, standards, customs and habits of the ruling majority may produce imitative types lacking in integrity and stability Mimesis, as pointed out by Arnold Toynbee, often passes over into travesty.

Secondly, we have the change of time scale for the whole community. The relationship between the Jewish community in Israel and history undergoes a deep transformation. The Tribes have to recover not only a common territorial location but also a common location in time. The field of the collective consciousness is being related not only to the surrounding space, but also to time and history. In this way environment and time, space and time fall into one, into a new space-time continuum. This new space-time continuum must be common for all the Tribes, and therefore it must reach back in time to the period preceding the Diaspora, as the Diaspora experience differed for each single Tribe. In this way the present Israel becomes the Third Commonwealth as a direct descendant of the Second Commonwealth, which disappeared with the Roman Conquest; and one Jewish civilization is created, extending from its beginning until its consummation in present-day Israel.

The *Umwertung der Werte* in Jewish history means the overvaluation of certain periods, the periods spent in the Land of Israel, and at the same time the under-valuation of another period, the period of the two thousand years of the Diaspora. The Diaspora experience is, in the Israeli's interpretation of history, derogated and denigrated. It is not regarded as Jewish history as such, but rather as world history centring on Jewish distress, affliction and humiliation. It is passive not active Jewish history, where Jews were the victims of history not the actors in it.

This means the re-interpretation and rewriting of the Jewish past from a new vantage point. This re-interpretation will show that the Jews, as exiles, led an aimless and meaningless life. This new interpretation must show that the hub of Jewish history is the New State of Israel. It is the epitome of all that the Jew has achieved up to now, and therefore must provide a new frame of reference for the historian. This is the new vantage point of a history which is being rewritten for teaching in Israel. The Diaspora becomes equivalent to shame and humiliation. People want a return to times of glory, of active life, heroism, struggle and creativity. Massada[1] is the new symbol of Israel.

[1] The last outpost of resistance in the Jewish war against the Romans.

There is a streak of romanticism in this approach, not without some affectation. This romanticism is especially nourished by the Polish Jews, who possess much of the Polish national romanticism. Romanticism, after all, went hand in hand with 'historicism', and Israeli society at present lives in a state of heightened historical consciousness, a consciousness of historical roots going back to the land of their forefathers, and a consciousness of historical responsibility.

In this process of reshaping the past, the Israeli historian is faced with the immense problem of fusing the secular with the sacred. This is a very hard and most embarrassing task for a secular historian versed in modern historical research. The Jewish past in the Land of Israel was for the most part sanctified history, as recorded in the Bible. And so the process of reshaping the past assumes religious undertones, merging with the religious thought of Judaism. This trend is nothing new in Judaism. It goes very well with the basic character of Jewish religion and of Jewish ideology. The Jews were always regarded as the 'most historical nation', meaning not only the nation with the longest uninterrupted historical record, but also a nation with a strong historical consciousness. The Jew always regarded history as God's province, believing that a Divine purpose runs through his long and painful experience. The Jew first developed the conception of hallowing history by raising and translating it into religion, and a great part of the Jewish religion is sanctified history.

A paragraph of the Passover Service reads: 'Every Jew should regard himself as if he had personally gone forth out of Egypt', and this is partially true. Thus history continuously shapes the Jewish mind. Judaism is not only a religion, but also a philosophy of history which reads into history God's will and purpose. And in the resurrection of the ancient State of Israel the Jew can find again justification for his beliefs, for his belief in Providence which has kept its promise to gather in the Tribes from all corners of the world. The religious Jew feels that his faith in the Promise has been fully rewarded. The secular Jew who has ceased to treat the Bible as a storehouse of divine revelation finds himself confused and perplexed, wishing to give credit for the Return to the nationalist movement, to the Zionist policy, to diplomacy and sheer effort.

This process of the reshaping of the Jewish past is not without protest from many quarters, not without pain and bewilderment. The Jewish immigrant finds himself alienated from his immediate past, and in fact from the historical experience of the last two thousand years. Two thousand years are simply wiped out as meaningless and worthless. It means that the process of reshaping the Jewish past to suit the Israeli society, involves the resurrection of time on the one hand, and its death on the other. It means a total revision of the time scale, of time notation and of time sequence.

There is one more aspect of the revision of the time scale in the Jewish historical consciousness. The time scale needs revision also in relation to the future. The glorious past must be confronted with the future. Massada is a symbol not only of the past but also of the future. It means not only a dedication to make the desert bloom, but also one to make sure that nobody and nothing will ever again drive the Jew from the Promised Land.

The Israeli Jews have to make up for this lost time. And in fact, judging from the experience of the Israelis during the last generation, no one can deny that they have moved very fast, as if to recoup this lost time. The first thing one can say about Israeli society is that it is baffling in its growth and creativity, as if all the bottled up forces and joys of self-expression and self-fulfilment had suddenly been let loose. The Israeli, with a heightened historical consciousness, cannot live only for the present. He has to justify his existence before the genius of history.

And in fact he has made history, turning Israel, to the astonishment of the world, into the dominant power of the Middle East, dominant not only in military terms but also in economic and technical terms. In previous economic periods, such a power would have built an empire, stretching from the Nile to the Euphrates, like the great empires of Islam. But the time of empire building on a local scale—with UNO and the two superpowers in control of world events—is over, and the Jews, with their ethnical exclusiveness, are no Empire builders.

No less baffling are the achievements of Israel in the internal development of economy, in terms of technology, irrigation, sanitation, town and country planning, road building, social services, etc.

In one generation, Israel has moved from the position of an under-developed country into that of a near-developed country, and what is even more significant has been able to give substantial help and assistance to other under-developed countries.

This hurried movement forward in terms of economics and technology does not go on without great strains and stresses, nor without danger for the future. Foremost among them is the danger of what is called Levantinism which is a product of this hurriedly made journey forward and which large sections of the population in Israel are in danger of. It means adopting the paraphernalia of the twentieth century without the real cultural values of the West. For large sections of the population, Western-ization is a process of form rather than of substance, consisting of the imitation of a culture for which they are little equipped by virtue of education, mentality or tradition.

Reviewing these two main hurried journeys in time, the one journey into history, stretching back two thousand years, and the other a journey forward in technology and economics, we can say that the main strains and stresses of Israeli society derive largely from the contradictions arising between these two jour-neys, both undertaken at a very great speed. The historical journey is an expedition into the childhood of the race which feeds itself on child's food; the journey in terms of technology and economics is a strenuous march into full maturity. The combination of childhood dreams with the prospects of the atomic age is no mean task. In fact it is a formidable undertaking, which has still to prove itself.

6.

Transformation of Identity and Self-Image

IT IS an old experience that the identity and self-image of a
person can be radically changed by a new location, by a permanent
change in residence. A man moves from, say, London to Tel-
Aviv, and his identity and self-image, self-evaluation and self-
placement are radically affected. To start with, his Jewishness,
whatever that may mean, which was repressed and depressed in
London, which consciously played only a small part in his
personality in England, now expands in depth and width, being
amplified and magnified out of all recognition. What was previously reduced, is now being restored to its normal size, or rather
becoming actually oversized. Let us assume the index of Jewishness in a Jew's personality as 100; in England it was perhaps 30,
but in Israel it is likely to be raised to 100, and in due time even
above that to an inflated figure of let us say 130. On the other
hand the 'Englishness' of the English Jew which was in England
highly developed becomes reduced and in due time may gradually
evaporate.

A Jew coming to Israel changes his language, his reading, his
aspirations, his allegiance, his friends, often his class, his work
and his hobbies, and in fact assumes a new identity. He reviews
his previous life in a new light, minimizing some parts which do
not seem to coincide with his present identity, while on the
other hand he enlarges and highlights other bits of his life which
he hitherto regarded as meaningless and unimportant, giving
them a new meaning and significance from the new vantage
point. He reshapes his past, he rewrites his biography, much as
an historian in a new revolutionary State rewrites the history of
his country from the vantage point of the new regime. Placing
himself in a new environment is for the immigrant a revolution,
a new vantage point in his personality, from which he reshapes
and reinterprets his past. His past is altered as much as his future
will be altered. His past is made to fit his new identity. What

could have been an embarrassment in England, is an asset to be proud of in Israel. His new mates, friends and neighbours ask him: has he been persecuted as a Jew, has he supported Jewish causes, has he been a Zionist, has he received a Jewish education, does he know Jewish literature and so on? A local pressman, if he were to interview him, would ask the same questions. And he also asks himself those questions, searching for every scrap of fact which can support his standing among his fellow citizens. In a way the new immigrant undergoes a sort of conversion, a conversion to become an Israeli Jew, a more nationalistic type of Jew.

The past needs reinterpretation also from the standpoint of his new social status. The immigrant does not fit into exactly the same social stratum in the new society as in the previous one. His new rank is usually below that enjoyed in his native country. While in England he might have been an independent shopkeeper or industrialist, in Israel he is more likely to become a wage- or salary-earner. In this respect also he has to reorientate himself and often assumes a new identity as a member of a new social class. In his native country he may have been Conservative or Liberal in politics, but in Israel he will be more frequently Labour, belonging to one of the four labour parties, mostly those in power. Here again he has to search in his past history for any sign of sympathy for parties and ideologies which have been basically foreign to him, but which he could have supported in a marginal way at one time or another, let us say in adolescence. He discovers in himself new potentialities and new allegiances.

Also his basic habits and customs undergo changes according to the requirements of a new climate, a new environment and new conditions. In this respect also he will be searching for all the pointers in the past which he could interpret as leading to these new habits, so as to keep the continuity of his personality intact. He might have had those habits in his adolescence or early youth, and now he remembers and resuscitates them, as points of reference in his personal history.

Often this new identity is simply regarded as the rediscovering of oneself, or the rediscovering of one's true self, or a coming back to the fold, or as a returning to one's earlier self in adolescence, when the ego was still very pliable, where one can discover traces pointing to various lines of development.

This metamorphosis of identity is often sealed by the shedding of one's own name and the assuming of a new Hebrew name A new name is a common experience in all kinds of conversion. In the Old Testament Abram was renamed Abraham when he was visited by Jehovah, and Jacob, after fighting with the angel, Israel; in the New Testament, Levi became Matthew, and Saul became Paul. Many settlers assume new Hebrew names, both family and first names to make a clean sweep, to underline the new identity, to assume a new image and self-image. A new-born man is emerging in Israel, so he does not even need to reinterpret his past, as the past is blotted out as insignificant or without meaning. 'Thou shalt be called Shraga not Alfred, and thy family name shall be Zahavi instead of Gold.'

To the miracle of Israel a new personal miracle is added, the emergence of a new personality for the immigrant. His self-definition is based on Israel, and the Israeli society with its values and standards becomes his new frame of reference and his new centre of values. In this he will be supported by Israeli society, which will try to provide him with new symbols for his new identity and new self-image.

The Hebraization of his name is what the anthropologists call a *rite of passage* which implies the repudiation of an old, and the assumption of a new identity. The psychologists and psychotherapists often call this transformation therapy or commitment therapy, when a man who was previously without faith and commitment assumes a new commitment, in this case a national Israeli commitment. Amongst Carl Jung's followers this commitment therapy would be regarded as a worthwhile and commendable experience. In support of this view I should mention here that several immigrants highly praised their new existence as a regeneration, as a creative re-creation of their personality, which gave a new meaning to their life.

As a new man the immigrant will be witnessing in himself certain psychological symptoms usually associated with youth. As a newly converted or rediscovered Israeli Jew, he is 'a baby' who needs education, training and guidance. He has a lot to learn, not only the language, but also the symbols, values and standards of a new society and new culture. In the Ulpan (a boarding school for new immigrants), where he will learn the language, he will also learn new songs, which he will sing in a group like children do. Actually an Ulpan is not only a school

of language but also an instrument of indoctrination and acculturation, and therefore it requires residence. In his own process of
rediscovery, he goes back to his childhood and adolescence, as
already said. He has to prove himself anew, as a young man does.
He has to achieve a position of his own, to acquire a niche of his
own, starting almost from scratch. He needs to mobilize all his
energy, he needs enthusiasm, and he starts with enthusiasm, with
hope for the future. He feels rejuvenated all round, until frustration and disappointment dampen down and mar his efforts. The
newness of his position excites him and he is full of wonder and
curiosity, like a child. He visits new places which may seem not
quite real to him, and like a child he discovers his new self in
this new environment. Others may address him in a way which
reminds him of his treatment in childhood; people speak slowly
to him and explain things to him. When he blunders or commits
an offence, he is forgiven because of ignorance. In fact he
experiences all the psychological symptoms of youth.

Of course, this process of self-transformation and self-definition
is not without internal struggles and opposition. It is often felt
as a betrayal of one's part, of one's self, of what was regarded
as Self. The question arises straight away, whether what was felt,
professed and believed in the past was genuine or only hypocritical
conformity, whether a man, who sheds his old identity, used in
the past to deceive himself as well as others? What was the
degree of his sincerity in the past, and where is the degree of
sincerity greater, in the old or the new identity? A certain
schizophrenia develops from this division and a sense of guilt
may also follow.

In this way we may find an explanation why so many good
Zionists and Israelis turn back, after a long time spent in Israel,
to their past, investing it with new emotional colours. Thus
Polish Jews, who can hardly now speak Polish, are suddenly
happy when they hear Polish spoken, and so the newcomer from
Poland can at once establish contact with older settlers from
Poland the moment he starts speaking Polish.

The past is shed at first, as it hinders the new identity, but
when that new identity is firmly established, there follows a re-
definition, finer and more balanced, in which the past is no longer
repudiated, but rather integrated in a truer way, forming a synthesis between old and new.

The transformation just now described may be complete: or it may be only selective and partial, tentative and incomplete, if the immigrant proceeds slowly and cautiously, and does not anticipate his full conversion. Complete transformation requires a special kind of personality endowed with great flexibility, an ability to bend with the wind, an ability to change course in mid-stream. Such a transformation makes great demands on the individual. Not only is there a problem of learning, but also a problem of forgetting, of the shedding of early acquired values and outlooks. In a way it is a new pattern of relations, a new relation to time and history, to place and geography. The immigrant defines the role of Israel and Judaism, and he defines his own role in relation to Israel and Judaism.

This complete transformation is easier for the very young and the very old. For the very young, because they have a small part of life to rewrite, and their commitment is not yet over-formed. For the very old, because their identity is really finished, and the new commitment does not matter much at the end of life. The most difficult task is for those of middle age as alienation from their former adulthood may involve discontinuity and anxiety about the obsolescence of a major part of their life.

The complete transformation is easier for non-assimilated Jews than for fully assimilated. It is also easier for those who come from culturally less developed countries than for those who come from centres of high culture. English, American, and German Jews find the process very difficult as well as painful, because they have been socialized and assimilated much more thoroughly than the Jews of other countries. They cling emotionally to their past identity, of which they are proud, much more strongly and for longer than the others. They are inclined to believe that their cultural heritage as linked with their past identity is of a higher value than the one they are going to acquire. And this painful process provides the explanation why so few Anglo-Saxon Jews venture into Israel. It is commonly assumed that the lack of Anglo-Saxon Jewish immigrants is due to the differences in standards of living. In fact, psychological hindrances may be of greater significance and importance. If somebody has an identity of which he is proud, if he has a past which is dear to him, if he is already committed to his own native country, he is not likely to throw all that overboard and become *Shraga Zahavi*.

Of course there are instances where the new immigrant does not shed his former identity and remains what he was, clinging tenaciously to his past. But, in that case, he will be alienated in the new country, and remain a stranger. I met a number of immigrants who felt that way. These were not in most cases voluntary immigrants, but rather compulsory ones, stranded on the shores of Israel by the stormy currents of history.

On the other hand, there are also cases where the new and the old identity exist together side by side, neither repudiating the other, but rather being superimposed one on the other, constantly shifting and expressing themselves with varying strength in different circumstances. In this way a new syncretism and a new amalgam of personality is formed, often not a very well integrated one. The immigrant 'keeps up with the Joneses', tries to reach the people around him, to learn to live with them without a feeling of isolation and alienation. At the same time he keeps his past to himself without trying to develop a new image or self-image. But such a position can easily produce anxiety, guilt and a split personality.

One very disturbing aspect of this transformation of identity is the transformation of the marginality of the new immigrant. In his own country, he often found himself on the margin of the dominant social groupings, but he was in the centre of Jewish affairs in that country. In Israel he often finds himself a marginal man all round, being on the margin of the dominant social groupings in Israel which are formed chiefly by the veterans and the old-established élite. Being on the margin of Israeli affairs is concomitant with being on the margin of Jewish affairs as well, and this he finds much more difficult to endure. It was easier to be a marginal man in the Gentile affairs, than to be a marginal man in Jewish affairs. His insignificance in this field is more hurtful.

One hundred per cent Israelism has not yet been achieved even by the Sabra and it is very doubtful whether it ever will be achieved; it is even more difficult for the immigrant to acquire such a complex of Israeli cultural values, which in many ways differ from those in the Diaspora.

The process of the transformation of identity would be easier, if Israel could learn to cherish the enriching complexity of the cultural values of the Diaspora.

7.

The Basic Myths of Israel

THE HORIZON of Israeli society is studded with a whole constellation of myths, both religious and secular. I use the term *myth* in the sociological sense, meaning sanctified or hallowed belief patterns accepted by society at large and referring to suprarational or supernatural events or relationships. It is a technical term which excludes any value judgements, i.e., any statement about the factual truth of the beliefs or of their social and moral value. Myths have both cognitive and evaluative elements with a strong emotional tone; they are related to religion, history or politics, and they are relevant to the life-interests of the community. They are often fused in complex ideological belief systems. They are almost blindly and to a large degree subconsciously accepted by the members of the community. National claims, needs or grievances are substantiated or justified by reference to those myths. They form, to use Talcott Parsons' term, 'an orientic framework', for the basic value orientations.[1]

The peculiarity of Israeli myths is the close fusion of national, historical and religious elements. A purely religious myth often has a historical wrapping, and also a political elaboration with a practical conclusion. Israeli myths refer primarily to the relationship between the Book, the Land and the people of Israel, and also to the relationship between Israel and the Diaspora. They proclaim the holiness of the three basic eternal elements of Jewish destiny, the Book, the Land, and the people of Israel, they proclaim also the priority of Israel over the Diaspora. Let us review some of the myths of Israel one by one.

The Myth of the Holy Book

This myth proclaims that the Bible is a Holy Book, linked in a supernatural way with the people of Israel who produced it, and with the land of Israel which nurtured it. As Ben Gurion said in

[1] Talcott Parsons *The Social System*. Free Press, Glencoe. New York 1951.

his article 'The Spirit of New Israel'[1]: the Book has been up-rooted from the Land and came back to the Land. The Land was given back not only to the Tribes of Israel but also to the Book, so that now a happy and normal relationship exists between the three elements in the Holiness of Israel. The Book forms the source for other myths, provides a central focus for the mytho-logical or mythical 'reality.

The Myth of the Holy Land

This myth proclaims a supra-rational relationship between the Land of Israel and the Tribes of Israel. The land was promised in the Covenant to the Tribes of Israel, and is a holy possession of the Jews. Their claim is eternal and sacred and they cannot be divested of their rights. Only possession was lost, as the Jews were exiled, not the ownership itself.

The Myth of the Redemption

This myth proclaims the redemption of the Land, of the Tribes and of the Book. The Land has been redeemed from waste and neglect as well as from occupation by foreigners who did not care for it or know how to use it. The redemption of the Tribes of Israel took place by the re-possession of their heritage. Equally the Book, as we said previously, was redeemed. Having been 'imprisoned in a material and spiritual Ghetto' (Ben Gurion), it came back into its own, regaining its natural habitat. This triune unity of the Land, the Tribes, and the Book will be the starting point for the Integral Redemption yet to come.

The Myth of the Continuity of Israel

The Jews of present-day Israel are the direct descendants of the ancient Tribes of Israel and there is an unbroken continuity between them. The Third Jewish Commonwealth as built now by Israel is the direct successor of the Second Commonwealth destroyed by the Romans. The ancient Tribes known as Israel are those who were bound by the Covenant, a sort of Holy Pact as described in the Bible.

[1] See *Israel: Its Role in Civilization*, ed. Moshe Davis, p. 21. Harper Bros. New York 1956.

The Myth of the Return

This myth proclaims that the conquest or reconquest of the Land is not a simple act of colonization but an act of Return. The Return of the exiles is similar to the first Return from Babylon. The Jews never fully relinquished the Land. They lived in the Land in such numbers as were allowed by the occupying Power. The Law of Return which is the basic Law of the State of Israel proclaims that every Jew has the right to settle in Israel and can immediately claim citizenship rights. As he only returns to his land, he can claim back his home and his ancient citizenship.

The Myth of Fulfilment

The prophecy about the restoration of the Tribes has been fulfilled, and the truth of the prophetic vision of the Bible has been fully vindicated. The State of Israel came into being as the fulfilment of Divine Prophecy, irrespective of the factors which worked to make this prophecy come alive.

The Myth of the Exile

This myth proclaims not only that those Jews who returned to the Land were exiles, but also that all Jews who remain outside Israel are in fact exiles. Their homeland is Israel, and their duty is in and for Israel. Israel, as the homeland, can claim the devotion, loyalty and support of all Jews in all countries. If they support Israel, they support only their home, to which they belong. From this follows the conception that Israel is part of the World Jewry and must be considered as such. In this light Israel becomes a financially, economically and culturally viable and strong State, as the resources which World Jewry can muster for Israel may be added to her own resources.

The Myth of the Special Creativity of Israel

The coming together of the three elements, the Book, the Land, and the Tribes, is bound to produce an extraordinary release of creative energy in Israel not dissimilar to the creative energy of the Second Commonwealth. Moses Hess, Herzl, Achad-Haam, Bialik, Weizmann, Ben Gurion and many others have often expressed this belief that the genius of Israel will flower again in fullest bloom the moment that the Tribes of Israel are restored to the Land. To quote only Achad-Haam:

If all these scattered powers were assembled within our borders and worked in the interest of our national culture, as was formerly the case, there is no doubt that this culture would be one of the richest and most original in the world.

The restoration would mean also the resurrection of the spirit and the soul of Israel. The Tribes which claimed their material heritage would claim also their spiritual heritage.

The Myth of the State of Israel as the Embodiment of Jewry

The State of Israel is the embodiment of Jewry at large. It is the natural representative, sponsor and defender of the Jewish people all over the world. This position was most clearly stated in the trial of Adolph Eichmann in Jerusalem, who was tried *inter alia* for 'crimes against the Jewish people' as defined in the Nazis and Nazi Collaborators Law of 1950. Israel is also a recipient for all the rights and claims of world Jewry *vis-à-vis* other countries. A country which owes something to Jewry at large, owes it to Israel. This claim was implied in the Jewish German reparation agreements. Germany owed restitution not only to the victims and their heirs, but also to the State of Israel which embodies and represents Jewry at large.

The Myth of the Founding Fathers

Two entirely different categories make up the Founding Fathers of Israel. The first category was formed by pioneers who prepared the ground for further waves of immigration, and by fighters for Israeli independence in the Arab Revolt of the thirties and in the War of Independence. The new State, the State as such (not the Return), has been paid for, as any other State, by toil, sweat and blood, and was born by the force of arms in an armed contest. The Day of Independence is celebrated proudly and gaily as the most important annual festival, and is the symbol of this victory which made the State possible.

The second category of the Founding Fathers was formed by the victims of the Holocaust, and survivors of the concentration camps. The State of Israel is the direct successor and inheritor of the Gas Chambers, of the Warsaw Ghetto and of the Jewish blood and tears which marked the reign of terror in Europe. The State of Israel not only inherited the human material surviving from the concentration camps, it not only received reparations from West Germany, but the whole recognition of its existence by the United Nations was bound up with the sympathy the world felt for these helpless victims. A sense of guilt for what was done in a Christian country has largely contributed to the re-emergence of Israel. The war of liberation was won not only by Jewish courage, determination and resourcefulness but also by a generous flow of volunteers and of help from all over the world.

And so alongside the pioneer and the hero appear also the victim and the martyr of the Holocaust as Founding Fathers of the new State. In the same decade the greatest triumph of Jewry, the establishment of a free and independent State, followed closely on its greatest tragedy, the annihilation of one-third of the biological stock in continental Europe. The National Day of Mourning for the victims and martyrs of the Holocaust, celebrated as a festival of mourning, and followed closely by the Day of Independence, which is celebrated as a festival of joy, are the outward symbols of this double nature in the conception of Founding Fathers. The mournful festival of Remembrance, which means remembering the event and making sure that it will never happen again, and the joyous festival, a sort of resurrection of the martyrs, the positive answer to the perpetual threat overhanging future generations, are closely linked with each other. The hero and the martyr form a unique ideological combination as the most significant and deepest symbols of national awareness. The hero figure calls for readiness and vigilance, while the martyr figure calls for humanity, compassion and world co-operation. Not far from the grave and monument of Herzl on Mount Herzl stands the monument to the martyrs, Yad Vashem on the Mount of Remembrance.

The Myth of 'Solving the Jewish Question'

Zionism as a movement was very largely nourished by antisemitism, and Herzl's programme for a *Judenstaat* sprang largely from the Dreyfus affair and Lueger's policy in Vienna. The return of the Tribes was only partly voluntary. About 80–90 per cent of Jewish immigrants came to Israel involuntarily or largely involuntarily, squeezed out or expelled or expropriated or sent direct from the concentration camps. With each wave of anti-semitism, Israel developed and flourished. If a new wave of anti-semitism broke out in the West or in Russia, Israel would gain a new lease of life, expanding both in population and in capital investment.

The myth widely accepted in Israel is that anti-semitism presents a permanent, although intermittent, feature of the Diaspora, which is going to be re-enacted again and again. It has nothing to do with social structure (as shown by the example of Russia), national character or politics. It has deeper sources which flare up from time to time. Therefore, Israel is a necessity as a haven and refuge for the Jewish masses, namely for those who will be persecuted in future. So it is obviously sensible for anyone who wants to prevent the persecution of his descendants, to settle in Israel. That is the only way to 'solve the Jewish question' once and for all.

The Centrality of Israel

This myth proclaims the centrality of Israel for World Jewry. Israel, which 'regards itself as the creation of the entire Jewish people' (as the Law of 24 November 1952 proclaims), may in turn re-create the entire Jewish people. Israel must be regarded as the hub of world Jewry, providing the basic focus of identification and self-identification for Jews everywhere. This aspect is most important in an age of increasing assimilation for Jews in the Diaspora. Israel is the answer to the search for new identity by Jews who find themselves in a vacuum following the weakening of the old religious beliefs. Israel is also the image maker for the Jewish people, presenting to the world and to the Jews themselves a new and genuine prototype of a rejuvenated and regenerated Jew, free from the servitude of the past.

The Myth of the 'Fuller Jewish Life'

The Jew cannot live a full Jewish life except in Israel. Anyone who wants to live a full and free Jewish life or what is often termed 'a fuller Jewish life' ought to settle in Israel. Anywhere else the Jew must find himself under restraint and can live only a partial Jewish life, compelled to compromise with the values of his Gentile environment. Only in Israel can he unfold his Jewishness to the full without concern for anything or anybody.

These are the main myths of Israeli society, all somewhat related and forming a consistent corpus of ideas and sentiments. As Bronislaw Malinowski said, 'Myth is not merely a story told but a reality lived . . . believed to have once happened in primeval times and continuing ever since to influence the world and human destinies'.[1] For the Jews who came to Israel, their myths were a living reality, and they largely influenced their lives and actions. Such myths were the 'idees-forces' of Fouilleé,[2] and they are active today in a hundred-and-one ways.

The Israeli myths are open to innumerable interpretations, messaianic-mystic, religious-traditional, political and cultural. For some the myths are a simple affirmation of fact; for others they are an expression of Authority, of the Divine Will; for yet others they are a derivation of tradition and national sentiments; for still others hallowed allegories of Jewish fate and destiny. However, for everybody, the myths form a shorthand record of the aspirations, ideals and ideas which have inspired and still inspire Israeli society.

Of course all myths can be easily misread, misunderstood and misrepresented. A study of myths demands not only great insight and familiarity with the ethos and the spirit of the people, but also sympathy and empathy. However, no one can misread the basic myths of Israel in one respect. The shorthand meaning of all the myths can be summarized in one belief, the belief in the uniqueness and miraculousness of Israel. This is the arch-myth of the Israeli society, an arch-myth which has considerable factual and historical support in the lightning speed of the emergence of the new State. The State was the outcome of innumerable small and large events, which no one could have expected or foreseen. It was born out of incredible coincidences, insignificant in themselves, but highly significant in their combination. Its survival hung for a long time in the balance. Paradoxically, the enemies of the Jews had a large share in establishing the State.

---

[1] *Myth in Primitive Psychology.* Kegan Paul. London 1926.

[2] Alfred Fouilleé, *La Psychologie des idées-forces.* Part of *Bibliothèque de philosophie contemporaine,* Paris 1893.

The Arabs themselves play also a large part in keeping the Jewish society strong and united. Also the State of Israel is founded on a site of which many miracles have been reported and accepted as such by millions of Jews and non-Jews outside Israel. In fact quite a number of Israeli myths are accepted almost at their face value by millions of Jews and non-Jews outside Israel. This is what is often called the Zion Mystique, a mystique centred around the Mount of Zion.

The myths recorded previously have considerable functional value for the Israeli society, both manifest and latent. First of all they are factors towards social and national integration, a means of forging the various mixed Tribes into one nation. They are elements of stability, for they form the foundation for basic value orientation of the society. Their functional value consists also in the justification of the State of its rights and claims in the struggle for survival with the Arabs, and in mobilizing the sympathy of the Christian world and other international support. They are also instrumental in forming Jewish opinion, and encouraging Jewish immigration and Jewish financial support.

Their functional value consists also in their creation of an atmosphere of optimism, that in spite of everything, in spite of all the perils and blunders and muddle within, Israel will win through somehow, at the last minute, saved from the abyss by Providence. One could say that Israel is a society of optimists, which may seem surprising to outside observers who might think that the bitter experience of the past would have created sworn pessimists. The optimism inspired by these myths is of great value just because Israeli citizens are faced with so many inherent dangers, insecurities and frustrations both within and without. It is the sort of blindness which enables a sleepwalker to stop on the edge of a precipice. This optimism is the heritage of a persecuted race and has a survival value as well as a spiritual quality ('rejoice!'), but in Israel it is much more pronounced than in the Diaspora.

This belief in the miraculousness and uniqueness of Israel provides an enormous challenge and opportunity and is instrumental in many ways. Even the Arabs themselves are not entirely free from this myth. Who knows whether the Arabs, who also believe in the Old Testament as the Holy Book, do not fear the hopelessness of their struggle against the fulfilment of Prophecy, which has to be accepted as the Divine Will. But this belief in the miraculousness and uniqueness of Israel has at the same time a considerable dysfunctional value, with many inherent dangers, pitfalls and drawbacks.

It may be a source of fanaticism, intolerance, recklessness and disregard of commonsense. The leaning towards fanaticism, a very old trait in Judaism, is an endemic feature of Israel. The reliance on Providence may lead to a disregard of the common rules of economic life (the so-called economic laws) as not applicable to the land of the miraculous. The mythology can be interpreted as a stricture on commonsense, rationality and practicality—and in fact, by many Israelis coming from backward countries, it is being interpreted in a crude and childish way.

Mythology can bring Israeli society into a climate of mental childhood. The tendency to go back in time to the childhood of the race is very strong, as the whole society has to go back in time to link the Third with the Second Jewish Commonwealth. Many features of Israeli society cannot be understood otherwise, but only by reference to the atmosphere of childhood, which is encouraged by Israeli mythology. Israeli society is a unique mixture of the very old and the very new, of the sacred and the profane, of reality and dreams, of fact and fantasy, of maturity and childhood, of the abstract-analytical and the demonic-visionary, of the acquisitive society and theocracy. It is not only a mixture in the sense of the combination of values but also in the sense of polarity, meaning by this that those values appear in a forceful, striking and dynamic form. And the dynamism of each of these elements seems to be not only strong but trapped within itself, i.e., unreleasable.

The irreligious, realistic, down-to-earth Sabras are not very happy about the weight of these myths on the shoulders of Israeli society. They have a very ambivalent attitude towards the value of those myths. They would like to develop the Israeli State as a down-to-earth society without excessive claims and without excessive responsibility, just like any other normal State. The claims which are imposed by the myths seem to them too romantic, too sentimental, too irrational and supra-rational, and they feel that no society can live up to the claims which they invoke. Such claims have bred only misery for Jews in the past, and they will lead into misery again. However, even the Sabras cannot divest themselves of one thing, the heritage of the Holy Book, and, once the Book is accepted, many other things follow. So the People of the Book cannot escape the grip of the high drama presented by the Holy Book on one hand and the Holy Land on the other.

The Jewish people in its long history was always moving along two parallel axes, quite opposite to each other, one along the axis of the greatest probability, the other along the axis of the greatest improbability.[1] The defeats, the persecutions, the expulsions were the events occurring along the axis of the greatest probability; the rescue, the revival, the renewal and the rejuvenation occur along the axis of the greatest improbability. Those who have wanted to destroy the Jews considered one axis only, convinced that the movement of Jewish history along this axis is the whole story. Therefore, they have regarded the Jews as an easy prey for their aggression, while the Jews themselves know that, while they can be easily defeated along this axis, there is always the other axis waiting for their renewal. Perhaps this consciousness, deeply ingrained in their minds, is responsible for the operation of the second axis. Only those who expect miracles get them. The Jews have a strong consciousness of directive history, which carries them along the axis of greatest improbability according to the sense and meaning with which they have endowed their history. Both apolcalypticists and millenarists have abounded in Jewish history, the former belonging to the first axis, the latter to the second.

The uniqueness of Jewish history comes from the simultaneous operation of these axes. The weakest and most powerless people shows the strongest power of survival and regeneration, the most humiliated and persecuted has great historical claims springing from the joint operation of both axes.

[1] I use here Teilhard de Chardin's terms for considering the history of mankind. (*The Phenomenon of Man*, tr. Bernard Wall *et al.* Collins. London 1959.)

8.

'Religionality' – The Nationalization of Religious Culture

IT IS POSSIBLE to discuss the nationalization of religious culture in Israel at two levels: at the official level of close unity between religion and the State and at the level of a spontaneous process of secularization of religion into what may be called 'Land-religion', in which veneration of the Land forms the focal point. The transformation of Jewish religion in Israel into what I call 'religionality', i.e., a religion merged with nationhood and closely linked with statehood, may be regarded as one of the most remarkable dialectical processes in Israeli society. Zionism was a secular, in fact an anti-clerical doctrine[1] which from the beginning invoked the hostility of the religious leaders, especially of the orthodox wing. But Israel, which was founded by Zionism, turned more and more into a religious State, i.e., a State linked organically with a dominant religion. This transformation has been brought about by the force of circumstances of Jewish life.

We can see a parallel to this development for instance in the process of urbanization. Zionism was primarily a rural and anti-

[1] Chaim Weizmann in his *Trial and Error* writes on p. 569, 'I think it is our duty to make it clear to them from the very beginning that whereas the State will treat with the highest respect the true religious feelings of the community, it cannot put the clock back by making religion the cardinal principle in the conduct of the State. Religion should be relegated to the synagogue and the home of those families that want it, it should occupy a special position in the schools; but it shall not control the ministries of State. . . . There will be a great struggle. I foresee something which will perhaps be reminiscent of the *Kulturkampf* in Germany but we must be firm if we are to survive; we must have a clear line of demarcation between legitimate religious aspirations and the duty of the State towards preserving such aspirations on the one hand, and on the other hand the lust for power which is sometimes exhibited by pseudo-religious groups.' (Hamish Hamilton. London 1949.)

urban doctrine but force of circumstances deflected Israel from its programme of rural development into a process of accelerated urbanization. Similarly the socialist programme of the pioneers became more and more deflected into nationalist channels and the socialist State became more and more capitalistic. The nationalization of the Israeli society was bound to affect both its socialist and religious culture.

This dialectical movement in the field of religion is primarily responsible for the strong contradictions and contrasts which characterize the Israeli religious scene. These are the contrasts between fundamentalism and growing secularism, between archaic legalism and living Judaism, between religious 'Statism' and religious party politics.

The problems of Jewish religion in Israel can be viewed perhaps more clearly under the following heads:

(i) Religion and the State of Israel
(ii) Religion and the Land of Israel
(iii) Religion and Party Politics
(iv) Religious Observance
(v) Religion and World Judaism
(vi) Religion and Social Class
(vii) The Secularization of Jewish Religion

(i) *Religion and the State of Israel*

The Jewish religion is the State Religion *par excellence*. Israel considers herself as a Jewish-nation State,[1] however, with this proviso that it is a State of those who profess Jewish religion not Jewish nationality. Religion is the only criterion of Jewishness. The definition of the Jew is based on elements of ascription with a combination of elements of profession (see next chapter 'Who is a Jew?'). According to the laws of Israel citizens may contract a marriage or divorce only before the religious courts of their own denomination. Jews must be married by a Rabbi, Moslems by a Kadi, Christians in their Church and so on. Mixed marriages are not recognized.[2] Civil marriages do not exist. The offspring

---

[1] The Declaration of Independence of 14 May 1948 speaks about 'the establishment of a Jewish State in Eretz-Israel'.

[2] The State of Israel is transgressing the Article 16. (I) of the Universal Declaration of Human Rights of 10 December 1948, according to which people have the right to marry irrespective of creed, race or nationality.

of mixed marriage contracted abroad, if the mother was non-Jewish, or was not properly converted by an orthodox Rabbi, is regarded as non-Jewish. The existing rules often force a father and his son to belong to two different ethno-religious communities as for instance in the case of a Russian-born family of the name Akbitz, whose son was considered against his will as non-Jewish because the mother was not formally converted by an orthodox Rabbi.

The Jewish religion has at its disposal the full power of the State. The two chief Rabbis, one for the Ashkenazi, the other for the Sephardic (Oriental community) are the dignitaries of the State. The highest religious authority is vested in the Rabbinical Council composed of the chief Rabbis and six associate Rabbis elected in an Electoral Assembly from a list of 42 Rabbis and 28 laymen. The Council exercises supervision over local rabbinical offices acting as rabbinical Courts of the first instance and also serves as a Court of Appeal from the rabbinical Courts.

The scope of activities of the State in the field of Jewish religious and communal life can be gathered from the schema of organization of the Ministry of Religious Affairs. Apart from departments for Moslem, Druse and Christian religion, it has three departments dealing with Jewish religious affairs: Rabbinate and Rabbinical Courts; Religious Councils; Department of Jewish Religious Affairs. The latter has six sections: (i) Religious Culture section, (ii) The Holy Places section, (iii) Contact with the Diaspora section, (iv) The Public Service section, which supervises the Kashrut (the observation of dietary laws) in the armed forces, hospitals and public institutions and also meat imports from abroad, (v) The Immigrants' section, which organizes the religious life of the settlers, (vi) The Religious Institutions section, supervising the religious schools and Yeshivot (Religious Academies).

We see how large is the range of the State religious regime in Israel. We may describe it as a regime of etatization and centralization. As religion and State are one, the centralization of the State brings about the centralization of the regime.

Many Israelis feel that the close link between the State and religion has a distorting and corrupting influence on religious life in Israel, not very different from the corrupting influence of power on any religion. A number of cases of corruption in which dignitaries of the State dealing with religious matters were involved, give support to this view.

The marriage between State and religion is hardly a love affair on either side. It actually breeds distrust on both sides and there are frequent clashes between the interests of the State and the Orthodoxy in whose hands the control of religious affairs is concentrated. The representatives of the State are conscious that the Jewish religion, as it stands at present, has not adjusted itself to the requirements of the State and frequently hinders its progress and modernization, while the representatives of orthodox Judaism are not happy with the State either, regarding it as a secularization of the sacred. Actually Jewish religion as it stands now was formed in the Diaspora, adjusting itself to the dispersion, and it is more alive in the Diaspora than in Israel.

The close link between the State and religion in Israel, or rather the complete identification of the two, is strongly criticized by the Jews in the Diaspora who have always been in the forefront of the struggle for the separation of the State and religion. The institutional arrangements in Israel appear as a reflection on the sincerity of their own struggle. However, any attempt to separate the State and religion in Israel would be fraught with very great difficulties. First, because of strongly entrenched interests and old-established myths and claims accepted by the majority. Second, because of the very nature of the State as the State of Jewish people, which potentially includes the Diaspora.

In a Jewish State, i.e., the State of the Jews *qua* Jews, the structural segregation of State and religion is hardly possible. In a Jewish State the Jewish religion becomes by the nature of things a dominant religion and a dominant religion in a society must somehow come to terms with the problem of power and responsibility. A dominant religion must wield the power and, having power, must merge with the political structure of society. A dominant religion must claim an exclusive jurisdiction over personal and family status and must be able to decide who is to be regarded as a member of the dominant power group. Coercion and the use of force are the very ingredients of the dominant religion. The Jewish religious situation in Israel is one of the best illustrations of the sociological thesis of the clustering of social institutions, such as developed by Talcott Parsons.[1]

[1] *The Social System.* Free Press, Glencoe. New York 1951.

(ii) *Religion and the Land of Israel*

The geographical location of the Jewish faith presents many strange paradoxes. Jewish religion originated in the Land of Israel. This location was favourable to the formation and development of the original Jewish faith as presented in the Torah (although not as presented in the Talmud which was the faith of the Diaspora). The question arises, does the same location favour the faith of the Israelis, does it strengthen their religious allegiance? The Bible stories come true in Israel where all the holy places can be seen and experienced. King David's tomb, Mount Zion, the Cave of Elijah, and all the well-known holy names assume the reality of existence. And yet! Religion means mystery, clouds of the unknown; the sacred comes very near to the secret, the sacrament to concealment. Not for naught was the inside of the holy tabernacle inaccessible. Holiness requires mystery, distance, inaccessibility. Familiarity breeds contempt. In this sense the Land contributed to the decline of religion in the traditional sense. The same applies to the influence of the Hebrew language. The average Israeli Jew understands every single word of his prayer and he often finds it somewhat dated, meaningless and irrelevant. A Hebrew youth often cannot swallow the prayer of thankfulness for being born a man, not a woman, or a girl cannot swallow a prayer of thankfulness for being born according to the will of God. It is not for naught that the Catholic religion fought for centuries against any attempt of vernacularization of its Latin prayers. The vernacularization of prayers has deprived them of a great deal of their magical power which was hidden in the sacred, unfamiliar language.

The Hebrew became the vernacular used not only for prayers but also for swearing and cursing, for military drill and street fighting. One can understand the negative attitude of the *Naturei Karta* (radical wing of the orthodoxy) against the use of the Hebrew language as the vernacular.

Religion in Israel has also a different function in Jewish life than in the Diaspora. In the Diaspora the synagogue affiliation is a means of identification, professing and claiming Jewish identity. In Israel the synagogue affiliation is of no consequence to Jewish identity. In Israel the Jew has so many other means and symbols of identification, through his participation in community life, in armed forces, and the Hebrew culture and language.

The geographical location has brought about the decline of the synagogue as the centre of Jewish life but on the other hand it has strengthened ancient, half-forgotten practices in ceremonial and ritual which may be regarded as a regression in religious worship. I refer here more specifically to the revival of mass pilgrimages to holy places and the revival of what might be called ancestor-worship in magical forms of prayers addressed to the holy ancestors requested to act as intercessors in heaven, with candles offered to them and little notes recording requests stuck in the crevices of the old burial stones. On anniversaries of death of holy men or on religious festivals one can see old burial places covered with little notes and candles which remind us of the atmosphere of Lourdes. Mass pilgrimages to holy places are arranged, often under the aegis of the Ministry of Religious Affairs and a pilgrimage to holy places or festivals is being more and more regarded as a religious duty. Since the recovery of East Jerusalem the pilgrimage at Succot time to the Wailing Wall is being proclaimed as a duty of every Jew, not only of every Israeli. This is definitely a regression of Judaism to much older forms of worship, often preceding the Bible itself, which states that Moses' burial place was kept secret in order to avoid the practice of sanctification of places and ancestor worship. This regression is partly due to the mass of illiterates and semi-illiterates which weighs heavily on the Israeli society. The use of charms, talismans and magical formulas abound among them. The fear of the 'Evil Eye' (*bli ayin ra*) is constantly expressed.

The impact of the geographical location can also be seen in the spread of the new secularized version of the Jewish religion, where the Land itself becomes the main object of religious worship, if we accept the definition of the Archbishop Nathan Söderblum of the 'religious man as one to whom something is holy'.[1]

(iii) *Religion and Party Politics*

Religion in Israel is strongly linked with party politics and presents also a major issue in political life. In the Diaspora the Jewish religion has hardly ever been linked with party politics,[2]

---

[1] Nathan Söderblum, late Archbishop of Upsala, *The Gifford lectures*, p. 21. Beacon Press. Boston.

[2] Franz Rosenzweig said appropriately: 'Religion has every reason to reject the clumsy service of the politician'.

except to a small extent in Eastern Europe, where the Chassidic Rabbis, with their large followings, were often misused as pawns in party elections by their Gentile overlords, especially in communal affairs in towns densely populated by Jews. In Israel the three religious parties: The National Religious Party, Agudat Israel and Poalei Agudat Israel have a fair following amounting to about 15 per cent of the electorate. In the last Knesset Election they polled 14·8 per cent of votes gaining 17 seats out of a total of 120. Yet in spite of the small numbers, with the fragmentation of political parties in Israel, they hold a key position in the balance of power, as they are necessary for the formation of a viable majority in a coalition government. They managed to exploit this position by driving hard bargains, securing for themselves the full control of religious affairs and all matters pertaining to personal and family status of the citizen. Religious affairs, the jurisdiction over personal status, births, marriages, divorce, right of citizenship, including the issue who should be regarded as a Jew, are in the hands of the representatives of the religious parties, who deal with them according to the Laws of the Talmud (*Halacha*).

The religious parties have not only control over religious and personal affairs but also form an economic-political estate with their own economic and social services and interests and enterprises exerting a sort of patronage over their members. They have considerable funds and no small influence in distributing staff positions in public services. They have their own housing estates, villages, schools and also Kibbutzim, in a way not dissimilar from other parties. They have also their own channels for transfer of Jewish aid from abroad, especially from the U.S.A. Considerable sums were also transferred from Germany under the Reparation Agreement, for causes controlled by the religious parties.

(iv) *Religious Observance*
The Jewish population in Israel can be divided, as far as religion is concerned, into three major groups:

1. *The Orthodox* with very definite strong beliefs, vociferous, very active, and well organized, politically. They often express themselves in violent assertions and actions, staging public mani-

festations, even riots, such as the recent riots about autopsy[1] or the stoning of cars on Sabbath in the orthodox quarter of Jerusalem. They live in, for and by their strongly knit religious communities. They represent a system of control of personal life by complete dedication to the precepts of the Law as basis of their behaviour. Their religious and secular life merge into one. They would like to subject Israel's secular life to the dictates of the Torah. The late Ashkenazi chief Rabbi of Israel, Dr Itzhak Herzog declared: 'We hope that with God's help the Law of our Jewish State will be based on the tenets of the Torah'.[2] Similarly Rabbi Yitzhak Meir Levin, leader of the Agudat Israel declared in Knesset 1950: 'Orthodox Jewry aspires to a Law that is based on the Law of the Torah and only that Law should dominate all aspects of life in the country'.[3]

The class composition of the Orthodox can be described on the Ashkenazim side as petty bourgeois, containing mostly small shopkeepers and traders, insurance brokers and artisans. The Orthodox avoid the working-class existence, which is very difficult to combine with their various religious duties, and try to be economically independent. Study and reading of the Torah and commentaries take a great deal of their time. They have large families with patriarchial ways of family life. They have communal ways of living with a strong sense of fellowship centred on the synagogue which is not only a place of worship and study but a social and welfare centre of the first magnitude. There is a considerable segregation of the sexes[4] and a puritanical approach to life.

[1] In an open letter the medical staff of Tel Hashomer Government Hospital in Ramat Gan, reacting against the violent campaign against autopsy stated: 'We, the doctors of Tel Hashomer, some of us Israel born and soldiers on active duty, feel we may have to go into exile until enlightenment comes again to this country, for only if that happens will we be able to return to work peacefully in our profession, without being pestered and humiliated'. Reported in *Jerusalem Post*, 14 May 1967.

[2] Quoted in *Legislation and Law in the Jewish State*. Yavneh. Jerusalem-Tel-Aviv. May 1949.

[3] Quoted in Joseph Badi, *Religion in Israel today*, p. 41. Bookman Associates. New York 1959.

[4] Dr Esther R. Goshen-Gothstein in the issue of the *Israeli Annals of psychiatry* (Jerusalem Academic Press). Survey on the orthodox women's approach to marriage.

Their philosophy is founded upon a crushing sense of sin. The first thing an Orthodox will tell you, when the tragedy of the Holocaust is mentioned, is that this happened because the Jews sinned gravely and did not keep all the commandments. The curses of Moses in Deuteronomy ('Behold I set before Ye this day a blessing and a curse. . . . If ye shall not hearken unto the commandments of the Lord our God. 11. 26–28') are frequently recalled. The Orthodox are overwhelmingly conservative. They have many qualities to be admired such as strong faith, dedication and purity of morals. There is practically no juvenile delinquency and no illegitimate births among them. They have a strong conception of social duty. They are drawn into a life of unceasing social activity with the idea of charity to their neighbours in the foreground. On the other side of the coin are fanaticism, intolerance and rigidity amounting to complete ossification and total rejection of secular education as invalid. Austerity, drabness, lack of aesthetic values are very common.

The Orthodox presented here in a generalized form combine a whole gamut of groupings, from moderate such as the Mizrachi and Hapoel Hamizrachi, to very orthodox such as members of the Agudat Israel, with their own schools and their own Chief Rabbinate, and to ultra-orthodox such as Naturei Karta which refused to recognize the State of Israel: 'Clanishness rather than unity marks the various orthodox groups'.[1]

The Orthodox form a minority which probably does not exceed 20 per cent of the population. In the last survey (1967) of the Institute for Applied Social Research in Jerusalem only 13 per cent of those questioned stated unequivocally that they *fully* respect the Jewish tradition, and moreover, only 8 per cent considered themselves unreservedly religious, attending the synagogue daily.

2. *The second minority group* comprises agnostics, atheists and those who are completely indifferent to religion. They present the majority of the educated section of the population and a large section of the former inmates of concentration camps. In the survey referred to, 62 per cent of those with secondary education declared themselves completely detached from religion. A very

[1] Joseph Badi, *Religion in Israel Today*, p. 41. Bookman Associates. New York 1959.

large number of those who vote for Mapam,[1] Ahdut Avoda and the Communists belong here. They are the rationalists for whom religion is past history. The religious festivals are accepted as national festivals. They oppose religious coercion as exercised by the religious parties but most of them do not oppose it actively or do not press their protest too hard. They know the difficulties implied in an atheistic approach to the Jewish State in Israel and to its links with the Diaspora and they also realize the emotional strength and appeal of the Orthodox population.

This group represents probably one quarter of the population. In the survey referred to 26 per cent of all questioned stated that they never enter a synagogue, even on the Day of Atonement. This section is growing rapidly with the spread of secondary and academic education.

3. *The third section* of the population, definitely the largest section in Israeli society, comes between the two extremes. In the survey referred to 48 per cent of those questioned affirmed respect for some part of Jewish tradition. About 40 per cent of all Israeli children go to religious schools. Those in this group are neither Orthodox nor disbelievers but on the border line between belief and disbelief. They accept the traditional side of Jewish customs and rites and frequent the synagogue on great festivals. They accept the basic claims of Judaism as a unique religion. They are not rationalists like the second group but lean to a certain extent towards Jewish traditionalism. They are recruited mostly from those who support Mapai and the Liberal parties. One could say that David Ben Gurion is a typical representative of this group, accepting the basic truth of the Bible and the claims of Judaism as a unique religion, the mother religion of all monotheistic creeds, but still expressing from time to time his doubts and disbeliefs, interpreting the Bible in the modern way. This group opposes the religious coercion exercised by the orthodox but in a lukewarm way, accepting the fact that in a Jewish state, i.e., in the State of the Jews, there is no real alternative to close linkage of the State and religion.

The three sections of the population find themselves in conflict.

---

[1] Mapam is opposed to religion and religious teaching. It was mainly due to the Mapam that the Declaration of Independence of 14 May 1948 omitted all reference to God.

There is an especially deep split between the first and second groups, which arouses great anxiety in public opinion as both groups hold militant views. The religious regime in Israel, its religious policy and its religious officialdom have very little support in public opinion. They are supported by a small minority against the wishes of the large majority. However the minority is protected by myths and traditions deeply embedded in Jewish consciousness and to a large extent by the nature of the State itself.

(v) *Religion and World Judaism*

There are many contrasts between Jewish religion practised in Israel and that practised in the Diaspora. There is no centralized rabbinical authority in the Diaspora countries, and where it exists it is rather a matter of administrative convenience without real control or power. There is no duty of other Rabbis or synagogues to obey its rulings. The religious life in the Diaspora has always been highly decentralized, one could say even atomized, and the centre of authority lies more with the distinguished laymen than with the Rabbis who have the status of a teacher and spiritual guide. Religious authority in Judaism is based only on superior learning and moral stature not on hierarchy and rank.

> In Israel today the rabbinate is rapidly developing into a firmly institutionalized and centralized Church imposing and exacting discipline on its members and facing the general body of laymen as a distinct power. This is not a religious development, but ironically enough the outcome of the emergence of the State. The latter has given rise and legitimacy to an established church.[1]

The two chief Rabbinates present not only a central authority but also exercise a strict central control of semi-authoritarian nature. Due to this control they manage to achieve a complete dominance of only one wing of Judaism with the total exclusion of all other wings. Only the orthodox persuasion is officially recognized as Jewish faith. The four other wings of Judaism, the Reform, the Conservative, the Liberal and the Reconstructionist, which form the big majority in the U.S.A., have practically no representation in Israel. The ecclesiastical authority which is in the hands of the orthodox Rabbis discourages in many ways, by

[1] Talmon, *op.cit*. p. 289.

fair means or foul, the other persuasions, primarily by underhand, unofficial pressure and threats. This has been most clearly revealed in the case of withdrawal of premises to newly formed congregations for progressive Judaism in Tel-Aviv (by Bnei Brith in January 1966) or in the case of withdrawal of premises to conservative congregation in Ashkelon by Wizo in 1966. There is a constant refusal of the Rabbinical authorities to grant the necessary licences to Rabbis of other persuasions. The conversions of non-Jews by Rabbis of other persuasions in the Diaspora are not recognized in Israel.

The religious authorities in Israel and the religious leaders in the Diaspora, especially in the U.S.A. as the largest Jewish centre, find themselves miles apart and the gulf between them is growing. The Rabbinical Assembly of America in its Report on the State of Religion in Israel (the so-called Blue Paper which appeared in Spring 1965) describes the situation in Israel as 'dinosaur-like inability to adjust to new realities', stating inter alia: 'The concept of religion in Israel has become equated with political parties and the country remains sharply divided between a parochial orthodoxy and a non-Jewish secularism'.[1]

'The American Friends of Religious Freedom in Israel', headed by Rabbi Ira Eisenstadt, the Reconstructionist leader and by Shlomo Katz, editor of *Midstream*, issued an appeal in Washington (April 1966) declaring that religious coercion places Israel in the position of 'emulating our oppressors, of mocking the effort of Jews everywhere on behalf of human rights. . . .'

In consequence the value of the Jewish religion as an integrative force in World Judaism may become considerably weakened and in due time may become a negative factor as the gulf between Judaism as practised in Israel and Judaism as practised in the Diaspora is constantly growing. In the Diaspora Orthodoxy is constantly losing its hold on Jewish masses and the other wings of Judaism are constantly expanding their allegiance, while those in Israel are completely excluded.

The other aspect is the intolerance which is shown by ecclesiastical authorities in Israel both *vis-à-vis* other wings of Judaism and *vis-à-vis* other non-Jewish religions, as shown for instance in the withdrawal of premises in the Sharon Hotel for a lecture by

[1] See the Blue Paper published as the Rabbinical Assembly Commission's Report to its Annual Convention.

a Christian Scientist. The Jews in the Diaspora who were for centuries in the forefront of the battle against religious intolerance, look with dismay at the intolerance of the official Ecclesia in Israel.

(vi) *Religion and Social Class*

The preponderance or rather the exclusivity of the Orthodox wing of Judaism in Israel can be explained historically as the preponderance of the Polish-Russian immigrants of lower middle-class origin. Max Weber expresses the view that, 'the specific nature of a religion is a simple function of the social situation of the stratum, which appears as its characteristic bearer' and in another context states: 'During the middle ages Judaism fell under the leadership of a stratum of intellectuals who were trained in literature and ritual, a peculiarity of Judaism. This stratum has represented an increasingly quasi-proletarian and rationalist petty-bourgeois intelligentsia'.[1] This is largely true up to today in Israel.

The dominance or rather the exclusivity of the Orthodoxy in Israel expresses the social and ethnical composition of its population. Israel is composed primarily of the remnants of the East European Jewry and the Oriental Jewry coming from the Arab countries. In all those countries the only representative wing of Judaism was the Orthodoxy with practically entire absence of all other wings. Those wings flourished in Germany and in Western Europe at large as well as in the U.S.A., but with the exception of a small remnant of German Jewry, the Western Jew appears in Israel in very small, almost insignificant numbers, and is being outdistanced in all matters of importance in the social life of the community. The Rabbi from the East European *Shtetl*, the 'petty bourgeois' and 'quasi-proletarian' is the characteristic bearer of Israeli Judaism. In his struggle against the majority (public opinion) he feels anxiety and insecurity, as the whole style of life is against him, hence his aggressiveness and hostility against everything which goes on in Israel today, his 'dinosaur' rigidity and clinging to the letter. The immobility of religious beliefs, the fundamentalism, the rigid and closed aggressive front against progressive forces is so much stronger in Israel because religion

[1] See his *Social Psychology of Religion*, tr. Ephraim Fischoff. Methuen. London 1965.

is there so much more endangered by those forces than in the Diaspora.

The Rabbis in Israel can be divided into three classes: the first consist of a small number of the Chassidic Rabbis who are endowed with charismatic authority. They are credited with qualities of sanctity and near magical power. They engender extraordinary devotion and hero worship. Their devotees keep their commands blindly as if coming from the Deity itself, expecting revelation, inspiration, guidance, often miraculous cures.

The Rabbi of the second category is a community leader, interested in political affairs and taking part in the political struggle. Chaim Weizmann describes him as follows:

> I have never feared really religious people. The genuine type has never been politically aggressive; on the contrary he seeks no power, he is modest and retiring—and modesty was the great feature in the lives of our saintly Rabbis and sages in olden days. It is the new, secularized type of Rabbi, resembling somewhat a member of a clerical party in Germany, France or Belgium, who is the menace and who will make a heavy bid for power by parading his religious convictions. . . .[1]

The Rabbi of the third category wields 'traditional power', to use Max Weber's terminology. His habitual workaday authority is based on customs and habits, on expectation and submission to what was always accepted as the rule of law. Often he is only an official who is simply carrying out the religious policies of the ecclesiastic and State authority.

The sociology of religion in Israel produces some variations from the phenomena observed in the West. In most Western countries one can observe the correlation between church allegiance and economic deprivation or class affiliation in the sense that church allegiance is primarily a middle-class affair, while the working class shows indifference or hostility to the Church. In Israel the class differences are crossed by ethnical differences, the manual working class in industry being largely recruited from the Oriental immigrants. The orthodox section of the population is largely recruited from the under-educated layers of the population, primarily from the lower middle class, quasi-proletarian and the Oriental proletarian classes. The mark of the middle-middle and upper-middle class status in Israel is religious indifference

[1] *Trial and Error*, p. 569. Hamish Hamilton. London 1949.

and agnosticism, and not the attendance of the synagogue. Religious indifference is also one of the marks of the higher educational status of the individual and his main aspiration is for intellectual and spiritual freedom, for the right to think for himself. A man who has discarded his religious allegiance is called in Hebrew *Chofshi*, meaning free, that is he is free from the yoke of the Law, a free thinker, a man who thinks for himself.

(vii) *The Secularization of Jewish Religion*

It would be wrong, in viewing the religious situation in Israel to concentrate exclusively on traditional Judaism, which may be called the rabbinical Judaism. No less important is the process of secularization of Jewish religion, which tends to develop a new brand of non-rabbinical Judaism. The two sections of Israeli society, the atheist-agnostic and the half-believers converge towards a new secular version of Jewish religion. The Land is worshipped as a sanctum, the Bible as a hallowed history. The circumcision and Bar Mitzva are universally observed as secular rites, all the religious holidays are observed as secularized festivals (as already explained in another context). The Sabbath is a day of rest. The belief in Israel as a spiritual power and the belief in the uniqueness and miraculousness of Israel are almost universal. All Jewish homes have a *mezuza* on the doorpost, treated more like a coat of arms, proving national identity.

The process of secularization of religion is of course not confined to Judaism. It is a process which embraces almost all religions and creeds (for instance the secularization of Christmas). Religion is not dying; it is too deep and too universal, it covers too essential a need to disappear from the range of man's experiences, but under the impact of science it undergoes a process of secularization, an adaptation to the present-day scientific culture, shedding its supernatural and ritualistic contents.

In the Diaspora countries the secularization of Judaism also takes place but assumes different forms from those in Israel. In the Diaspora, especially in the U.S.A., the secularization expresses itself in cultural and social forms, as feelings of belonging and fellowship.[1] The Jewish identity is not given up; it is felt as

[1] Oscar Handlin, *The American People in the Twentieth Century*. Harvard 1954. Will Herberg, *Protestant, Catholic, Jew. An Essay in American Religious Sociology*. Ancor Books. 1960.

sui generis religious identity but the religious identity is expressed in folkways, modes and customs, in social work, in philanthropy, in supporting Jewish causes, in help to Israel and other pro-Israel ventures.

In Israel the secularization of Jewish religion follows the general process of nationalization of society. Jewish religion is almost identified with nationhood. No one can be an Israeli Jew in terms of nationality without being a member of Jewish religion and vice versa.

The secularized version of Judaism in Israel is not entirely without supernatural elements. The Invisible Hand shaping the destiny of Israel, the fulfilment of Prophecy, the sanctum of the Promised Land and the Bible are still there. God cannot be separated from the Holy Land of Israel, as only the idea of Godhead can grant it the halo of holiness, and no Jew would accept the idea that the *Eretz Israel* is not a holy land. The secular version of Judaism in Israel is almost entirely centred around the Holy Land.

The secularization of Jewish religion in Israel is at present highly weighed with nationalism and this is its greatest danger and handicap. But all the same it is an extremely interesting development which can assume various forms and is potentially a phenomenon of great import for the future.

It can in due time become a new version of a non-Talmudic, non-Rabbinical, non-legalistic Judaism which is nourished by the soil of Israel. It can claim all prophetic messages arising from the Land of Israel, including the message of the Jew of Nazareth, as in the secular version there is no room for the argument of apostasy or heresy.

9.

Who is a Jew?

STRANGELY enough the question: Who is a Jew?, became one
of the basic issues of the Israeli *Kulturkampf*, stirring up passionate
controversy. Are the Falashas (a small group of Ethiopian Jews
living North of Lake Tana) or Bene Yisrael (Hindu Jews) or
Cochini-Indians—Jews? Are the Karaits (those who cling to the
Old Testament only, rejecting the Oral Tradition and the Talmud)
Jews? Are Evangelical Jews (those who profess Jesus as Prophet
of Israel and accept the Synoptic Gospels) Jews? Is a half Jew
on the paternal side to be treated differently from a half Jew on
the maternal side? What is decisive: blood, religion, nationality,
culture? And how, and who shall determine them? Can a man
who claims Jewish nationality, even a Zionist, but not of Jewish
religion be accepted as Jewish? What of conversions? Should
only formal conversions conducted by competent orthodox
Rabbis be accepted or all formal conversions also by reform
Rabbis, or informal conversions as well?

All those questions have arisen during the long history of the
Jews, but only sporadically without great significance and consequence. They had a different complexion at times when Jews
had no State authority, no country of their own and no status
and privilege to confer, only yellow badges, contempt and
persecution. In Israel they have assumed a different meaning, as
Jewishness in a Jewish State confers status, rights and privileges.
In the Law of Return the right to immigrate to Israel and automatic, immediate citizenship is granted to the Jews. Service in
the armed forces is reserved for the Jews, privileged positions in
Civil Service and many industries linked with security are held
by Jews only. The Jews have also a different personal status in
regard to marriages, divorces and so on. In Israel conceived as
a Jewish Nation State, full citizenship can only be enjoyed by
Jews, so it was inevitable that the question arose: how to define
a Jew.

The theory of Zionism, as developed in the Diaspora, proclaimed that the Jews are a nation, not simply a religion. Weizmann engaged in endless debate with the British Jews, pursuing this point and condemning the British and American Jews for rejecting the claim of separate nationality. But strangely enough in Israel no such official claim is made for defining Jewish identity. For the purpose of defining the personal status in marriage and divorce, in service in the army, in the Law of Return, etc., the Zionist theory is discarded. A man who claims to be of Jewish nationality but without Jewish religion is not accepted. The Jewish identity is accepted as a religious identity, as defined in Talmud. The Law of Return itself does not define the term 'the Jew', but leaves this to the Minister of the Interior and in the last resort to the Courts. The Ministry of the Interior which adjudicates the right of citizenship in the issue of passports, and the Ministry of Religious Affairs which deals with personal status of citizens, accept the principle of the *Halacha* (the law of the Talmud) that Jewishness is an ascriptive value not to be shed. A person born of a Jewish mother is Jewish for all time, while a person of a Jewish father and a non-Jewish mother is not to be received into the Jewish community. Conversions are accepted when carried out by orthodox Rabbis only.

In the famous case of Mrs Eitani, a local Councillor in Nazareth and a member of Mapai, the wife of a Jew and mother of Jewish children (anyway of children who regard themselves as Jews), who herself came to Israel in 1947 from Germany as a Youth Alija ward and a Jewish child, the Minister of the Interior withdrew her Israeli passport, cancelling her citizenship under the contention that she was born of a non-Jewish mother, although her father was Jewish and she suffered as a Jew in Germany. As she was unable to show a document of valid conversion, she had to be regarded as non-Jewish, therefore had no claim to automatic citizenship under the Law of Return. Public opinion was outraged and after a great deal of public protest and also from Mapai whose member she was, the Minister had to retreat, conferring again the right of citizenship on Mrs Eitani, but not on the basis that she was Jewish by right but on account of an old principle of British law (taken over by Israel) called *estoppel*, whereby the authorities are prevented from depriving a person of a right which has once been granted by mistake in good faith.

In that way the principle of the ascriptive quality of Jewishness by birth from a Jewish mother has been upheld.[1]

The Israeli courts also follow this principle[2] in most cases, but in the famous case of Brother Daniel, a Catholic Monk, who claimed citizenship under the Law of Return, as a son of a Jewish mother, the Court rejected this principle, declaring that since Brother Daniel was a Christian he would not be regarded as a Jew by Jewish people. The Court argued that the term *Jew in the Law of Return* should be given 'a secular meaning', that is, 'as usually understood by the man in the street . . . as it is understood by the ordinary plain and simple Jew'. In fact this interpretation is also based on a common principle accepted in the Talmud called 'the majority rule', meaning accepting the interpretation of a term in the way the majority of people interpret it.

So the gates of Israel are not really open to all Jews, but only for those who are regarded as Jews by the Orthodox or in another interpretation 'by the ordinary, plain and simple Jew', if such a figure exists.

However it is very doubtful whether 'an ordinary, plain and simple Jew' has any clearer and more definite notion of the term

[1] It is ironic that Ben Gurion, who was, more than anyone else, responsible for the present state of religious legislation in Israel, had to experience the full effect of this legislation on his own family, when his grand-daughter, Miss Galia Ben Gurion was refused registration of her forthcoming marriage by the Haifa Rabbinate (February 1968) on the ground that her mother is unable to produce a valid certificate of conversion by an orthodox Rabbi. The Haifa Rabbinate stated: 'We have no doubt that Mrs Mary Ben Gurion, became a convert to Judaism before her marriage took place in England, but we wish to be sure that an orthodox Rabbi approved of her conversion'. (Reported by *Jewish Chronicle*, 1 March 1968.)

A common joke in Israel says that according to the *Halacha* Krushchev's grandson is a Jew, while Ben Gurion's grandson is not.

[2] The matriarchic principle for Jewish identity, based on a wilful interpretation of one passage of the Bible, goes against the grain of the whole Bible and militates strongly against the patriarchic principle of the Jewish people, regarded as descendants of Abraham, Isaac and Jacob and his sons, and not of Sarah, Rebecca, Rachel, Leah and their maidservants. The succession of Levites, Cohanim and other Tribes goes by father, not mother. God is the Father not the Mother of mankind. The whole Hebrew language bears strongly the imprint of patriarchalism. It is Fatherland not Motherland, it is father not mother of invention, the highest mercy in the Bible is expressed as the mercy of fathers to their sons not the mercy of mothers to sons, etc.

Jew than the sophisticated student of Jewish problems, be he a theologian, anthropologist, psychologist, sociologist or historian. Each of them would discuss for hours on end this question and defend his own answer from the point of view of criteria accepted by him after long study of the problem. For the theologian, orthodox, reformist, liberal or reconstructionist, there is a large field for disagreement on this subject. For the anthropologist, who would concentrate on physical characteristics of Jews living in a certain area, for the psychologist who would concentrate on Jewish mental characteristics, Jewish consciousness and awareness, for the sociologist, who would concentrate on characteristic features of Jewish culture, for the historian, who would concentrate on historical experiences of Jewish action and reaction, the field of disagreement on the subject of what is Jewishness is no smaller.

'Jew' is of course a term and as such subject to semantics. When we ask a person why he thinks himself to be a Jew, we may get a series of different answers. A may say: because I am of Jewish religion, meaning confessing the Jewish religion or born to Jewish religion without professing it. B: because I am of Jewish nationality, whatever that may mean, for instance having national aspirations. C: because I am of Jewish race, whatever that may mean in the context of a certain geographical region. D: because I was born to Jewish parents, whatever Jewish may mean in this connection. E: because I identify myself with Jewish values or suffered for a Jewish cause, actively or passively. F: because everybody regards me as Jewish.

If you ask Gentiles why they regard a given person as a Jew you might also get a series of answers which vary greatly.

If you ask an historian what is the nature of Jewish identity, whether the Jews are a nation, a religion or a culture, he would say that in various periods and countries they presented all those identities to a degree. They must be regarded as a space-time category. They turn from one identity to another according to the impact of external and internal events. They have a different awareness, cohesion and loyalty, when they are persecuted and when they are free and treated on equal terms; different also when they appear in mass in a given territory and when they appear in small numbers. Their awareness is also different according to the different notions of human groupings and loyalties at a given time. Nationhood is a very recent, nineteenth-century notion, which did not exist in antiquity or the middle ages. When the ancient Israelis lived in the Land of Israel, there was no notion of nationhood, although we would be inclined to regard them as what we now class as a nation. Apart from present-day Israel, where the Jews are turning into a nation, the Jews were never a nation like the English or German or French are. For long stretches of their history they were a distinct group because they lived mostly in ghettos. In Eastern Europe the Jews lived in a mass, segregated from the rest in closely knit communities, speaking their own language, and so we can say they had some ethnic characteristics, and call them a nation, rather stretching the term. But in Western Europe the Jews were definitely not a nation, and whenever someone wanted to treat them as such, they protested. As an historian I would say—continues our historian—that the term 'Jewish' should always be used with more specific connotation. One has to state which aspect of Jewishness one has in mind. One can often read that Spinoza or Disraeli or Marx were Jewish. They were Jewish only in a sense, not in a sense that Einstein or Freud were Jewish. They did not regard themselves as Jewish, they were not regarded as Jews by other contemporary Jews, or by Gentiles, except those who were hostile and critical of them. An historian would say that there is no such thing as Jew in a generic term. A generic term 'Jew' is an abstraction, i.e., it exists only as a mental construction. There are Israeli Jews, American, English, Polish Jews. They all may have certain common characteristics but they also show significant differences which cannot be overlooked. Jews have inter-married and inter-bred and there are a thousand and one marginal cases, where no one can say to what degree a person is Jewish or not. So much for our historian.

The attempt to define 'Jewishness' in clear cut, definite terms must be regarded as abortive. There is no such thing as Jewishness *per se*. There are religious Jews who profess Jewish religion of various brands, there are national Jews who live in strongly knit communities, speaking one of the languages of the Jews, there are racial Jews who have distinct somatic characteristics recognized as Jewish in a given geographical region, and there are cultural, spiritual Jews. Every Jew and every Jewish community has his or its own awareness of Jewishness according to his or its experience, both personal and collective. As a mental concept, 'Jewishness' is dynamic and changeable and undergoes transformation according to the experiences, notions and conceptions of a given age. The notion of nationhood may in a hundred years' time drop out of usage and be replaced by other wider loyalties. We cannot expect permanency or universality of a mental concept. Universality cannot be expected either in applying the notion to all situations or in terms of its acceptance by all. Whatever definition of a Jew we may advance, it will certainly not be accepted by all, by the Orthodox and Reform Jews, by atheists, by the assimilated, by nationalists and Zionists, by filosemetic humanists, by anti-semitic racialists and by Communists. A Jew is not only one who regards himself as or is aware of himself as being a Jew but also one who is regarded and treated as a Jew by others. One could term them 'active' and 'passive' Jews. Millions of passive Jews have been subjected to persecution throughout the ages and they have often been regarded as heroes or martyrs in Jewish history, while millions of active Jews led a life of security and comfort. Millions of passive Jews became active Jews when they were awakened by persecutions (Moses Hess and Herzl were among them). The 'Yellow Badge' became for many passive Jews a badge of honour which brought them into the camp of active Jews.

The nature of Jewish identity is as great a secret as the nature of the 'I' of the individual. The 'I' in itself is unfathomable and it presents itself as a thought series or a mental concept. The consciousness of the 'I' goes back in the past, as a series of memory pictures, is felt as the present and extends into the future. In his 'I' consciousness man is what he thinks he is and partly what other people think of him. The notion that his identity as a particular individual could be held in question by others is for the individual simply absurd. He knows that he is what he is, although he cannot define it. 'I am that I am' a man can say of himself similar to the famous phrase recorded in the Bible for Jehova.

The same applies to the 'I' of the Jew *qua* Jew. It can be considered as a mental concept related to past history as well as to the present and the future. It can be based on the personal or collective experience of a family, Tribe or Jews at large. It can be based on what the Jews think of themselves or what other

people think of them. It can be based on fleeting and changeable
impressions or on deep theological, historical and sociological
disquisitions.

The Israeli search for a definition of the 'Jew' must be puzzling
to many and must gladden the heart of the anti-Semitic racialists
all over the world, as they were also searching in their own way
for their own purposes for a definition of the Jew. This definition
is actually needed in two cases only, when discrimination of Jews
is practised and the Jew has to be kept out, and when privileges
are to be conferred on Jews and the non-Jew has to be kept out.
In the Diaspora the Jews are not interested in the definition of
this term. On the contrary, they resent it as a manifestation of
anti-Semitic discrimination. Whenever, in any country, Jewish
identity has to be declared and the definition of this identity, as
in Hitler's Germany, is appended, it is clear that the definition is
only an instrument of discrimination against the Jews. In Israel
the boot is on the other foot and the non-Jews or half Jews or the
not formally converted resent the definition of this term for the
same reason.

The great Jewish writer of the last generation, Sholom Ash
in his *What I Believe* said, 'God be thanked that the nations have
not given my people the opportunity to commit against others
the crimes which have been committed against it. I say, God be
thanked, because had that opportunity been given it, who can
doubt that it would have conducted itself against strangers in
the same manner as the other people.' Now Israel has the opportunity. . . .

The Israeli search for definition of the Jew is instructive also
in another respect. It shows that in spite of the Zionist ideology,
which has inspired the creation of Israel, the answer to the
question, 'who is a Jew?' can be given only in religious terms,
whatever the actual meaning of this may be. It cannot be given
in ethnical or racial terms. So in the controversy between Israel
and the Diaspora on the nature of Jewish identity, Israel herself
gives, in fact, the same answer as the Diaspora. But the religious
identity does not necessarily mean the archaic identity of the
Halacha with its notion of the rejection of half Jews who are not
born of Jewish mothers. The religious identity can be interpreted
in a restrictive way or in a liberal, humane and generous way by
opening its gates widely to all who regard themselves as Jews

and who are willing to share the fate and destiny of the Jews in Israel or anywhere else.

Even in the Talmud one can find many opinions and rulings of the sages, among them Maimonides, to support such a liberal attitude, and those sources were inter alia quoted by the Attorney-General of Israel, Justice Haim Cohn in his report written in 1959 at the request of the then Prime Minister, Mr Ben Gurion. In *An Anthology of Medieval Hebrew Literature*[1] I found a very interesting *Responsum* of Rabbi Soloman Ibn Adret on 'What shall be the status of people who claim to be Jews?' (*Responsum* II. 16–17) which reads as follows:

> From the tone of your question, wherein you say 'and they have been living with us for some time as full-fledged Jews, carrying out all religious observances', it appears that since they do not know their father's Hebrew name, you doubt whether they are really Jews. But whatever their origin, their status is fixed. If they claim to be Jews, no one has the right to investigate their past record, and they are to be accepted as full-fledged Jews just as we accept Jews of most distinguished birth. No one has the right to say to a Jew: 'Prove that you are a Jew'. . . . Even if a man claims that he is proselyte, that is that he has been converted by a properly constituted Beth Din (Rabbinical Court), he is to be believed.

Israel would be very well advised to follow this *Responsum* and to be content with a simple declaration which would enable all those who regard themselves as Jews and wish to share their life and destiny with Israel, to do so. Her liberality in this respect would be very well rewarded, considering that most of her potential immigrants are to be drawn from Russian or English-speaking countries, where the percentage of mixed marriages is very high. The answer to the question, 'Who is a Jew?' should be left to the consciousness and conscience of the individual.

---

[1] Abraham E. Millgram, *Abelard Schuman*, pp. 215–16. New York 1961.

10.

Specific Versus Generic Anti-Semitism

To Jews complaining about conditions in Israel I have often said, 'At least you have solved the Jewish question for yourself, there is no anti-semitism here', to which has come the curious reply, 'No anti-semitism here? What about Sabras, they can be as anti-semitic as any *goy*'. And at this we would both laugh. The orthodox Jew may say that he feels more embarrassed to put on a *Shtramele* and *bekeshe* (his traditional Sabbath garments) in Tel-Aviv or Haifa than in the Jewish quarters in his native town.

Of course what is called Jewish anti-semitism is not a new phenomenon and as an act of self-hatred and self-contempt it is not confined to the Jewish minority only; it is very well known especially among racial minorities all over the world. Self-hatred and self-contempt absorbed from the values of a dominant majority has been described and analysed by sociologists and psychologists. Dr Theodor Reik described it very convincingly on the basis of self-analysis as well as his analytical experiences with Jewish patients in Europe and the U.S.A.[1]

The Jews have always been engaged in self-criticism, fault-finding and self-flagellation. They indulged in it, following the ways of the Bible, which called the ancient tribes of Israel 'stiff-necked people'. The astonishing thing about the 'chosen people', who have to carry the message of Jehova, is that it is described as a most sinful nation, a nation full of weaknesses and failures, which falls down again and again. Jewish chronicles present a gloomy picture of a corrupted nation whipped and castigated by Lawgivers, Judges and Prophets. The same attitude among the Jews goes on even at present. Speak to the Orthodox about what happened in Europe and he will be the first to tell you, 'It is because of our great sins'.

[1] Dr Theodor Reik, *Listening with the Third Ear*. Pyramid Publications. New York 1948.

Ben Gurion writing in his Preface to the biography of Chaim Weizmann, says about Herzl, 'He had no idea of the faults of the Jewish character. Even if he had, he would never have dared to criticize them; for he was not one of their kind and would have been chary of giving offence. Weizmann was the exact opposite. . . .'[1]

The fact is that not only Weizmann[2] but the whole Zionist Movement regarded as their first task the elimination of shortcomings and failures in the Jewish character as brought about by persecution and the status of inferiority in the Diaspora. Zionist literature is full of disparagement and detraction of the Diaspora Jews.

All national literatures and nearly all serious recorders of a people's life alternate in their use of the glasses, but no other literature has the schizophrenic quality of the Jewish—from the Bible down to our own day. The Jewish people loves and hates itself, admires and despises itself, with pathological intensity.[3]

This schizophrenic attitude still goes on in Israel, where everything is criticized and the Jewish character comes for critical self-appraisal, which can be more openly conducted than in the Diaspora. The criticism is often conducted systematically under the heading of the Diaspora distortion of the Jewish character. Such and such a character trait was acquired in the Diaspora and should be discontinued in Israel. We are now free and we should behave like free people.

In the young generation self-hatred and self-contempt is

---

[1] *Chaim Weizmann. A Biography by Several Hands*, ed. W. Weisgal and Joel Carmichael, p. 1. Dial Press. New York 1944.

[2] In his last days in hospital Chaim Weizmann intimated to his life-long friend Meyer Weisgal as follows: 'What hurts me most, as I lie here helpless, are the serious mistakes which are being committed before my eyes in this country. We are small people, Meyer, exceedingly small in number. But we are at one and the same time a great people; an ugly and yet a beautiful people; a creative and a destructive people; a people in whom genius and foolishness are commingled in equal quantities. Through our obstinacy we are capable of breaking through any barriers and breaching any wall; but the breach in the wall is always liable to swallow us. . . .' Quoted in Samuel Shihor, *Hollow Glory. The Last Days of Chaim Weizmann, first President of Israel*, p. 236. Translated from Hebrew. Thomas Yoseloff. New York 1960.

[3] Maurice Samuel, 'The Road from Motol' in *Chaim Weizmann, op cit.,* p. 63.

definitely on the decline and the tendency is rather to reach far out in the opposite direction.

However, when one speaks about 'Jewish anti-semitism' in Israel, one has in mind not the generic but the *specific* anti-semitism, i.e., directed against specific types or Tribes. It has often been observed that a Jew coming to Israel stops being a Jew and starts being a Pole, Englishman or American. Professor Harrod R. Isaacs of the Centre of International Studies at the Massachusetts Institute of Technology published in the *New Yorker* (September 1966) the result of his research on the position of American Jews in Israel, saying *inter alia* that the American Jews are looked on in Israel with malice, envy and sometimes grudging admiration, that the American Jews who were in the U.S.A. 'Jews', in Israel in turn became 'Americans'. This phenomenon is in fact not confined to Americans in Israel but is shared by immigrants of all nationalities.

The American Jews are not very popular in Israel, displaying qualities which are, to say the least, not endearing to other Tribes. But the German Jews are also not popular with the American Jews, or in fact among any other Tribes. And the Polish Jews are also not popular with the American, German, French or English Jews. The Rumanian Jews are disparaged by all other Tribes, the Moroccan or Algerian Jews are widely sneered at. Many tribes have nicknames of denigration, such as *Jekkes, Galicianers, Litvaks, Kozaks*. I have heard English Jews fulminating against the German or American Jews and the Americans against every other Tribe.

Is it surprising? We have to take into account the long sojourn of the Tribes in various countries with different political, social, economic, cultural and linguistic backgrounds, and their different experiences. The Bible described the Jews who, freed from Egyptian slavery, came into the Promised Land as 'Mixed multitudes' (*ereb rab and asafsuf*), what might be called a mixed crowd. The crowd of the Second Exodus is even more mixed. It has come from more than seventy countries with as many different languages. It has come mostly from lower middle class or proletarian or semi-proletarian backgrounds. Many of the immigrants were just freed from slavery in the concentration camps. This mixed crowd in the Second Exodus has done wonders in a few years in Israel. They have done as well as the mixed crowd of the First Exodus, but still the handicaps of the mixture, especially the inner frictions and tensions, have not been overcome.

The mutual dislike of the German and Polish Jews, or American and European Jews is just a reflection of the dislike of the German and Polish Gentiles or of American and European Gentiles. As the German Jews styled themselves on the Ideal type of German and absorbed a great many German characteristics, while the Polish Jews styled themselves on the ideal type of the Polish gentleman, acquiring a great many Polish characteristics, it is not surprising that there is mutual antipathy between the two Tribes. The same rule applies to all other Tribes.

Professor Stanislav Andreski in his *Elements of Comparative Sociology*[1] tries to explain the existence of anti-semitism by the presence of sadistic elements, or lust for power or the fight for good places and good things in life. As sadistic elements or the drive for power are to be found among Jews as anywhere else, as the fight for good places and good things in life occurs among Jews in Israel as anywhere else, and what is foreign is often misunderstood and treated with suspicion, so it is not surprising that suspicion, discrimination and favouritism are also not absent in mutual relationships of the Tribes. In fact the term *protekeja* (favouritism) is on everybody's lips in Israel and one can hear a great deal about it. But of course favouritism, suspicion or malice are not principles or rules of behaviour for the community as a whole or for the majority and they are not to be found in organized or semi-public relationships. On the contrary discrimination is seriously disclaimed and frowned upon and in fact dealt with in public and semi-public policy and the principles of fairness and inter-Tribal equality are adhered to in the majority of cases. But the actual forces tending to favouritism are not easily overcome and it will take time before the mixed crowd becomes homogeneous socially as well as culturally.

The inter-tribal frictions and misunderstandings are a source of disillusionment and disenchantment for those who came to Israel in order to enjoy a 'fuller Jewish life'. They expected a feeling of complete brotherhood and fellowship with the rest of the Jews but instead they often met with suspicion and misunderstanding. They could rely mostly on their own 'nationals', who meet together in private and public gatherings, developing

[1] Weidenfeld and Nicholson. London 1964.

their own associations and newspapers. Professor Isaacs in the survey already referred to suggests that for every American who stayed in Israel five have returned to the U.S.A., but again this figure is not dissimilar from the percentage of German, English or South African Jews who left the country, or from an overall percentage of voluntary immigrants with means, who left. It is estimated that of the second wave of immigration, the so-called Second Alija (the immigrants of the turn of the century) only 20 per cent stayed in the country. One can say that the immigrant with means who came voluntarily and who can settle somewhere else, in the majority of cases does not stay in Israel for long. Of course there are various other reasons apart from inter-tribal frictions, such as economic (difficulty in finding a job or difficulties of very sharp competition) or social reasons (annoyance at the bureaucracy), or cultural reasons (difficulties with the language) or religious (affiliation to a Reform Synagogue is impossible, and the legitimacy of one's marriage or children may be questioned by the Orthodox Rabbis). But all the same the inter-tribal animosities form an intangible background for disenchantment.

Actually Israel is geared more to the life of the proletarian and lower middle class, and the proletarian and lower middle class members feel more at home in Israel than the higher ranks. The proletarian and the lower middle class man stays, while the member of the upper-middle class rarely immigrates to Israel, and when he does he often goes back.

And here one has to refer to another kind of 'Jewish anti-semitism', which consists in the animosity and lack of understanding between the ghetto Jew and what you may call the liberated Jew, the Jew of the open world. By ghetto Jews I mean those who lived in more or less confined and cramped Jewish quarters which comprised a closely knit community with a very intensive life of its own. By the liberated Jew I mean the Jew who lived outside those quarters in close contact with the Gentile world and moving freely within it. The two types get on each others' nerves, they do not understand each other and rather look down upon each other. The liberated Jew accuses the ghetto Jew of narrow-mindedness, muddle-headedness and lack of manners, while the ghetto Jew accuses the other of snobbishness and standoffishness. Most immigrants to Israel came either from East European ghettos or the Moslem ghettos. The immigrants brought with them the atmosphere of the ghetto, which is gradually disappearing but it has not yet entirely disappeared. Actually the great danger for Israeli society is that it can turn into a large cosmopolitan ghetto, which may appear a contradiction in terms but which paradoxically enough has a vestige of reality in Israel.

Similarly to a ghetto, Israel covers a relatively small and circumscribed area, fenced off from the surrounding inimical environment, with a very intensive life within. Israel is rapidly developing into a City State with a network of suburbs, a sort of modern conurbation. (About 40 per cent of the Jewish population lives in Greater Tel-Aviv.) Small local issues are often inflated to national dimensions, and local and national issues have a very similar character. The Cabinet often deals with problems which in other countries are dealt with by the Borough Councils. Petty problems, individual jealousies and rivalries such as are usually encountered in local politics, consume much of the Cabinet's time.

However, the other side of the coin is Israel's cosmopolitanism. People gathered here from all over the world. It was reported that the President of Iceland, Mr Asgeir Asgeirson on his official visit in Israel in May 1966 was able to speak Icelandic with one of the citizens of Israel. Jewish communities from India, China, Burma, Ceylon, from the Pacific Islands, from all over Africa settled in Israel. Israel is a small community of nations. So narrow parochialism, the outcome of confinement and smallness is counterbalanced by cosmopolitanism, based on an immeasurable richness of human material, which tends to keep an open window on the world by multi-lingual journals, books, films, lectures and exchange visits.

However, this rich human material is being hastily lumped together and interlocked, in a small, very confined space, fenced off from the outside. And the danger exists that Israel could in due time develop a ghetto-like atmosphere, similar to the atmosphere from which most of the immigrants came. By a hurried, intensive uniformity Israel may produce a type of cosmopolitan ghetto Jew, wearing a 'coat of many colours', born and bred in a very closely knit community with a very intensive life within.

A completely different and novel aspect of anti-semitism is

the anti-Jewish hatred of the Arabs. This hatred has of course a rational and factual basis in the struggle of two nationalities, but of late it has become overgrown with an enormous super-structure of irrationality in a blind hatred and will of destruction. It is hatred concentrated against the State but also directed against Jewish society at large, overspilling into hatred against indivi-duals. Of course not all Arabs, perhaps not even the majority of Arabs living in Israel experience active feelings of animosity and ill-will towards the Jews. But the animosities are constantly being inflamed by outside propaganda. Archbishop George Hakim, head of the Greek Catholic Community in Israel has declared (in the January 1967 issue of *Ramzoz*, the organ of the Mapai Youth) that '75 per cent of the Arabs in the country are anti-Israel'.

The anti-semitism of the Arabs has a different character to the anti-semitism of the Diaspora. The anti-semitism encountered by the Diaspora Jew was coloured by contempt and stigma, dis-paragement and constant faultfinding. It affected the self-respect of the Jew and his sense of dignity. It spilt over to his conscious-ness as a sort of poison, as a factor of disorganization of person-ality. It had a many-sided background, partly racial and religious and partly economic, social and cultural. The anti-semitism of the Arabs is a political hatred concentrated on one point, the loss of the land and dispossession. It lacks racial or religious background. It is not tinged with contempt, slight and abuse. It is the other way round. It is tinged with the feeling of the superiority of the Jew, his achievement against great odds. The Jew is admired; he appears in the eyes of the Arab almost as a near superman, who managed to conquer the land against the greatest odds, and against overwhelming numbers. The Arab's attitude produces in the Israeli Jew not the feeling of inferiority but rather the feeling of superiority. The Arab hatred actually sustains the Jewish community, presenting a great challenge, bracing the muscles and the will-power, the will to resist and survive. Without the Arabs' hatred Israeli society would have fared much worse.

The phenomenon of 'Israeli anti-semitism' as described is not a reflection on the Israeli Jew, it is rather a reflection on 'the human condition'. Does the Englishman like the American and vice versa, and does the Frenchman like the Italian and vice versa? Does the German like anybody else and vice versa? Does the Pole like the German or the Russian and vice versa? They have to live with each other in peace and amity, and co-operate if they can, but their feelings are outside their control. And what nation is free from sadistic impulses, from resentment, suspicions, power lust, selfishness and greed, which are the motors operating behind all the 'anti-sentiments'. Maybe the psychologists will teach us in due time how to overcome those sentiments or dispose of them at birth but the time is still far off.

The 'anti-sentiments' in Israel are at present still very strong and they are mostly the unfortunate heritage of the past. The Israeli Jews allow themselves to dwell too much in the past, in the past persecutions, discrimination and slaughter of the Jews as the victims of all the evil forces in the world. There is a case for taking out the sting and bitterness of old memories of a whole nation, for the sake of its sanity and balance, as much as there is a case for taking out the sting and bitterness of individual memories, with which the psycho-analyst is dealing. From not forgetting to not forgiving, from not forgiving to revenge, from revenge to hate, from hate against one to hate against many, from hate against many to an overall hatred against the world and to an overall atmosphere of hate in one's own society—this is an almost automatic progression. Hatred, it has been observed a thousand times, cannot be confined because it is a frame of mind. It is bound to spill over in attitudes to one's own citizens, as hatred is often inverted, turned against oneself. That is what might happen if Israel is not careful in controlling the anti-attitudes and anti-sentiments, if she dwells too much in the past, cultivating the atmosphere of grievances and wrong. The danger for Israel is even greater, due to a very intensive life confined in a small fenced off space.

The phenomena of 'Jewish anti-semitism' in Israel throws considerable light on the problems of anti-semitism in the Diaspora. Let us take for instance pre-war Germany. Germany had many waves of immigration of Jews. There were native German Jews settled there for centuries, but there were also Polish Jews, Russian Jews and Rumanian Jews who had come more recently. The German Jews were not conspicuous, they were thoroughly assimilated, and their identity not very noticeable. But the Polish Jews in Germany had acquired many characteristics of the Poles, and the Russian Jews those of Russians, and the Rumanian Jews those of Rumanians. They were conspicuous and noticeable and to the German they were repellent, as they represented some of the characteristics of nations which they despised in addition to specific Jewish characteristics even more despised. They aroused feelings of hatred in the Germans. And this was reflected in turn on the position of the German Jews in Germany. It was not surprising that the German Jews looked askance at the immigration of foreign Jews to Germany, regarding them as factors of anti-semitism in their country.

Exactly the same problem existed in Poland. The Polish Jews, rooted for centuries in the country, were tolerated much more than the Russian, Lithuanian and Ukrainian Jews squeezed out of Russia by the Tsarist government.

From this we can learn that anti-semitism is a complex phenomenon which reflects not only hostility to Jews *qua* Jews, but hostility to foreigners *qua* foreigners, especially to those foreigners whose characteristics are exhibited by foreign Jews. The hostility to 'foreign' Jews persists even in Israel but of course the foreign Jews, as we said previously, lose, when they come to Israel, the character of Jews and take on the character of their previous nationality.

As the Jew is moving constantly from one place to another, he is bound to engender the feeling of strangeness and foreignness. The mobility of the Jew—and the Jews are perhaps the most mobile of all nations in all respects both in horizontal and vertical mobility—breeds resentment and suspicion. Having no security in himself, he can hardly give the feeling of security to others. In this sense Israel, as a resting place for the Jew, has a great contribution to make to the fight against anti-semitism in the Diaspora. But her lasting and most significant contribution can be made only when she has been able to overcome the atmosphere of anti-sentiments which has grown in her midst as a result of the terrors experienced by the last generation in Europe. What I called the specific Jewish anti-semitism is nothing but part of the atmosphere of anti-sentiments which was allowed to grow in Israel.

Part II

status and stratification

1.

The Two Israels

THE TWO Israels, the Israel of the European-American Jews (for short the Europeans) and that of the North-African and Asian Jews (the Orientals) are not a sociological invention; they are a very potent and disturbing reality. No problem has more tortured the conscience of the country than that of *Israel Bet*. The ethnic division forms a uniquely complex pattern in which several other divisions overlap, demographic, social, economic, educational, cultural and religious.

The Europeans and Orientals present two different, easily recognizable physical types. Medical research carried out in Israel (*inter alia* by Professor Green on Gaucher's disease and other metabolic diseases) suggests also two different genetic strains, prone to different hereditary diseases. The structure and movement of birth and death rates, infant mortality, causes of death, fertility rates, age composition and age of marriage, all differ widely from one group to another. They have also different levels of education, different religious attachments and interests, religious rites and customs. They have a different occupational and class structure and a different ratio of active population. They have, of course, different levels of income.

One could say that the two Israels present two different worlds, not two sub-cultures in one society but two different cultures, each with its own standards, values, attitudes and patterns of social relationships. They live in the same geographical space but do not move in the same social, cultural and psychological space. Nor do they move in the same time category; one belongs to modernity, the other to the distant past. One represents the economic and technical capacities in differential affluence, the other biological capacities in differential fertility. One is dominant politically, socially and economically, the other biologically. One echoes Christian civilization, the other Moslem civilization. They both have a strong awareness of their differences, not only in terms of mere otherness but also in terms of clash of values and interests. They are both aware that the State left in the hands of one of them would assume a completely different structure, identity and image than if left in the hands of the other. Resentfulness can be encountered on both sides. One side speaks about Levantinization, being afraid of the ever-rising biological tide of a semi-educated mass touched by a technological and economic civilization; the other speaks about the domination of an alien civilization of European or rather East-European provenance, being afraid of a second-class citizenship.

Both are afraid of a caste-like structure similar to the caste-like structure existing in Western countries with a significant proportion of coloured population. There exists in Israel a syndrome of ethnical underprivilege, similar to the syndrome of the colour problem in the U.S.A. or in contemporary Britain, made up by excess poverty, excess unemployment, excess share in slum housing, excessive share in underpaid menial jobs, undereducation, etc.

Let us first of all consider the size of the problem. At the end of 1964 the Jewish population numbered 2,239,000. Of those 643,000 were immigrants from Asia and Africa (28·7 per cent), 714,000 from Europe and America (31·9 per cent), the remainder 881,000 (39·4 per cent) were born in Israel. Among the latter (the Sabras) those whose fathers were born in Asia or Africa formed the majority. We can say that at present there is a full demographic parity between the two strains, but the trend in favour of the Oriental strain is unmistakeable. The European population is weighed down by older age groups, while the younger age groups are in a majority among the Orientals. For instance in the age group up to fourteen there were in 1964 94,000 Oriental children against 31,000 Europeans, a ratio of 3 to 1 in favour of the Oriental group. It means that the Oriental population will have in due course a considerable majority.

Oriental girls marry earlier than European girls. About 17 per cent of the Oriental girls married at the age of fifteen or less against 1½ per cent of the Western girls. The gross reproduction rate of the Orientals is almost twice as high as that of the Europeans (according to the computation of the Central Bureau of Statistics—2·24 against 1·16 in 1963). The average size of family of the Orientals is (1961) double that of the European families (4·3 children against 2·1).

The Oriental population not only shows a higher rate of natural increase, but also it is more settled, showing a much lower percentage of emigration from Israel. Emigration of Europeans is four times as high as that of Orientals. In the period 1952–61 the Orientals formed 15·0 per cent of the total emigrants from Israel, while the European emigrants—63·8 per cent (with 21·2 per cent of Israeli-born). The Oriental stays put, while the European, who has greater opportunities to settle somewhere else, leaves the country in greater numbers.

Now let us consider the occupational structure. Most of the Oriental population can be found in unskilled or casual employment among building workers, agricultural wage-earners, dockers and porters and workers in heavy industry. In farming the percentage of the Oriental population varies from 10·6 per cent to 24·3 per cent (the percentage of their engagement in farming varies with the date of immigration to Israel), while of the European population the proportion lies between 7·1 per cent to 12 per cent (in farm labouring the ratio of the Orientals is much higher). Construction workers, quarrymen and miners make up 12 per cent to 16·9 per cent of the Orientals and 6·8 per cent to 10·3 per cent among European immigrants. On the other end of the scale professionals, scientists and technicians made up between 3·2 per cent to 5·3 per cent (1963) among the Orientals, and 11·9 per cent to 21·1 per cent among the Europeans. Also more Europeans than Orientals have more than one job.

The average income of European families is about 45–50 per cent higher than that of Oriental families. The European veterans (the pre-1948 immigrants) had an income of 775·4 I£ per month, compared with 532·1 I£ earned by the Oriental veterans. The European new immigrants (post-1947 immigrants) earned 600·2 I£, compared with the Oriental new immigrants' 467·7 I£.

The percentage of working wives among the Orientals who could contribute to the family income is considerably smaller than among the Europeans, primarily owing to larger families and also to a greater incidence of illiteracy. The percentage of Oriental working women aged 18 to 34 among those who immigrated since the inception of the State was (1963)—30·9 per cent of all women in their respective age groups, compared with

40·7 per cent of European women. In older age groups the disparity is still greater until it reaches, in the age group of 55 to 64, the ratio 1 to 3½ in favour of the European working women.

The ratio of working population among the males varies also considerably from age group to age group. The Oriental male starts working early but he drops out from the actively engaged population in greater numbers later on. In the age group of 14 to 17, 41·9 per cent of the Orientals are already at work, compared with only 26·9 per cent of the Europeans. In the age group of 18 to 34, 81·1 per cent of the Orientals are working compared with 77·1 per cent of the Europeans. In the higher age groups the ratios are reversed. In the age group of 25 to 54, 94·4 per cent of Orientals are actively engaged against 97·8 per cent of the Europeans; in the age group 55 to 64, 77·1 per cent of the Orientals against 92·3 per cent of Europeans; among those over 65 the ratio is almost 1 to 2 in favour of the Europeans.

From the comparison of active population one can see that the Orientals are more prone to the conditions of what is called *Lumpenproletariat*, men without distinct occupation or employment. They appear also in greater numbers in what is known as the hard core of unemployment. Altogether they are more prone to unemployment. The percentage of the Orientals among male unemployed was almost twice as high as that of the Europeans (in 1964, 53·8 per cent of the total number of unemployed were Oriental immigrants against 27·9 per cent of European immigrants).[1]

The incidence of criminality is also greater among the Oriental than among the European immigrants. The rates for serious offences committed by immigrants from Africa (North Africa) are 13, from Asia 10, from Europe and America 5 (per thousand of population).[2] Juvenile delinquency is much higher among the Oriental than among the European population.[3] 'The street-corner boy' hanging around on the pavement with a doubtful future ahead of him is more often than not the child of an Oriental family.

The under-education of the Orientals expresses itself in various

[1] All figures given in this chapter, if not otherwise stated, are from the *Statistical Abstract of Israel*, 1965

[2] Shlomo Shoham, *Criminality in Israel*.

[3] *Juvenile Delinquency in Israel*. Ministry of Justice 1956.

ways, in the incidence of illiteracy, in school attendance, school performance and relative scarcity of academic degrees. The percentage of illiterates among the Oriental population in 1963 amounted to 31·8 per cent against 2·8 per cent of the Europeans. Among Oriental women illiteracy reached 43·6 per cent against 3·9 per cent among European women.

The Oriental child does not have the same chance of education as the European child. The so-called free educational system in Israel is only free in principle with many supplementary fees which rise in the higher grades. The Oriental parents are not as interested in their children's education as the Europeans are; they cannot help them in their homework, they cannot spare their earning power. The discrepancy in educational chances starts right at the nursery school (kindergarten); the European child is sent to the nursery school at the age of three, the child of the Oriental family which is not so well off, usually starts at the age of five. In the primary schools (the statutory school-leaving age is fourteen) the Oriental child heavily outnumbers the European child but he often goes straight to the bottom of the form. Where there are two streams, as for instance in Beersheba, the second stream consists mostly of the Oriental children. After primary schooling the education of the Oriental child is mostly discontinued. The percentage of pupils in secondary schools from Oriental families amounts to only 17·8 per cent (1963/4–1964/5); the discrepancy increases with each higher grade. Among first degree students in academic institutions their percentage declines to 12 per cent (1963/4), and among the second and Doctor degree students, to 6 per cent.

Housing is perhaps the biggest and the hardest problem in the syndrome of underprivilege. The Jewish Agency allocates to both European and Oriental families the standard 2½ room flat, discriminating, if at all, to the advantage of the Europeans, arguing that in order to attract Jews from the affluent societies it has to offer better housing conditions. However, the same standard flat means for the large Oriental family overcrowding with two, three or four persons to each room. The majority, namely, 62·2 per cent of the veteran and 67·4 per cent of post-1947 immigrants among the Oriental population occupied in 1963 accommodation with two or more persons per room, while the respective figures for the Europeans are 20·8 per cent and 33·6 per cent. This overcrowding with swarms of children quickly turns the housing estate into a slum. The Oriental population lives mostly in separate quarters, villages or estates (*shikunim*). Sometimes on one side of the road live the European families while on the other side the Orientals. One can see at once the differences in appearance and amenities. The *shikunim* of the Oriental families are easily recognizable by their gloomy houses and sombre roads. The contractors and builders of the new estates complain that if they sell one house or flat to an Oriental family, they can hardly sell the remainder to the Europeans. The contempt and disapproval from the European neighbourhood is evident and leads to reluctance to allow European children to mix with those from the Oriental quarter. The distrust often affects the relationship of the children themselves. Discrimination is sometimes unconcealed, as for instance in the case of the House Committee (*Vaad Habajit*) in a block in De-Haas Street in Tel-Aviv, where the committee refused to sanction the transfer purchase with key money of three flats to three prospective buyers from Yemen, on account of their country of origin.

However, in spite of all this, the two Israels are coming closer to each other as time passes. They meet together at many points, and cultural, social and demographic contacts are on the increase. Inter-marriage, the greatest healer of this division, is on the increase. The percentage of European brides marrying Orientals was 4·3 per cent in 1953 and it gradually climbed to 6·5 per cent in 1963; the percentage of Oriental grooms marrying Europeans climbed from 7·5 per cent to 8·9 per cent. Oriental grooms have greater attraction for European girls than Oriental brides for European boys, which is almost a normal phenomenon for all minorities or underprivileged strata. The Central Bureau of Statistics in Jerusalem has worked out an index of attraction of marrying couples between the two Israels, accepting the level of I. as meaning that all marriages are between people of one and the same community (for instance within the Oriental community only or within the European community only), while zero means that there is neither attraction nor rejection, as though no community division existed. According to this computation the index of attraction dropped from 0·81 in 1955 to 0·73 in 1963. This means that the attraction increases between the two communities, but it still has a long way to go to reach the point zero, where marriage would be entirely determined by chance without the pull of any bias or prejudice on one side or the other. Actually the attraction to marry within each Tribe, not only within the European or Oriental section, is considerable, although it varies from Tribe to Tribe. The Yemenites are attracted in the highest degree by Yemenites only, showing the highest index of attraction, 0·82. After them come North Africans, the Iraqis and the Persians. The Orientals are much more clannish than the Europeans. The German Jews, the Czech and the American show the lowest index of attraction (0·26, 0·16, 0·12 in that order).

The Oriental peoples voice many grievances and resentments. First of all they resent their political under-representation, what is often called second-class citizenship. Out of 120 seats in the Knesset they command only 23 seats, out of 18 members of the Cabinet, 2 members only. In the Jewish Agency they have only one member of the executive and not even one director of the departments (1966). A similar position obtains in the Histadrut and political parties at large. Radio and journalism are almost entirely in the hands of Europeans.

Even greater resentment arises from the fact that they have lost the middle class or lower middle class positions which they held in their country of origin to become to a very large extent a proletarian or semi-proletarian class in Israel. In their country of origin 43 per cent of them were traders, agents, salesmen, administrative and clerical workers. Only 5 per cent of them were employed in farming or construction and very little unskilled manual work was done by them. Now they have been forced into farming, labouring, building, and unskilled or semi-skilled industrial work. The Oriental Jew was able to hold his own in competition with the Arabs but he is unable to compete on equal terms with European Jews. He resents being assigned the position of hewer of wood and drawer of water.

Resentment arises also from clash of mores and customs. The sex morality is more permissive among the Europeans. A Yemenite would say, 'Even prostitutes in our country were not dressed as indecently as the European girls dress over here'. The Orientals have lost their status, often in their own families, especially if the wife had to go to work. The adolescent son does not show the obedience and respect which is due to his father according to the traditional mores. The Oriental would say, 'When I spoke to my father I had to stand up and show my respect. Here my boy laughs at me. He is sitting while I am standing.'

Resentfulness is felt at the irreligiosity of the European Jews. Except for the small section of the Orthodox, most Europeans are either atheistic-agnostic or religiously lukewarm, while most Orientals feel deeply about their religion; they take offence, seeing the Law being disregarded by the European co-religionists. 'What kind of Jew is he if the injunctions of the Torah do not mean anything to him', the Oriental Jew would ask.

The educated Oriental is more vocal about his grievances, trying to take advantage of them. Any failure to obtain a position or a job or university place is attributed to ethnic discrimination. Individual blind spots, greed and private interests are woven into collective generalizations and prejudices. The actual strains and disparities are conducive to hostility but they are additionally aggravated by partisan pressures. Some political parties try to channel the discontent and grievances of the Orientals for their own benefit, as the *Israel Bet* is becoming more and more important at a ballot box. General anxieties, whenever an economic recession occurs, which is always harder on the unskilled, are easily exploited. Regular publications such as *Bama'archa* ('In battle') in Jerusalem add fuel to the issue.

Israel Bet is torn between two tendencies, one of assuming and valuing its cultural inheritance, and the other, simultaneous, tendency of disowning and rejecting it. The Orientals want to keep their faith in their own idiom; they reject the idea of their cultural inferiority. Their art and culture are appreciated and cultivated, especially their music, singing, dancing and traditional crafts; on the other hand they are eager to disown and deny their heritage and to assume European customs and mores. The Oriental is often apologetic about his country of origin. A Moroccan would often claim, 'I am from the South of France' an Iraqi would often present himself as *jelid Haaretz*, Israeli native. In order to succeed the Oriental has to imitate the Europeans, on the other hand it is difficult for him to part with his past.

Moreover, the Oriental resents the equation of unity with uniformity, the enforced Europeanization, which is often implied in the fact that most teachers are recruited from the Europeans. European ways in school, the Oriental argues, often produce automatically what is called the backwardness of the Oriental child. The Oriental child at home imbibes values and standards which are out of step with those at school, and often clash violently with them. The intelligence of the Oriental child is of a different quality which would suggest that a different approach would bring out the best in the child, while at present he is simply pushed back to the bottom of his class.

The Orientals are not quite sure whether to lodge a claim to their identity or not. Their very identity is questioned. They are dissatisfied with the public image of themselves and they are not sure what is to be their identity. What are they? What are they to be? The Europeans promise them oneness at the cost of their identity. Is that what they want? Do they want to give up their separate identity? Their main ally is time; time is definitely on their side. And they are also more in harmony with the landscape of the country and with the demographic structure of the region. In the past, when they left the land of Israel, they still remained in the same region, and now having returned to Israel they stay where they are.

Both sections have a sense of guilt. Since time immemorial the Jews refused to think in terms of national and ethnical stereotypes and treated men as individuals on their own merit. Now they have fallen into alien traps of making distinctions between men according to ethnical and racial labels. The hope is expressed that Israel will mature towards her own vision, which will do away with national shiboleths and tribal labels in the spirit of mutual tolerance and cordial fellowship.

For the time being the differences seem to be dominant if they are measured by the outcry of resentment that is to be heard. Prosperity, which came in the last decade to Israel, did not heal the wounds of the division as might have been expected. On the contrary, Europeans are able to make better use of the opportunities offered by rising affluence than the less adaptable Orientals. The percentage of professionals, scientists and technicians among the Oriental immigrants (who came to Israel since 1955) fell from 4·4 per cent in 1961 to 3·2 per cent in 1963, while the percentage of those engaged in building, mining and industry has increased from 38·1 per cent in 1961 to 40·6 per cent in 1963. The Oriental is increasingly characterized as a manual worker while the European takes over professional and administrative work in Israel. This is going to raise serious problems as the ethnic differences are set into the class structure. However, in the Six-Day War both sections proved equal to their task and their differences did not seem to matter in their comradeship on the battlefield.

The syndrome of underprivilege of the Oriental Jews in Israel throws some light on the colour problem in the West. It shows that the syndrome of underprivilege is not due only and entirely to colour prejudice and colour discrimination, because very little of it exists in Israel, but it has some deeper roots in the historical past of the people, who suddenly enter an area of more developed civilizational forms, in which they have to compete with more sophisticated and better equipped social groups. Their handicap cannot be obliterated by providing mere equality of opportunity or even by the brotherly advances of a more fortunate relation, like those often offered by other Tribes in Israel. When two civilizations of unequal level of development meet in a single area, a gulf similar to the one existing between them in their natural habitat, will be expressed in different levels of welfare, culture and social relationships at large, on their new meeting ground. The gulf will fill only gradually in generations to come until all the traces of former differentials are wiped out.

2.

Stratification and Status Distinction

ISRAELI society presents a mosaic-like fine stratification (often called the Israeli social rainbow) with various scales of status and prestige based on many diverse criteria. Some are ascriptive statuses linked with countries of origin, especially European or Oriental origin, others with greater or shorter length of residence in the country, level of education, religious practice, party membership, skill and occupation. A number of them are crossing each other and overlapping. Some are relics of the past, others have functional value. Some are factors of integration, others are divisive; some are perpetuating tensions and conflicts, encouraging envy and snobbishness, others are operating as checks and balances.

A relic of the past is the caste-like division of Jewish society into three broad tribal layers, the Cohens (priests), the Levites (the old Temple servants), and the remainder, the rank and file. Each of those Tribes have a definite role in religious life and their rights and duties are observed up to now and adhered to in the sphere of marital status, as administered by the Rabbis. The status of the Cohen carries a certain degree of prestige among the orthodox section of the population, but none among the secular Jews.

Also a relic of the past are statuses centred on *baalebatiut* (the well-to-do household family) and *jichus* (descendance from a good family). They are still operative in Israeli society to a certain degree but more so among the orthodox section of the population. They are a straight inheritance from the *shtetl* (the Ghetto), which was ridden 'by appalling social discrimination'.[1] A 'tatten's kind' (a son of a well-to-do father) still confers status and prestige not to be compared with that of a descendant of a workman or

[1] Maurice Samuel, 'The Road From Motol'. In *Chaim Weizmann. A Biography by Several Hands*. London 1960.

craftsman. The sons and grandsons of the 'big shots' enjoy prestige and positions of influence. Family-property origin plays a part in all kinds of social relations in Israeli society, especially among the Orthodox.

A very important division in Israeli society is based on the length of residence in the country. There were various waves of immigration, each with a character of its own. There were the pioneers, voluntary, semi-voluntary and forced immigrations. The first wave, as it is called in Hebrew *Alija* (ascendance) began in 1882 and lasted up to the end of the nineteenth century. This was the immigration of the *Bilu* (from the initials Beth Jacob Lecha Unelecha—O house of Jacob come ye and let us walk in the light of the Lord—Isaiah) and *Hoveve Zion* (The Lovers of Zion). Most of the immigrants were financed by Baron Edmond de Rothschild. The oldest settlements in Israel such as Rishon-le-Zion (The First in Zion), Petah Tikvah (The Door of Hope), Rosh Pinah (The Corner Stone), were founded by them. Many of them succumbed to the diseases of the swamp and the desert and very few, if any, survive up to the present day.

So the highest status is at present accorded to the Second Alija (1904–14), who are regarded as the Pilgrim Fathers of Israel. They are classed as veteran pioneers. However distinction is made between those who settled on the land and middle-class veterans who settled in the towns. The immigrants of the Third Alija, mostly from Russia and Poland, who took immediate advantage of the Balfour Declaration (1919–23) are also often classed in this category, although their prestige is just a fraction lower. The Fourth Alija (1924–6) from Poland under the influence of fiscal reforms of the Government of Grabski, which severely hit the Polish Jewry, belongs to the semi-voluntary immigration and their members are in a category of their own with a prestige below that of the previously mentioned groups. The Fifth Alija, the so-called German Alija in the thirties, was an enforced Alija and those immigrants have much less prestige. The lowest status is accorded to the post-State immigrants, from European camps and from Arab countries, who were forced to leave their country of origin and had nowhere else to go.

The basic distinction at present, observed in most statistical surveys, is between pre-State immigrants, who are called veterans in the larger sense (*Vatikim-Seniors*), and post-State immigrants who are called *Olim* (the immigrants). The immigrants of the last five or six years have a status of their own and they are called *Olim Chadashim* (the new immigrants). When a veteran hears an immigrant complaining about the conditions in Israel he would say to him, 'You have no idea what we have been through for your sake. You came when the table was already set and yet you grumble.'

The veterans enjoy certain privileges in getting a position or in keeping a job whenever redundances are considered. The right to a job through a Labour Exchange or the order of dismissals in redundancy in establishment is based on a point system, in which family responsibilities, seniority in a workplace or the depth of unemployment, play the most important part. However, length of residence in the country is also marked by a number of points. On the other hand the new immigrants are helped in other ways, in getting an apartment, in tax exemption, exemption from customs duties, credit facilities, in job reservations, etc.

The occupational structure of the veterans differs considerably from that of the immigrants. Higher grades are mostly occupied by veterans and lower grades by immigrants. For instance the administrative, executive, managerial and clerical staff among the European veterans make up 26·2 per cent of their labour force, while among European post-State immigrants (1948–54), 18·1 per cent and among European immigrants since 1955, 11·7 per cent. At the other end of the scale, manual workers form the big majority among the post-State immigrants. The immigrant has to accept what is left, after the best positions are taken, and not in big towns but mostly in developing areas.

The level of income of veterans is much higher than that of immigrants. The total monthly gross income (in 1963–4) was among Europeans 775·4 I£ for veterans, against 600·2 I£ for post-State immigrants; among Orientals 532·1 I£ for veterans, against 467·7 I£ for post-State immigrants. Especially great is the gap in income from wages and salaries. The gap is greater among Europeans, as their scale of grades is greater, while the Orientals concentrate mostly on manual labour. Also the adaptive qualities of the Europeans are greater than those of the Orientals, as they present the dominant, tone-giving section of the community. As the majority of the post-State immigrants came from the Orient, the two divisions, the division between the veterans and immigrants and the division between the Europeans and the Orientals to a certain degree overlap.

The veteran and immigrant sectors are also somewhat geographically divided in different zones of settlements. Rehavia in Jerusalem and North of Tel-Aviv or Mount Carmel in Haifa are settled by veterans, while the fringes of the towns are settled by new immigrants. New towns such as Beersheba, Dimone and Eilat in the South, or Nazareth and Kirjat Shmone in the North are settled by immigrants.

Another important scale of statuses is linked with levels of formal education which also serve as a basis for social segregation and for selection in occupational structure. Formal education both as a collective key for social groupings and for occupational choice is of crucial significance in Israeli society which values educational standards very highly. This was true of Jewish society in the Diaspora, but even more so in Israel, which has to rely on education as the basic instrument for socialization and integration of the new society, as well as for preparation for its occupational structure. Education is the key to a unified nationhood.

The criteria of formal education are the basis for the distinction of five separate layers of Israeli society, which in the Israeli civilian labour force appear as follows:

First we have the illiterates with no schooling whatever, who form about 16 per cent of the total Israeli labour force (1963).

The next layer are the semi-illiterates with a smattering of a primary school education, with one to four years of schooling, forming 8 per cent of the labour force.

The popular education layer consists of those who have between five to eight years schooling in primary education, making up about 34 per cent of the labour force.

The secondary education layer consists of those who have completed between nine to twelve years of schooling. They form 31 per cent of the labour force.

The highest layer is formed by those with university or equivalent education with thirteen plus years of schooling, who make up 9 per cent of the labour force.

Those are the five social layers in terms of formal education. Social groupings based on common interest, leisure time activities, friendship and fellowship circles are primarily related to those five basic levels of education.

We see strong contrasts in this stratification, as about 1 in 4 is illiterate or semi-illiterate and about 40 per cent are those with high school or university full or partial education. However, there is a strong tendency towards a more even spread of education. In about 10 years time, 5–8 years of schooling should be universal, while at the highest level, university education is rapidly expanding. The Israeli is a man of strong intellectual bent, and a well-equipped bookcase is an essential part of most homes. The consumption of books and periodicals per head of the population is one of the highest in the world and most masterpieces of the world literature are already translated into Hebrew. The strong pressure for higher education already produces more scientists, technologists, architects and lawyers than can be absorbed within the country. Israel is likely to develop a considerable export of brains to other countries. Already the universities and Technion are producing brain power for export as many Israeli students leave for post-graduate courses and of those a considerable number do not come back. Many more Israeli students leave for the U.S.A. than Jewish students from America come to Israel.[1] This is a considerable dilemma for the Israeli society, as expanding higher education means in fact the encouragement of the brain drain abroad which is equivalent to a negative selection of the population. The resolving of this dilemma may be sought in a forceful development of a science-based industry, which could absorb the scientific manpower of the country.

Religious practice is another focus of statuses. As described in another context religion in Israel is a source of considerable social tension arising out of the refusal of the Rabbinical authorities to accommodate themselves with greater liberality to the changing times and living conditions in Israel. This tension expresses itself in mutual disapproval of the two broad sections of the population. The Orthodox Jew regards the secular Jew as a 'goy', who betrays the values of Judaism, while the secularists who form the majority look upon the Orthodox as an obscurant ignoramus and a sort of archaic relic. That religion and education, and more definitely orthodoxy and education do not go together, are firmly established convictions of the secularist majority in

[1] Out of 35,000 registered unemployed in February 1967—630 had academic degrees.

Israel. In fact the Orthodox appear in small numbers among the professional and scientific staff. They are more often encountered among the small independent traders, salesmen, insurance agents and among the middle and lower echelons of clerical employment in private and even more frequently in public service. We can say that the Jewish religion in Israel in spite of Sombart and Max Weber, is definitely not conducive to the growth of capitalism; the religious Jew appears in greater numbers in more economically backward areas such as Jerusalem or in the slums of Tel-Aviv; he belongs mostly to low income and low or middle status occupation. The Orthodox is in a much weaker position as a competitor, as he is bound by his many religious duties and practices and spends so much time on the study of the Torah, on prayers, community life and charity duties. He is not only isolated from the secular community at large but he also isolates himself, not approving of others and not being approved by them. He forms a sub-culture in Israeli society, living in enclaves or self-imposed ghettos, similar to the *Shtetl* from which he emerged. Not only in towns but also in the country there are religious enclaves in separate villages, which stress very much their separateness from their secular surroundings. The Orthodox often protest, send petitions, stage public demonstrations, keeping alive their 'minority complex' from the Diaspora. They form a section of Israeli society which is the least affected by the general atmosphere of freedom, national independence and pride of sovereignty. They form also the best organized pressure group in society.

An important focus of status in Israeli society is linked with party membership, the standing and the degree of activism in the party and the exercise of political power through party membership. Being a socialist or a liberal or a *Herutnik* or a communist confers a status of its own. A man committed to a certain ideology is classed a progressive or reactionary, a man furthering or hampering the new society and its social integration. In Israel those distinctions are very important, as politics play such a big part in Israeli society and the Israeli is a political man *par excellence*. The distribution of wealth and income, especially of contributions from abroad which form such a big part of revenue, the distribution of licences, subsidies, credits and tax exemptions, is governed to a large extent by political power and by what is often called party key. The power élite or the political class are the activists in the politically dominant parties. The political élite in Israel is fairly cohesive and homogeneous, recruiting itself mainly from the Second or Third Alija and ethnically from East European stock. The key appointments in the public and large semi-public institutions and offices are made mainly from this stratum. It subscribes to a certain ideology which can be described as a mixture of socialism and nationalism with a latitude of doctrinal and practical interpretations in shifts of emphasis between several parties. It is a small and self-recruiting oligarchy. The oligarchies of most parties are composed of the East European veterans. They are recruited in great numbers from Kibbutzim and collective Moshavim, whose members are political men of the purest breed.

Now we must consider the class structure of Israeli society. Israel was formed by the middle classes of Eastern Europe or the Middle East. The Western Europeans and the Americans form a very small minority. These middle classes were predominantly lower middle classes with a sprinkling of semi-proletariat. The special characteristic of Israel is that the pioneers who were recruited from the lower middle class came to Israel with an established socialist ideology and a working-class ethos. This ideology and working-class ethos have been taken over as the official ideology of the political and social élite and supported by the mass of wage and salary earners, who in recent years (1964) formed about 70 per cent of the total manpower in Israel. The middle-class mentality of the former merchants, traders and artisans has not basically changed but it is super-imposed by *sui generis* working-class ethos and ideology.

This middle-class mentality expresses itself perhaps best in the ethos of house ownership. Israel is a society of house owners. The ethos of house property is part of the general ethos of society. Every man should have his own house, or apartment, a roof of his own over his head, every man to be his own landlord. This idea was put into practice in Israel. There is hardly any modern society where this idea was translated into reality to such an extent. About two-thirds of the 625,000 householders in Israel own their house or apartment. Only one-third are tenants in privately owned dwellings and among these about 15 per cent are in rent-controlled tenancies, which are equivalent to self-owned property (the occupant of a house or flat acquired by key money can sell his rights on payment of one-third of the selling price to the owner of the rent-controlled house). The overwhelming majority of immigrants of five years' standing own their house or apartment.

The wish to own house property has considerable impact on the saving habits of the population, as the savings are mostly directed to acquiring a new and better house or apartment, and equipping it. Savings turn automatically into investment and they give strong encouragement to the building industry and allied trades. The house or apartment—together with a car and holiday abroad has become the main status symbol.

Now let us consider in some detail the actual class composition of the population as seen from its occupational structure. Here we have to distinguish between town and country. The socio-economic pattern in the two environments is entirely different and it is very difficult to discuss them under common headings. Since 86·3 per cent of the Israeli population live in towns, the stratification of urban society is of the first significance.

At the top we have the class of large-scale employers and the very rich men which we may compare with the upper class in Western European countries. There is no Jewish aristocracy in Israel. The Barons, the lords and millionaires do not settle in Israel. Israel gathered small men, who had been rejected or squeezed out, most having had a marginal existence in their country of origin. But some of them have shown special initiative, enterprise and skill or cunning and have worked themselves up to the position of millionaires (a hundred new dollar millionaires are reported for Tel-Aviv) or to the position of large-scale employers, factory owners, owners of chain stores, large housing estates or extensive citrus groves. Those are mostly of European veteran origin. Political power and influence and rise of land prices had their share in making those millionaires. The complex policy of subsidies, premiums, import and export licences, land lease and land sales, as well as contributions from abroad, have created a climate conducive to 'get rich quick' shifts in population. There is a layer of *nouveaux riches*, which is to be expected in all developing countries with high immigration. Their standing and influence is not very high, they have little self-confidence and may experience feelings of guilt, as they made money out of Israel, while others made contributions and sacrifices for the country. They have developed their own strong professional bodies such as the Manufacturers Association; they belong mostly to the Liberal parties and Herut. They have no tradition of being a separate class but they are developing class consciousness through mobilization of their defences against what they regard as the onslaught of socialism. They are the defenders of Israeli capitalism, but in fact very weak defenders and not very convinced about the righteousness of their cause.

In their struggle against socialism they are supported by two other layers of employers and self-employed men, one middle layer of medium and small factory owners, of successful business men, of owners of insurance and trading agencies, art galleries and tourist agencies; and the lower layer of self-employed artisans, shopkeepers, salesmen, agents and traders of all kinds. Those three layers form the independent classes, by and large supporting the business interests, defending what is often called the policy of free enterprise. They formed, together with members of private co-operatives who have a somewhat similar ideology, 18·9 per cent of the civilian labour force (1963). They are a contracting layer, declining from 22·6 per cent in 1955 to 18·9 per cent in 1963. They represent the element of profit in the Israeli society.

Now we come to the working classes in Israel. The term working class is applied to all those who work with brawn or brain without 'exploiting' others, i.e., without employing others or without being middlemen or business men. Two classes of people are excluded: employers and self-employed middlemen in all walks of life. A shop assistant is 'working-class', but a shopkeeper, even if he does not employ others, is not. Accordingly all wage and salary earners up to the highest rank of management are 'working-class', as are all self-employed and all members of co-operatives in 'productive' work. The Israeli working class contains all those who are bound by the social idea of productive work, by the aspiration to build a new working-class society, in which everyone will earn his living by working with brawn or brain without exploiting other peoples' labour through employment or by trade. Moreover, the working-class so defined has a common organization in the Histadrut (the General Federation of Jewish Labour) which plays an enormous and decisive part both in shaping the individual worker's life and in general labour relations and labour conditions. We may call the working-class all those who are actual or potential members of the Histadrut. The working-class concept is thus institutionalized in a central organization, whose main aspiration is the building of this new working-class society.

The working-class consists of two distinct layers, salary earners and wage earners. They are in many ways subject to different institutional arrangements, so as to constitute two different social classes. They are organized in separate Trade Unions and in most work places also in separate Workers' Committees. They have different status, different stability of employment, different rights and duties. Wage earners are on the clock; they are, by and large, hourly rated men, paid only for the number of hours actually worked, with arrangements for overtime and part-time work. Salary earners are paid by the month irrespective of the number of hours worked. The two layers have different arrangements for sick pay, holidays, the length of working time, seniority, promotion, dismissal and compensation for discharge. While in theory the myth of the redeeming qualities of toil and sweat should give the manual worker a higher status in society, in fact it is the other way round, as in both status and actual terms of employment and level of wages, salary earners are favoured over the wage earners.

Among salary earners themselves we have to distinguish between two distinct strata, one which we may call the professional class, the other the clerical class.

The professional class is made up of professional managers of enterprises in private, public and semi-public positions, the higher echelons of the civil service, armed forces, the Histadrut and the Jewish Agency, doctors, lawyers, architects, technologists, scientists, university teachers and artists of repute. They form the élite of the country; most of them have university or similar education. They are very highly organized in professional bodies which protect their interests. They are typically 'organization men'[1] and committee men, bent on collective decisions and believing in the mystique of organization. They are well aware of their new role and position in society. They are mostly responsible for the new mental climate of society with its leaning towards technocracy, rationalization and planning. They are the epigones

---

[1] William H. Whyte, *The Organization Men*. New York 1957.

and heirs of the pioneers. The pioneers of yesterday became the organization men of today. They are the most dynamic stratum of society. The professional, scientific, technical and related staff (apart from executives and managers) expanded between 1955 and 1964 from 10.4 per cent to 12.3 per cent of the civilian labour force. They regard themselves as 'workers' and are active members of the Histadrut. They are the backbone of the labour movement. They are mostly recruited from the veteran European population. They have secured a high standard of living, own very comfortable apartments, run cars, take their holidays abroad, and send their children to university.

The clerical class is made up of the administrative and clerical staff of middle and lower echelons in private, public and semi-public employment: civil servants of middle and lower grades, school teachers, policemen, technicians without a higher degree, foremen, supervisors, hospital staff without a degree. They represent the element of bureaucracy in Israeli society. Max Weber believed that the specific nature of the bureaucratic mechanism 'develops the more perfectly the more the bureaucracy is de-humanized . . . '. The bureaucratic mechanism in Israel is highly developed (not only in the State apparatus, but also in private industry and politics[1]) and is also highly 'de-humanized'. It labours very heavily under mountains of paperwork, reports, statistical records, forms and questionnaires overloaded with meaningless questions, starting from the name and religion of father and mother and continuing in this vein, all in several copies, to make sure that none of these precious data will ever escape the future historian. The Israeli bureaucrat trusts no one and keeps asking: 'What, how, why, and why not?' The 'why not' is of course in line with all the perennial Jewish jokes in the Diaspora. He writes everything down and is greedy for more and more information. Documents, records, testimonials are requested and produced and then taken to the next room to be shown to the supervisor, as he does not like to take responsibility on himself. As the supervisor is also not very sure, he advises caution. Procrastination is the rule and this produces queues beleaguering every office in Israel.

With all that, one must admit that the Israeli bureaucracy has

[1] The new Labour Party has a central committee of 450 members and a secretariat of 187.

many handicaps which should modify our harsh judgement on its efficiency. It started with no tradition. It has to contend with the general insufficient mastery of the Hebrew language. There are no official norms and rules which are often changed from case to case. General distrust, casuistry and an excessive bent for legalistic interpretation is shared by the whole of society.

The civil servant not only frustrates others but is also the most frustrated person in the country. He wants to achieve something but he is up against the inertia of an immense apparatus which weighs him down and paralyses his movements. But he has the security of life tenure, and if he is a sadist or if he wants to give back what he himself experienced in the past, he has full opportunity to do so. His standard of living is below that of the professional class but still very comfortable. Most of them have full or part high school education or at least full primary education. They are recruited mostly from the veteran Europeans, however with a considerable admixture of the Oriental population. Some of them are from Orthodox families. The Israeli bureaucracy is often described jokingly as Talmudic-socialistic bureaucracy. They regard themselves as workers and are members of the Histadrut. They are much more strongly organized than the manual workers.

The two strata, the professional and the clerical classes, jointly represent 28·3 per cent of the civilian labour force and are expanding rapidly.

Now we come to the manual workers in mining, manufacturing, building and transport. These one may call workers in the strictest sense. We have here several gradations of status according to grades of skill and experience (in most branches of industry up to six grades), stability of employment (permanent, or temporary workers, weekly or daily paid), and seniority in the workplace (there are workers who can be dismissed only after the whole factory has been closed down). They are predominantly of Oriental origin and many among them are post-State immigrants. However, in old establishments such as, for instance, in the cement factory Nesher in Haifa or Shemen belonging to the concern of Histadrut, the staff of manual workers consists predominantly of European veterans. On the other hand the building workers or workers in heavy industry such as Yuval Gad in Migdal Ashkelon, making pipes and tubes, or in new factories such as Alliance

(Tyre Factory) in Hedera are mostly Oriental new immigrants.

The manual workers are organized in separate unions of the Histadrut but they are under the patronage of the power élite of the Histadrut parties. Their voice in the councils of the Histadrut hierarchy does not carry great weight. The degree of democracy in the workmens' unions is not very high, owing to the low standard of education. Because of this, there are numerous illegal strikes and a great number of illegal Workers' Committees.

The workers in different industries can be divided into categories by status and conditions of employment. We have the building workers who work very hard under the exacting conditions of the Israeli climate. Most of them are recruited from the thirty to forty-five age group. Younger workers have other opportunities and do not care for jobs in building. If a young single man finds himself in building, he often plays at the job, working for a month and then taking an unofficial holiday for a fortnight. Men above fifty are also rarely to be found among building workers, although in road building one can see occasionally very old men with their long white beards who have to accept heavy jobs because they cannot find anything else. By and large a building worker in Israel cannot continue for long at his full capacity. Many foremen and contractors, whom I interviewed, asserted that in Israeli conditions a man cannot continue at full capacity in his trade longer than 10–15 years, others estimated 15–20 years. Only a few thought that he could continue much longer, provided he took good care of himself, led a reasonable life, took annual vacations and was of a strong constitution. The level of intelligence of unskilled labourers is generally speaking low. Most of those whom I interviewed have never heard about socialism or communism, but they know what the Histadrut stands for. Most of them live in overcrowded conditions. They are reasonably well off when working but they suffer from spells of unemployment.

The building industry once engaged the finest workmen in the country, the pioneering youth. It was regarded as the aristocratic trade, providing the admission card to all the leading positions in the Workers' Movements. Most leaders of the movements were once building labourers. Now the position is reversed. At present the ratio of unemployment among building workers is very high owing to the stoppage of immigration.

The industrial workers fall into two categories, one in crafts, the other in industry. In crafts, that is in establishments using little mechanical equipment and employing up to ten men, a fair number are unorganized. The workers rarely have the protection of a collective agreement and rarely get full social benefits. In industry the situation of the worker is different. A job in industry is highly appreciated by the Israeli worker. The worker is at a bench out of the sun and a stool is provided where possible. The job is relatively well paid, gets the highest social benefits with a high degree of job security. Speaking to men at the labour exchange one often hears, 'To get into a factory, you need *protektzia*' (someone to back you up).

The type of worker, his situation and conditions vary greatly with the size of the establishment. The larger the establishment the better his position, the stronger his organization, the greater his self-reliance, the more pronounced his class consciousness. In larger establishments the worker faces professional management, in smaller establishments an owner or group of owners. In larger establishments his relationships with the management are institutionalized, while in smaller establishments they remain strictly personal.

Next we have two more layers of urban population, the Lumpenproletariat and the supported population. The Lumpenproletariat or what the American sociologists call the *underclass*, a mass of nondescript people beneath social visibility, who often combine great passivity with violence and parasitism, consists of men of shady occupations, drunkards, gamblers, peddlers, professional beggars, those who live by their wits, part of the criminal classes, prisoners or those committed to institutional care. Those form not a negligible stratum of society. The number of economic offences has risen steadily since the inception of the State with the post-State mass immigration. Thefts dealt with by the police for the first time, have risen in 1949–64 from 7,237 to 35,382, housebreakings from 3,330 to 17,136, causing damage to property from 719 (1950) to 5,232, fraud and forgery from 327 (1950) to 2,887. This is a very considerable economic criminality in such a small community. It suggests a considerable layer of the parasitic class in Israel. The permissiveness of Israeli society, combined with charity socialism and a large number of illiterates with ineffective acculturation, has produced a parasitic class not dissimilar to that encountered for instance in Latin America.[1] This could become a danger to Israeli society, if it is not energetically counteracted in time.

The supported population forms a not insignificant layer, which of course is not confined to urban population only. The number of Jewish families in the care of Social Welfare Bureaux has risen considerably during the last 8 years (1955–6 to 1962–3) from 65,506 to 101,300. Out of these, regular economic assistance was received by 25,700 families, while other material assistance by 30,000 families. In the last year (1966–7) owing to the stoppage of immigration and the deflation policy of the Government the number of families which have to fall back on public assistance has considerably increased.

Now let us review the social stratification of the Jewish rural population. First of all we have to divide this population into two separate sections which are hardly comparable, the private sector on the one hand and the co-operative and collective sector on the other. In the private sector we have a small number of farming estates and plantations usually run by contracting firms undertaking farming work for land owners. The owners of large estates rarely live in the rural settlements. They are mostly resident in towns, regarding the plantation as their capital investment.

Next in line we have a whole gradation of private individual farmers living in villages. Their status differs considerably with the size of their holding and also with the size, location and seniority of the village. Less than half the total live in Jewish veteran villages and are very well off. The remainder live in new Jewish villages (post-State) or in Arab villages, in difficult, often precarious conditions. A large number are agricultural labourers, who are the lowest paid workers in the country, although they are organized in the union of agricultural wage earners as part of the Histadrut. They vary considerably in status, pay and stability of tenure. In 1964 there were five grades among agricultural workers with a range of rates of 20 per cent. As regards the stability of tenure they were divided in several grades, such as permanent monthly workers, permanent daily workers, partly employed workers guaranteed about 150 to 200 working days per year, seasonal workers in the strictest sense with a guarantee

[1] Stanislav Andreski, *Parasitism and Subversion. The Case of Latin America.* Weidenfeld and Nicolson. London 1966.

of 100 to 150 working days a year, and finally temporary workers, those who are called men on the Labour Exchange, taken on and shed according to passing needs. The large majority of agricultural workers are recruited from the Oriental population and there is a constant drift from this class into urban settlements. Altogether the Jewish population in all villages, both Jewish and non-Jewish, totalled 78,000 persons, equivalent to 3·5 per cent of the entire Jewish population in the country (1964). Two-thirds of the villagers lived in large villages exceeding 2,000 inhabitants, approaching already the urban type of settlement.

Below the status of villagers are the members of temporary settlements, such as immigrants' reception centres, *ma'arbarot* (temporary immigrant settlements) and immigrant homes. At the end of 1964 there were three settlements with 1,400 persons (0·1 per cent of the Jewish population).

Now we come to the co-operative sector of the rural Jewish population. The members of the Kibbutzim, 80,900 strong, form 3·6 per cent of the entire Jewish population (1964). They have a very high status of their own, a significance and influence far exceeding their small numbers. They form the power élite in the country, being political men *par excellence*, penetrating deeply all the major labour parties, which are dominant politically in the country. They regard themselves as working class, actually an avant-garde of the working classes, but they are in fact a property owning class, as members of a property owning and prosperous integral co-operative community, which safeguards them a high standard of living. They form the aristocracy of the rural population, well fed, housed and clothed, well educated, well serviced with cultural amenities, with full security. They form an enclave in the rural environment, standing apart in most respects from the rest of the rural population. The property of the Kibbutz, except for personal belongings, is owned collectively. A member who leaves is in principle not entitled to 'withdraw any private belongings or money which he may have turned over to the Kibbutz when accepted as a member, unless such a return was specifically provided for in a written agreement between him and the Kibbutz'.[1] However the practice varies from Kibbutz to Kibbutz and from member to member.

---

[1] Harry Viteles, *A History of the Co-operative Movement in Israel. A source book*, Book One, p. 32. Vallentine-Mitchell. London 1966.

There are two slightly different models of collective Moshavim. The *Moshav Shitufi* (collective smallholders' settlement) was organized in 1935 by the immigrants from Bulgaria and *Kfar Shitufi* (collective village) was organized in 1933 for German immigrants. Both models come very near to the model of Kibbutzim. However, they are less thoroughly collective. While production is collective, consumption is private. The *Moshav Shitufi* differs from the Kibbutzim in three main respects:

First, every member of his family lives in his own house on a building site of about a quarter of a dunam. But the family may not use this land to raise produce for the market. The members —men, women and their children—work only in and for their respective Moshav Shitufi. The Moshav Shitufi provides a common dining-room and kitchen facilities only for unattached members. Some of the Moshavim Shitufim have joint laundry facilities and club-rooms.

Secondly, a Moshav Shitufi fixes the same allowance for adults, children and dependants, irrespective of the kind of work to which the members are assigned. Married women are expected to work outside their homes from two to four hours daily, depending on the size of the family. Members may spend their allowances as they choose, but only at the local community store. In special cases the committee of the Moshav Shitufi may grant permission for purchases outside. Differences in spending habits are reflected in home furnishings, clothes and in the amount of credit balances which members have with the Moshav Shitufi.

Third, a member leaving a Moshav Shitufi may take the families' possessions and also receive his credit balance, including his share in the refundable capital, reserves and other funds of his Moshav Shitufi.[1]

Kfar Shitufi is a similar model with a slightly smaller measure of collectivity; it permits private trading, generally limited to certain categories of goods.

The population involved in collective settlements of both models is very small, comprising about 4,200 persons in 21 settlements, equivalent to 0·2 per cent of the Jewish population in the country.

Far more numerous and far more typical for the rural scene of Israel are the Moshavim of a non-collective type. In 1964 there

[1] *Ibid.*, p. 34.

were 346 such settlements comprising 119,600 persons, or 5·3 per cent of the Jewish population. They are organized also on two slightly different models. One is called *Moshav Ovdim* (labour small holders' settlement) which is the oldest model going back to 1921, when the first such settlement Nahalal was formed. The second is *Moshav Olim* (immigrants smallholders' settlement) formed in 1948 for post-State colonization, primarily by the Oriental population. There is no joint farming, except during the first few years of membership and then only as a convenience and not on principle. Both production and consumption are entirely private, and only the purchase and use of agricultural equipment and marketing of the produce are carried out on co-operative basis. There are also educational and communal services provided in the settlements. The economic status differs from member to member. As a whole the members of Moshavim of the non-collective type have a much lower standing in society than the members of the Kibbutzim and the collective Moshavim. By and large they have also lower educational standards, a smaller interest in politics, and also a lower standard of living and equipment. Both Kibbutzim and Moshavim are organized in groups affiliated to political parties and are part of the Histadrut's economy.

Reviewing the social structure of the Israeli society, we can say that there is a considerable fragmentation of society. Society has not yet reached the maturity of full integration; it is still a society in the making. There is a considerable division into separate segments, fairly closed institutional sub-systems, very well organized in themselves. The parts seem to be greater than the whole, to use Aristotle's dictum in reverse. There is a certain lack of balance between the degree of integration of parts with that of the whole. The citizen can hardly be reached by direct approach from the centre; he can be reached most effectively through his own organization.

The society which started with an almost egalitarian social structure became in the course of development and with the rise of affluence very widely diversified, and the gulf between rich and poor widened considerably. We are witnessing the emergence of Jewish plutocracy in Israel. The prim upper and middle class suburbs spring up at the same time as the slums decay. We can speak also about the escalation of status distinctions in society. The strong status consciousness of the basically middle-class Jewish society proved stronger than the socialist and pioneering ideology which proclaimed the nobility of the physical toil of the worker and the peasant. This is most clearly reflected in the inferior status of the wage earner compared with the salary earner and in the very low status of the farm labourers. In the working classes themselves strong privileged positions have sprung up, firmly protected by various institutional arrangements. The Oriental wage earners turn more into a social class of their own.

The crystallization of class consciousness takes place mostly around the employer-employee relationship. On the other hand there is a very considerable social mobility of population. The transition from one class to another is relatively easy but the main ladder is provided almost exclusively by education.

The most disturbing aspects of class distinctions in Israel is the flight of European Jewry from farming and manual work which is being carried out increasingly by what is called Israel Bet. But in farming and manual work there also emerges Israel Gimel, i.e., the Arab worker who is more frequently assigned the role of a hewer of wood and drawer of water. In increasing numbers the Arab agricultural worker appears, in Jewish villages, to carry out the work of the Jewish farmer who takes a job in better-paid occupations in the towns. The same applies to building and roadwork and other manual unskilled jobs as well.

The ghost of the Diaspora occupational distortions start haunting again the Israeli Jewry. With the increasing numbers of the Arab population, rising affluence and technological and scientific developments, the spectre of the division between Israel Alef, Bet and Gimel, may turn into a threatening reality.

3.

The Process of Urbanization

THE INTENTION of the pioneers to build a strong, progressive and thriving rural community in Israel has been considerably deflected by economic and political realities, and by the general modern trend towards industrialization and urbanization. The Jew, since Roman times, has been predominantly an urban type. Now the whole world, and more so the Western world, is undergoing a process of acclerated urbanization and Western man is becoming a predominantly urban type. English and American societies have a residual rural population of 4 to 8 per cent. Trade, commerce and services which were once the speciality of the Jews have become the main occupation of Western man. The same trend is now reflected in the occupational structure of the Israeli society.

First of all we see a constant shift of the working population from primary industries (farming, fishing and forestry) to secondary industries (mining, construction and manufacturing). In the decade 1955–64 the proportion of workers in primary industries declined from 17·1 per cent to 12·5 per cent while that in secondary industries increased from 29·0 per cent to 33·6 per cent.

In the so-called tertiary (service) industries we see the expansion of certain sections at the cost of others. The professional scientific and technical staff increased from 10·4 per cent to 12·3 per cent; the administrative, executive, managerial and clerical staff from 15·8 per cent to 16·0 per cent; general services, sport and recreation services from 10·4 per cent to 12·1 per cent. On the other hand transport and communications reduced their share from 6·0 per cent to 5 per cent and commercial services, previously overstaffed, declined sharply from 11·3 per cent to 8·5 per cent.

So we can speak about the process of industrialization on the one hand and the process of bureaucratization and professionalization on the other. If we add professional, scientific, technical, managerial and administrative-clerical staff, we arrive at the overall figure of 28·3 per cent of the civilian labour force. It means that between 1 in 4 and 1 in 3 are engaged in more or less professional work, a percentage not far below that of workers engaged in secondary industries. There is strong pressure to increase the scope and range of salary earners in administrative, scientific and managerial positions.

The process of industrialization and bureaucratization, goes hand in hand with the constant urbanization of the country. The flight from country to town has reversed the trend of the pioneering age. In spite of persistent colonization planned by the government and deployed with great resourcefulness, the rural settlements are constantly losing their population. Overall, in 1963 rural settlements lost 8,167 men and 7,064 men in 1964, while the towns gained in balance 13,476 in 1963 and 9,696 in 1964. The Kibbutzim and Moshavim have lost the largest numbers. The Kibbutzim lost on balance 2,883 persons in 1963 and 2,387 in 1964, the Moshavim 2,349 and 2,413, in the same years.

The Jew, a typical urban dweller in the Diaspora, is again attracted to the town. It is often reported that the Jewish villager takes a job in the town, hiring an Arab worker to till his land. This practice has been many times condemned by the press but it still goes on. If the villager cannot hire an Arab worker, he leaves the land in the hands of his wife or another member of his family, taking up a more remunerative position in town. More and more Arab labourers are replacing Jewish farm workers.

At the end of 1964 out of a total population of 2,239,100 Israeli Jews, 1,944,400 lived in urban settlements and only 294,600 in rural settlements. It means that about 87 per cent are urban Jews with all the characteristics of urban dwellers. Except for the members of Kibbutzim (81,000) and Moshavim Shitufim (the villages of a collective type with a small population of 4,000), the countryman is rather looked down upon as a sort of country bumpkin, who cannot enjoy full cultural life, as for instance offered by Tel-Aviv.

Almost two-thirds of the Jewish population in Israel live in the three conurbations, Tel-Aviv, Haifa and Jerusalem, which are constantly enlarging their boundaries. Additional conurbations are springing into being along the coastal plain, Natania, Hedera, Ashdod, Ashkelon.

Also new towns are growing rapidly. Already 16 per cent (about 250,000) of Israel's population (1964) lives in twenty-one new towns. The biggest towns such as Beersheba, Ashdot, Elat, Arad, Afula are already fully established important regional centres, but they themselves suffer from constant and severe exodus to old towns. The attractions, subsidies, tax exemptions and assistance offered by the government (in 1963 11·6 per cent of Jewish families in new towns were drawing regular public assistance compared with the national average of 4·4 per cent) are not sufficient to keep the population in areas not attractive from the point of view of trade, employment, education and leisure. The new towns populated to a large extent by poverty-stricken Oriental immigrants (according to an estimate 80 per cent are below the poverty line)[1] are undergoing a further process of negative selection, losing the youngest, the most enterprising, the most skilled and educated elements to old-established towns. The new towns have a very difficult struggle to maintain the standard of their services and appearance, as the new buildings, mass produced or pre-fabricated soon turn into slums.

There is a heated discussion going on in Israel about the planning of new towns, their architecture, their aesthetic qualities, the density of housing development and its pattern[2] Many think that the landscape is spoiled by mass produced concrete four- or five-storey buildings and feel that at least an effort should be made to adjust architecture to the landscape and not to reproduce the American style shanty towns which soon turn into slums. Especially in Galilee it is somewhat depressing to see the square miles of ugly, unimaginative concrete of undressed stone boxes, devoid of privacy and grace and unblessed by adornments. Men somehow feel cheated, facing the hallowed land pulverized by bulldozers.

In spite of all the handicaps and disabilities, Israel's achievements in the field of town planning and resettlement are remarkable and in many ways impressive. The shortcomings can be explained by the haste and cheapness of materials necessary to get quick results with small means to meet the needs of the greatest mass immigration in modern history. The lack of any

[1] United Israel Appeal Estimate.
[2] Erika Spiegel, *New Towns in Israel. Urban and Regional Planning and Development*. Karl Kramer. Stuttgart.

local style is understandable. 'No style can be created synthetically. As long as Israel's culture and society are in a state of flux, no original style can be evolved. But the more this country crystallizes its culture and specific way of life the nearer it will come to a true local style.'[1]

What is striking in Israel is the speed with which an artificially created new town becomes an organic living town with a character of its own. The most striking example is Tel-Aviv itself which started its life as a town planning exercise on the sand dunes at the beginning of this century and which has grown rapidly into one of the biggest centres on the Mediterranean Coast. No one would believe that this is an artificially created town. It is now half a port and commercial centre and half holiday resort and tourist centre, half Levantine, half European, half dignified with character of its own and half slummy and shabby, half modern town wrecked by the invasion of cars and lorries and half village, changing, vanishing and reconstructing. It started as a fantasy of town designers and turned into a nightmare of town planners. Tel-Aviv is the best expression of the permissiveness of the Israeli society.

The effects of this permissiveness combined with the distortions of a rapid urbanization are already appearing, in the form of slums and overcrowded housing as well as soaring land prices. The urban semi-proletariat, called Lumpenproletariat, is already established with its full share of crime, juvenile delinquency and prostitution. There are groups of misfits and vagrants in each of the three great cities. Nightclubs and bars of uncertain reputation have sprung up in numbers. The contrast between poverty and luxury in large towns is too apparent and nowhere more obvious than in the contrast between North Tel-Aviv with its luxurious villas and South Tel-Aviv with its slums. On the other hand the towns can boast of marvellous cultural and educational institutions including theatres, concert halls, libraries, art schools, lecture halls and evening colleges.

The ideal of the veteran pioneers to obliterate the contrast between town and country has up to now remained unfulfilled. The contrast is as great in Israel as anywhere else (apart from the Kibbutzim). The Jewish urban and rural populations have not

[1] A. Yaski, 'Architecture in Israel'. *Israel Economic Forum.* Vol. X. 1–2. p. 31.

only different socio-economic environments, but also different demographic and cultural characteristics, as if belonging to different biological strains. The birthrate (1964) of the Jewish population in towns was 21·7 per thousand, in rural settlements 26·6. The difference is partly accounted for by the greater number of the Oriental population in rural settlements. The birthrate in the Kibbutzim, whose members are mostly Europeans, approaches that of the town (22·2). However, in the Moshavim, where the Oriental population is represented in greater numbers the rate is very high (29·2).

The mortality rates do not differ substantially from town to country. They are a little lower in rural settlements (5·1) than in towns (6·2). The rural population has a younger age composition which may account for the slightly lower mortality rates. However, infant mortality rates (per 1,000 live births in 1964) are much higher in rural settlements, 27·4 against 23·3 in towns, as hospitalization and the standards of personal care and hygiene are higher in towns. Again the Kibbutzim are the exception. The contrast between the Kibbutzim and the Moshavim in this respect is most enlightening. The Kibbutzim with 17·9 have the lowest rate of infant mortality in the whole country, while the Moshavim have a very high rate of 28·9. Large villages have a still higher rate (39·1), which is more than double the Kibbutzim, but still lower than the Arab villages (48·1).[1]

The stability of marriages differs also between town and country, similarly to the experience of countries of the West. The rates of divorce (per 1,000 mean population in 1963) are almost twice as high for urban settlements (1·1) than for rural settlements (0·6). Again the exception are the Kibbutzim, where divorce rates are almost equal to the rates in the towns (1·0 for husbands resident in the Kibbutz and 1·1 for wives resident). The Moshavim have exceptionally low rates of divorce (between 0·3 and 0·4), i.e., one-third of the town rates.

The economic backwardness of the rural settlements expresses itself in many ways in the standard of housing, in possession of durable goods, in the level of personal services and so on. In 1964 43·2 per cent of rural families possessed electric refrigerators against 75·5 per cent of urban families, 64·2 per cent a gas cooker against 88 per cent of urban families, 3·1 per cent a private car

---

[1] See *Statistical Abstract of Israel for 1965*.

against 7·7 per cent, 1·5 per cent a motor cycle against 4·0 per cent of urban families. Of course if the Kibbutzim were excluded the gulf would be much greater.

The contrast is seen also in the level of personal services which are available in the town and in the country. In towns the man-power devoted to personal services amounts to between 6·4 to 9 per cent, while in Moshavim 1·6 per cent, in other rural settlements, except Kibbutzim, 3·6 per cent of their respective man-power. In the Kibbutzim the percentage reaches 22·7 per cent which is the highest in the country. This shows the level of affluence reached in the Kibbutzim, where the educational, cultural and medical services are most fully developed. The Kibbutzim are also an exception in rural settlements as far as the occupational structure is concerned, showing a relatively high percentage of active population engaged in industry and crafts (18·6 per cent against 4·9 per cent in Moshavim) and also a very high percentage in public business and personal services (36·6 per cent against 12·3 per cent in Moshavim). The majority of the members of the Kibbutzim are engaged in services and industry, while only 39·6 per cent work in agriculture as against 74·6 per cent in Moshavim.

The Kibbutz is a showpiece of Israeli rural life. It shows the way to overcome rural backwardness, and the way is unique. It is the way to fight environmental backwardness by progressive-ness and selectivity of high standard human material. Place first-class men in backward environments, and equip them with first-class tools (the Kibbutzim have the most technically advanced productive equipment) and after many years of courageous, persistent and ingenious struggle, they will convert backwardness into a showpiece of progress and achievement. The unique com-bination of agriculture with manufacturing and a tourist industry is an additional help.

The ideal of Israeli society of converting the village into a first-class community and obliterating the difference between country and town, safeguarding a common level of infra-structure for the whole country, and counteracting excessive urbanization, has so far not been achieved. For a while it looked as if the Kib-butzim were the main ladder for uplifting the whole rural life of Israel, setting a model to be followed by others. But, as pointed out in another chapter, the Kibbutz movement is in retreat and the model is far from being an effective example of achievement for the rural life of the community as a whole.

The Kibbutz was able to create its proper climate, own socio-economic environment. It transformed the rural backward area into a highly progressive, sophisticated and affluent community. But the Kibbutz is an enclave in the rural environment, not linked organically with the rest. The social links of the Kibbutzim with the rest of the rural area are very slender. One can say the Kibbutz keeps itself to itself. The close links of the Kibbutz are with the centre of Jewish society, not with its rural environment. The Kibbutz did not penetrate deeply into the rural scene of Israel; it was unable to carry its message to other rural communities. The Kibbutz turned its back on the Israeli village, it turned itself inwards. There was no outward growth of the Kibbutz movement. This may be the reason why it lost its dynamism.

In a way the situation of the Kibbutz reflects the position of Israel in the whole region. Israel created in the Middle East a highly progressive, sophisticated and almost affluent socio-economic environment, resembling that of a West European community. This was, as in the Kibbutz, due primarily to the high quality of its human material combined of course with the high rate of capital investment. But similarly to the Kibbutz, Israel remained isolated from its neighbours.

4.

The Lessons of the Kibbutz Experiment

THE KIBBUTZ is the showpiece of Israel's creativity and its most significant contribution to 'social engineering' in modern times. The Kibbutz has attained world wide fame, drawing a constant stream of observers and social students who are attracted by its striking non-conformity in the Western world which gives a challenge and a hope. The enormous literature which has grown around the experience of the Kibbutzim often presents claims for the institution which seem out of proportion to its actual task and role. These claims are partly due to the zeal of the Kibbutz members and partly to the enthusiasm of their protagonists and friends. The Kibbutzim are engaged in an incessant process of self-analysis and self-scrutiny, as well as self-presentation. This process is of course not peculiar to the Kibbutzim; it is shared by the whole Israeli society. If self-awareness and self-criticism were accepted as an expression of a complex and sophisticated society, Israel would be credited with the highest degree of complexity and sophistication. This self-awareness is in itself a powerful factor in the self-transformation which has taken place in Israel since its inception.

Even more so the Kibbutz members are extremely self-conscious, subjecting themselves to a constant stream of surveys, enquiries, reports of commissions, councils and organized symposiums.[1] This may be so because the Kibbutz members try to read in their experience a meaning far transcending their existence. Is it a mission? Is the philosophy of the kibbutz a new philosophy, a new secular version of Judaism? Does it carry a lesson for the world, being an answer to the malaise of the industrial society? Is it a model to be followed by the underdeveloped nations? And while arguing about the answers, the Kibbutzim conduct their ideological and political feuds among themselves, splintering into factions and sects, often splitting a workable, well-prospering

[1] See Harry Viteles, *A History of the Co-operative Movement in Israel.* Book Two. *The Evolution of the Kibbutz Movement.* Vallentine-Mitchell. London 1966.

Kibbutz into two separate units (like two Ein Harods, or two Givat Haims), on some fine points of social philosophy, which must be observed out of concern for 'the soul of their members'. In spite of all the exhortations, exertions and attempts, the four main movements of the Kibbutzim have not been able to achieve unity in thought or action.

Although the claims made for the Kibbutz experience are excessive, the experience as such is a boon for the social student. It carries a lesson for the world both in its positive and negative aspects.

The Kibbutz is a multi-functional institution with many contradictory features. It is a cross between a large estate and a village; it has traits of both a large family and a monastery; it has the air of a labour camp as well as a holiday resort. It displays also characteristics of a training camp, a summer school and a first-class educational establishment. It has something of the utopian-like communistic early settlements in the United States but it has also some features of a military camp of the Teutonic Knights fighting on the border against the Slavs. It has something of the character of a permanent discussion group and a Jewish Congress, a first-class political unit. For all its features as an integral collective, it lays stress on the free development of personality, encouraging all sorts of artistic and cultural activities. In the Kibbutz the full personality can grow and reach its full stature, and the potential artist can express himself and directly reach his audience. For all its egalitarian ideology, the Kibbutz members acquire something of the status of the landed nobility, staffing the highest positions in government, Histadrut and officer corps. For all its modernity, the Kibbutz is part of the larger process of archaization of Israeli society, of the archaic turned modern.

The idea itself is ancient, springing from primitive communism which has survived in a rudimentary form throughout the ages. It has been attempted many times; in monastic communities, in ancient times on the same soil by the Essenes, and in recent times many similar experiments were undertaken in Europe, Australia, Japan[1] and the New World.[2] However, such an institution has

[1] David W. Plath, 'The Fate of Utopia. Adaptive Tactics in Four Japanese Groups.' *American Anthropologist*. October 1966.

[2] Henrik Infield, *Utopia and Experiment, Essays in the Sociology of Co-operation*. Praeger. New York 1955.

never been attempted on such a massive scale as in Israel. The Kibbutz 'represents the only perfect, integral, all-embracing co-operative to be found anywhere in the world, there being in fact nothing to compare with it on such a mass scale'.[1]

One can say that the Kibbutz represents a new attempt to create a work community in the strictest sense, a community which not only works but also lives together, bound by common life interests. It appeals to an archtype in our thinking and feeling coming from those ancient times when people worked and lived together .in closely knit communities. It is an attempt to link highly developed technological economy with archaic forms of village life by creating a rural or rural-industrial village held together by bonds of common ownership and common pro-duction, a community of comradeship, mutual help and under-standing. When I visited the Kibbutzim I felt the presence of the shades of Charles Fourier and Robert Owen. But equally the Kibbutz has developed historically out of economic necessities in response to the circumstances and environment in early Palestine.

Lack of water, swamps and insanitary conditions; scarcity of land available for Jewish cultivation and of funds; the need for defence against Arab attacks; the competition of cheap and more experienced Arab labour; the feeling of loneliness and isolation in a new country; the need to prepare for further waves of immigration: all these were factors in the development of this form of co-operative settlement. Jewish farming could not have been developed on individualist or capitalist lines, even had the pioneers been free from socialist ideas. In those pioneering days there was no prospect of profit or security of investment, only messianic hopes and idealism. Nevertheless socialist ideology was a distinct factor in the development of the Kibbutz.

The Kibbutz as it has arisen in early Palestine is therefore a blend of ideology and necessity. It has developed organically and spontaneously out of the Palestinian soil but it is all the same a purposeful, rationally designed ideological product with a strong political character.

Kibbutzim are groups with a similar economic, social and since about 1951 a common political ideology that voluntarily decide to

[1] Dr Walter Preuss, *Co-operation in Israel and the World*, p. 78. Jerusalem 1960.

establish integral co-operative communities in accordance with the
Abbe Morellet's principle (*Code de la Nature*, 1755) that each should
labour for the community 'according to his ability and share according to his needs'. There are no wages except in kind and services.
The Kibbutzim combine co-operative ownership of all property
(except personal belongings), purchasing, production, marketing,
consumption (including housing), rearing and educating children,
cultural, recreational and other services. Everyone in the Kibbutz
enjoys the same rights and assumes the same obligations. Hired
labour is taboo in principle but has been and still (1964) is used by
not a few Kibbutzim in workshops and to a smaller extent in
agriculture.[1]

Some of the principles of the Kibbutzim are best described by
quoting Josephus' and Philo of Alexandria's descriptions of the
Essenes' settlements.

From Josephus[2]:

They are despisers of wealth, and a thing to wonder at among them
is their community of goods; it is not possible to find any one
among them possessing more than another. They have a law that
those who enter the sect should turn over their property for the
public use of the Order, . . .

The overseers of their common property are elected and chosen
by the whole body, each with regard to his special functions.

Among themselves they do not either buy or sell, but each gives
what he has to one in need, and receives something useful from
him in exchange.

In everything else they do nothing without instructions from
their overseers, but these two matters are left to their own free
will, giving help and (deeds of) mercy; for to assist the deserving,
whenever they ask and to supply food to those who need, these
things are left to themselves to decide.

Gifts to relatives may not be made without permission of the
stewards. They know how to use righteous indignation, but anger
they control; they are champions of loyalty, ministers of peace. . . .

Admission is not immediate for those who become enthusiastic
for the sect. They lay down for him the same way of life for a year . . .

From Philo's description of the Essenes Order one may quote
the following passages which equally apply to the Kibbutzim:

[1] Harry Viteles, *op.cit.* Book I. *The Evolution of the Co-operative Movement*,
pp. 31–2. Vallentine-Mitchell. London 1966.
[2] *Bellum Judaicum* II. viii, 3, 4, 6 and 7.

First of all, they live in villages, avoiding cities because of the law-lessness which has become inveterate among city dwellers, knowing that from association with such there comes a deadly influence on their souls . . .

. . . there is a single treaure for all common disbursements, a common wardrobe, and common food, when they hold their com-munal meals. Among no other people will you find such things as having a common roof, a common life, and a common board more firmly established in practice . . .[1]

Thus, sharing each day a common life and a common table, they are content with the same conditions, being lovers of happy frugality, shunning luxury as a disease of soul and body.[2]

Very much the same things can be said about the Kibbutzim which have inherited the ethical though not the religious spirit of the Essenes.

A very important principle of the Kibbutzim is complete voluntarism both in joining and leaving. The Kibbutz regards itself as one big family whose members are adopted. A member can join only if accepted by the community, i.e., by a majority vote of the Assembly, but they can also opt out if they want to. The Kibbutz provides not only necessities and comforts of life but also friendship, a most important item in present-day alienated civilization. A new member must fit in not only as a manpower unit, but also as a member of a community, sharing its way of life, its interests and its cultural standards. This of course elimi-nates a great number of potential candidates for membership. 'We have to live with a new member', the old Kibbutznik would say. So one year probation is regarded as a minimum. A Kibbutz is a venture not only in economics but also in education and culture. It is an integral co-operation, most integral of all the forms of co-operation.

Other principles of the Kibbutzim are anti-authoritarianism and anti-disciplinarianism. There is no leader in the Kibbutz. The Charisma rests with the Kibbutz. The authority is shared and rotated. No prestige, no power and no incentives are attached to managerial functions. The Assembly of Members has to enlist for service those who will be in control of the affairs of the Kibbutz. The Kibbutz relies on the self-discipline of its members.

[1] *Quod omnis probus liber*, XII. 76, 86.
[2] *Hypothetica*, 11. 11.

The mobilization of work incentives is based on work schedules for teams of workers under elected supervisors but the incentives rely primarily on the complete identification of members with the community and free acceptance of the work schedules. Therefore, they assume the high morale of the members and a genuine, spontaneous cohesion, not enforced from outside but from inside. This high morale, organic cohesion, full identification, high standard of education and culture and high standard of social awareness, are the necessary prerequisites for the success of the Kibbutz. The Kibbutz may help to create a new social man but the new social man is a built-in assumption, the prior requirement of its success. Human material of the right kind must be available to start with. Without this material the Kibbutz cannot begin its work as incubator for the new man.

Now let us consider the dynamics of the Kibbutz movement from its origin. The Jewish pioneers from East Central Europe at the turn of the century returned to their ancient land with a special message that work, by which they meant manual work, can be a great blessing, a blessing both for the people of Israel and for the land of Israel. They were late disciples of Rousseau, as well as disciples of Tolstoy who preached the return to the land and to the simple village life. They returned to the Land in the strictest sense, to work with the land, to enjoy its blessing, to enjoy the daily contact with the soil. They rejected work with figures, abstractions, speculations; they longed for simple work and a simple life. When Aaron David Gordon left Russia (1903) at the age of forty-eight to become a pioneer in the desert of Palestine he wrote:

> ... all that we wish for in Palestine is to work with our very own hands at all things which make up life, to labour with our own hands at all kinds of work, at all kinds of crafts and trades from the most skilled, the cleanest and the easiest to the coarsest, the most despised and the most difficult.

And in another context:

> Work will heal us. In the centre of all our hopes we must place work; our entire structure must be founded on labour.[1]

The pioneers from East European ghettos came to Israel with

[1] Aaron David Gordon, *Selected Essays*.

ideas which underlined also the value of land as a symbol of space and freedom. Those values were derived directly from the anti-thetical experiences of ghetto life. Kurt Levin in his *Psycho-Sociological Problems of a Minority* (New York 1935) based his sociological field theory on his study of the restricted 'life-space' of the Jewish minority in the Diaspora. The boundaries of the ghetto imposed a strict limitation on the movement of the Jews, forming barriers, closed and confined walls. The biological space for movement and change, for personality and group was restricted, creating a state of high tension both for the individual and the group. This was the background from which sprang the most significant social experiment in Israel.

The first two Kibbutzim were founded in Kineret (1908) and in Dagania (1909), as a spontaneous response to a dire challenge as it presented itself to Dr Ruppin, the director of Zionist Settlement Office, when he was dealing with a serious labour conflict on a publicly owned farm on the shores of Kineret (the strike of the Jewish workers and unrest of the Arab workers). These first two Kibbutzim proved very successful and soon other settlements followed. Already in 1923 there were 13 Kibbutzim, some of them fairly large communities such as Ayelet Hashachar, Kfar Giladi and Ein Harod which today form 'historic showpieces of the Kibbutz movement'.[1] Their number increased steadily to 47 in 1937 with membership equal to 4·3 per cent of the Jewish population. The big leap came in the period 1936–47, when the number of Kibbutzim rose to 115, with membership amounting to 7·5 per cent of the Jewish population. That was the peak of their development, their heroic, pioneering and most creative stage.

After the inception of the State, the Kibbutz manpower started to decline, at first in ratio to the Jewish population, then also in absolute numbers. The Kibbutz membership has declined from 8·4 per cent of all manpower in November 1955 to 4·9 per cent in 1964 and in absolute numbers from 48,800 to 41,600 persons.[2]

The decline of the Kibbutzim appears not only in quantitative terms. We can witness a certain sluggishness and tiredness of the whole Kibbutz movement; actually the Kibbutz movement finds itself in an atmosphere of crisis and loss of self-confidence in the

[1] Dr H. Darin-Drabkin, *The Other Society*, p. 70. Gollancz. London 1962.
[2] *Statistical Abstract of Israel.* Jerusalem 1965.

future, more so in the last decade between the Suez Campaign and the Six Day War. Many councils of the Kibbutz movement dealt with this problem. Already in 1958 Mr Jaakov presented the background of the Kibbutz crisis in his pamphlet *The Kibbutz on Trial* to the Ninth General Council of the Kibbutz Haartzi.[1] In 1959 D. Rubner discussed the possibility of halting 'the vanishing future for the Kibbutz' in the movement of the Kibbutz Hameuchad.[2]

Martin Buber in an interview with A. H. Elchanani in 1959 expressed his disenchantment with the Kibbutz movement in the following way:

> In the course of time the hopes and dreams vanished. It is as if the ideology faded and withered. It seems as if this freshness of life has been cut off from the Kibbutz Movement.[3]

The decline of the Kibbutz movement is due to many factors, some indigenous, others exogenous or partly exogenous, as some of the factors operate simultaneously in society at large and in the Kibbutzim.

Routinization and Aging

Certain erosion of the original spirit and enthusiasm has taken place. Both the institution and the pioneers have aged. Fifty years of a basically idealistic institution is already old age. Disenchantment, routinization, formalization, friction and strain follow the realization of an idea. The revolutionaries of yesterday became the Establishment of today and the imaginative and the inspiring of yesterday became routine and boring. The pioneers became disillusioned and somehow they were unable to impart their original enthusiasm to their sons. When one asked a veteran kibbutznik, whether the new generation has the same enthusiasm, he answered, 'They take it for granted, it all fell into their lap ready made'.

With the passing of time all kinds of structural strains, usually underlying life in a collective, start to appear. There is the strain of boredom and monotony arising from seeing the same faces and hearing the same voices and arguments for so many years.

---

[1] Harry Viteles, *op.cit.*, Book II, p. 653.
[2] *Ibid.*, p. 651.
[3] *Ibid.*, p. 653.

There are strains arising from the forming of separate cliques to which different prestige status is attached (the clever ones and the morons); strains arising from the existence of black sheep or destructive personalities; strains arising from co-existence of three generations with different outlooks; strains from having to carry on with individuals with whom one has fallen out; strains from conflicting directives of various elected organs of the Kibbutz. With the passing of time a veteran Kibbutznik feels that he has no longer any alternative to remaining in the Kibbutz for life, that his marriage to the Kibbutz became in fact indissoluble. All those strains become more pronounced with the passing of the years.

Already in the enquiry made by the Hebrew University Staff to the question: 'Did you derive satisfaction from your work in 1955? only 55 per cent of members replied that they were satisfied with and enjoy and wish to continue their present work.[1]

Growth of Capital and Managerial Complexity

There are considerable changes within the Kibbutz imposed by technological developments and expanding economy. They require new adjustment and certain deviation from the anti-bureaucratic, anti-managerial, anti-authoritarian and anti-disciplinarian character of the early Kibbutzim. The Kibbutzim acquired considerable property and capital equipment which required proper maintenance, elaboration of work schedules, development of managerial responsibility, and managerial skill which could not be shared by all the members. Not all the members were interested in management, not all members could follow the technical details, the complex accounts or the requirements of the managerial technique. The managers had to be trained for the job and a great deal of authority had to be delegated to the experts. New modern technology required planning and planning itself imposes its own controls and regulations. The larger the Kibbutz, the greater the complexity and the greater the reliance on experts and organizers. Modern technology requires work schedules and time schedules; the machines are 'masters' not only in factories but also in Kibbutzim. The large Kibbutz involuntarily moves towards a pyramidical structure, in which the actual power

[1] Garber Y. Talmon, *Differentiation in Collective Settlements*. Reprint from *Scripta Hierosolymiana*. Vol. III. 1955.

becomes more and more concentrated at the top. A great many functions are also becoming more and more reserved to the central organization of the political movement operating for a series of Kibbutzim.

Disenchantment With Socialism
The Kibbutznik lost his enthusiasm not only for the collective but also for the creed which brought him into the Kibbutz. Socialism also has lost its pristine beauty. When the Kibbutznik looks at the Soviet Union from which many pioneers at least partly derived their inspiration, they see a Leviathan of bureaucracy and authoritarianism, not to speak of anti-Semitism. Socialism or Communism has certainly not proved itself the longed for Redeemer.

The Emergence of the State of Israel
Much of the programme and many functions which the pioneers set for themselves have been taken over by the new State of Israel. Education, defence, social security, development of agriculture, political guidance of the society, all those objectives are now in the hands of the State. The State is now the embodiment of the general will of the Jewish society and has pushed into the background all the voluntary organizations. All voluntary organizations in Israel suffered from the emergence of the State. Military service and contribution towards social welfare are no longer based on voluntary principle; they are being enacted and enforced by the State. (We can see here the similarity of the decay of voluntary welfare organizations in England since the development of the Welfare State.) This decay of voluntary principle affected especially the Histadrut, the Jewish Agency and the Kibbutzim, the largest and the most important voluntary organizations in Israel.

The Rise of Affluence
When one asks a Kibbutznik whether the same general atmosphere reigns now in the Kibbutz as previously, his answer is, 'No, of course not. It is all due to the affluent society, to the affluent society around us and to the affluent society within the Kibbutz.' He may also add, 'Equality in affluence is not the same as equality in austerity'. The general materialistic spirit in Israel,

due to affluence, is gnawing at the bones of the Kibbutz movement. Proximity to commercial and urban centres with their
innumerable motor cars make the Kibbutz members, especially
the younger generation, more prone to outside influences.
Affluence has brought about an enormous increase in travel
overseas, and the Israelis want to explore the world and to study
abroad. When a young Kibbutznik goes into the army, he often
does not come back to the Kibbutz.

The spirit of affluence raises claims in the Kibbutz itself, claims
for comfort and ease similar to those enjoyed by the educated
urban population. It also raises claims for privileged treatment
for some sections of the members, for instance for veterans, in
regard to housing or length of holidays or holidays abroad. The
German reparation grants which many Kibbutz members received in large sums raised new problems of possession. Many of
the members offered them to the Kibbutz but some have refused
to do this. It looks as if the tyranny of possessions has come back,
and with it the appetite for ease and comfort, while the love of
austerity has receded.

Trend Towards Intellectualism

The trend towards intellectualism started to reassert itself from
1948. The myth of the redeeming qualities of manual labour now
belongs to the past. The special attraction of the abstract and of
brainwork at large, the attraction of study and research, is again
taking hold of Israelis. Since the inception of the State there is
an enormous demand for professional, technical and scientific
work. The future of Israel, its industry and export capacity, is
seen in scientific and technological advances in industry based on
highly trained manpower. The proportion of manual workers in
the working population is declining rapidly, a phenomenon
shared by all countries affected by the new technological revolution. Manual work itself is mostly carried out by the Oriental
section of the population as well as by the Arabs. The enormous
increase of academically trained youth, common to all industrial
countries,[1] has gathered momentum in recent years with the
founding of the new university in Tel-Aviv, the university college

[1] 'The academic population in Britain will reach in 1970 about 19 per cent
of the respective age groups, in U.S.A. about 30 per cent of its college age
population are in the colleges'. (1965).

in Haifa, the university college in Beersheba, the expansion of the University Bar-ilan, etc. Large numbers of Israelis are studying abroad. In the U.S.A. alone (1966) there are 2,000 students and another 1,500 graduates in various jobs. This trend has affected the general atmosphere of the Kibbutzim and considerably diminished its sources of supply for new membership.

De-politization

Politics was always the field of the greatest interest for the Jew. His tragic experiences made him politically conscious because conflagrations, wars, revolutions, change of regime meant often for the Jew loss of status, expropriation or expulsion. But in the last decade, with the rise of affluence and relative political stability in the interlude between the Suez campaign and the Six Day War the Jewish population lost a great deal of interest in politics and all political parties in Israel complained about the relative apathy of the average citizen. This may also have affected the attraction of the Kibbutzim as a political institution. A Kibbutznik is a political man *par excellence*. Being free from most cares and troubles which beset an ordinary man, his needs and wants taken care of by the community, he turns attention and interest to the community itself and to society at large. The Kibbutznik lives for and by the community. This is the background of the extreme politization of the Kibbutz life. The interest and cares of the community are his in a most real and strict sense. After all, men must have problems and questions to solve, and the lack of personal problems invites collective problems.

The Kibbutz has made an enormous contribution to Israel's political leadership. Members of the Kibbutzim are leaders of the ruling parties in Israel, also in Histadrut and in all institutions of any political importance. The Kibbutzim themselves are divided in groups affiliated to political parties. The biggest affiliations are to Mapam (in 1964, 74 Kibbutzim with 28,000 members belonged to Ha Kibbutz Ha Arzi), and to Mapai (1964, 76 Kibbutzim with 25,000 members belonged to Ihud Hakvutzot ve Hakibbutzim); the third biggest affiliation is Ahdut Avoda (in 1964, 58 Kibbutzim with 22,000 members belonged to Hakibbutz Hameuhad); a few Kibbutzim are affiliated also to the religious parties and to the Liberals. So the Kibbutzim themselves are important political institutions. When the membership of a

Kibbutz splits in political allegiance, the Kibbutz can no longer exist as one unit. In that case it has to undergo a division so that two Kibbutzim emerge as separate units, each affiliated to a different political party. This is what happened to the oldest Kibbutz Dagania, which has split into two Kibbutzim, Dagania Alaf and Dagania Bet.

The Decline of Agriculture

In the last decade farming itself has become a declining industry in Israel. This is due to the development of farming technology and the rise of productivity. Tractors and other machines, improved farming methods, are displacing manpower. The labour force in agriculture, forestry and fishing fell in Israel from 15·0 per cent in 1955 to 10·6 per cent in 1964 of the general labour force and it is still declining.

The Kibbutzim are trying to develop industrial plants and services. They build factories for processing agricultural produce and other industrial plants, they also develop tourist services, hotels and catering. But communal hotel work is not the same as communal farming. Communal farming keeps men together close to nature, communal hotel work isolates them and brings them in daily touch with tourists who have a different mentality, a mentality which can be infectious from the point of view of a Kibbutz ideology.

Kibbutz factories bring the Kibbutznik in touch with wage labour which must be employed to a large extent because of shortage of manpower in the Kibbutz. This again raises many awkward problems of social and psychological nature. Most Kibbutzim feel that the workers employed in their factories are being exploited in the same way as other workers employed in private establishments. So most of the Kibbutzim pay what they regard as 'surplus value' (according to the Marxist theory of value) into a special fund administered by the central organization of their movement and devoted to the absorption of immigrants (*Keren Klita*). This is a sort of conscience money to overcome the feeling that they exploit other peoples' labour and it is also meant as a deterrent against excessive extension of the employment of wage earners. The mutual relationship of the Kibbutz members and wage earners raises also awkward social problems. The members of the Kibbutz represent the skilled or supervisory staff, while the wage earners are mostly unskilled hands. There are also considerable cultural differences which are often combined with language barriers, in addition to considerable differences in their attitude to work. When you ask a Kibbutznik whether there is a difference between the attitude to work of a Kibbutnik and that of a wage earner, his answer is short and simple: 'We work for ourselves, while they do not'. When a Kibbutznik comes in contact with the wage worker he feels his class superiority in all terms, he feels as if he belonged to a sort of managerial and property-owning class, while the wage earner is the proletarian in the textbook form.

The Oriental Immigration

The almost complete stoppage of the Western immigration and the large expansion of the Oriental immigration in the last decade has dried up the source of supply of the potential membership of the Kibbutzim. The Oriental immigrant, who is untouched by the ideals of socialism and co-operative movement, finds the idea of Kibbutzim completely alien to him. In the Kibbutzim he appears mostly as a wage labourer in the Kibbutz factories. The two groups, the members of the Kibbutzim and the Oriental wage labourers work in close proximity; the physical distance between them can be measured in yards, but the cultural and mental distance is almost unbridgeable. They represent two different worlds which do not understand each other. The wage earners cannot understand the Kibbutznik; they regard him as odd and abnormal, haughty and exclusive. The Kibbutz life looks in their eyes grotesque and bizarre. Not understanding the essence, the mythos or the ethos of the Kibbutz, they distrust it, they feel that there may be some catch in it, especially when membership of the Kibbutz is offered to them to catch the children; 'They want me to work for nothing, just for my keep', they report on the event. The members of the Kibbutz try to explain to the wage earner the ethos of the working class, its calling and mission in the world but all that falls on deaf ears. The Kibbutznik is a political man as we said, while the wage earner presents also here his greatest contrast. He is full of personal problems, cares and troubles. He thinks only about his family and himself, about his home, about food and the amenities of life which loom large on his horizon, beset as he is with hardship and deficiencies.

The decline of the Kibbutzim is an extremely interesting socio-logical phenomenon on many counts. First of all it is a showpiece for the process of aging of institutions. Institutions are subject to aging as much as man, institutions simply wear out. Any insti-tution in order to survive must justify its existence every day anew. The dialectical process presented by Marx is just an expression of this process of aging. The initial energy is spent and if the energy is not renewed or does not come from new sources, the institution affected is subject to decay.

Another interesting lesson is the part played in the life of an institution by the institutional environment, by the society at large. The institution is subject to the forces operating in the whole nation, to its general atmosphere and to the whole insti-tutional setting. The institution must be in harmony with this setting and with the general atmosphere prevailing in a given society. A capitalistic society does not allow the growth of a collectivistic structure within the society.

The other lesson of the Kibbutz experience is that the force of technology and economics is far stronger than that of ideology. The force of ideology deprived of its backing in technology and economics, soon fades out. The Kibbutz was an economic, social and technological necessity for Israel in her pre-State existence. The Kibbutzim were once the backbone of the new country in political, military, economic and educational terms, but the State has now a much broader foundation resting on its network of statutory institutions and arrangements. The Kibbutzim are still very useful; they provide the adornment of Israeli society but they are rather relegated from the centre to the more marginal spheres.

The other lesson of the Kibbutz experience is that in order to survive, an organization needs to develop. It is not enough to stay put; the organization must show a dynamic growth, com-parable to the rate of growth of other forms of social-economic organizations. The Kibbutzim have to compete with other forms of agricultural production, both co-operative and private, not only in real life but also with public opinion. The Israeli economy and the Israeli society have grown since the inception of the State at a very quick pace, while the Kibbutzim have showed a very low rate of growth and at last complete stagnation.

The decline of the Kibbutzim does not mean that their existence is in jeopardy. It means that they are moving down in the scale of importance to the country as a whole. The future of the Kibbutz is linked with its power of adaptation and adjustment to the new requirements of the Israeli society, its new psychology, technology and economics. Its future will depend more specifically on its ability to develop the industrial side of the Kibbutz activity, and to develop a rural-industrial ideology, suitable for this expansion.

Even more so the future of the Kibbutzim will depend on the future value orientations of the Israeli society. Will the pioneering spirit, which declined considerably in the decade between the Sinai Campaign and the Six Day War, come to life again under the impact of the great emergency, so triumphantly overcome in military terms but not yet in terms of peaceful achievement?

The other very important question for the Kibbutzim is: will Soviet Russia open her frontiers for the emigration of her Jewish citizens to Israel?

Were the answers to be yes, the Kibbutzim could look forward to a new lease of life with a prospect of important, new contributions to Israel's future.

5.

The Histadrut – Integral Trade Unionism

THE STUDY of Histadrut, *The General Federation of Labour in Israel*, is essential for the study and understanding of Israeli society. It plays a decisive part not only in the life of the 'workers' but also a major part in the political, social and economic life of the country as a whole. In the pre-State period, which is called 'the State in the making' it was besides the Jewish Agency the main centre of authority and power in Jewish society, and even now it is one apex a of triangle of power, the two others being the State and the Jewish Agency. The kingdom of the Histadrut, as it is often called, is still a state within the State. Its peculiar position within the State expresses well the nature of the Jewish State as a *sui generis* cluster of Estates. The Histadrut is an Estate with many functions which in other countries are reserved for the State. The Jewish Agency which deals mainly with land settlement, town planning and absorption of immigrants is also an Estate and is based on The World Zionist Organization. The Kibbutzim can also be classed as an Estate with many functions performed independently such as the provision of police, schools, welfare and health services, registration of births and deaths. The political parties themselves form a kind of Estate with their own rural settlements, housing estates, welfare services, insurance, etc. The co-operative principle which is the basis of Jewish society has been built into the very structure of the Israeli State which is divided between many separate realms. Marx, in his vision, foresaw 'the withering away of the State' with the advent of socialism. Israel can claim an interesting practical implementation of the withering away of the State by assigning a great many functions normally performed by the State to other institutions which are practically outside its authority.

The Jewish doctrine sees the authority of the State in a minor key, as something subservient to the needs of society. The Jews are rather distrustful of the power of the State and try to circumvent and limit it by hedging it with many other institutions. This was the result of historical development both in the Diaspora and in Israel itself, as the major Estates preceded the formation of the State (the Histadrut by twenty-eight years). The power of the State is now on the ascendant as all the Estates are gradually being encroached upon by the State but this process is far from complete and may never be fully accomplished.

Like the Kibbutzim and the Jewish Agency, the Histadrut finds itself on the defensive since the inception of the State. Some of its functions have been taken over by the State, such as the provision of labour exchanges, hospitals, industrial injuries insurance and industrial training. Also new labour laws passed over the years have considerably narrowed the tasks of the Histadrut. Collective bargaining, conciliation and mediation, limitation of hours of work, annual holidays, discharges and redundancy payments, apprenticeship and youth employment, employment of women and maternity protection, protection of wages, protection of health of workers, all these are regulated by legislation and the Histadrut-backed collective agreements simply repeat the provisions of the legislation. There is great faith in the value of labour legislation for regulating labour conditions and labour relations which may in future further restrict the field of activity of the Histadrut. The Minister of Labour already has the power to extend the collective agreements beyond the contracting parties to cover a whole line of industry.

The principles on which the Histadrut is built can be described as follows:

> (i) multi-functionalism,
> (ii) politization,
> (iii) centralization,
> (iv) universality of membership,
> (v) the combination of the status of the employer and employees' representative,
> (vi) the grass-roots in Workers' Committees.

(i) *Multi-functionalism*

One may compare the integral trade unionism of the Histadrut with the integral co-operative of the Kibbutz. Like the Kibbutz, the Histadrut is an original, unparalleled creation of Israel and it has attracted as much attention outside Israel. The Histadrut is a multi-functional body in Trade Unionism as the Kibbutz is in co-operation. All functions of Trade Unions which can be listed anywhere in the world, in the West as well as in the East, appear together in the Histadrut. It has many similarities with the American Unions which develop their own economy, banking and insurance. It has many functions similar to the Unions in Soviet Russia, which provide health services, convalescent homes, holiday centres, social and welfare services and take part in productivity drives.

The Histadrut is a Trade Union but trade unionism is not its primary concern. Only a minority of its activities and funds are devoted to trade unionism. The Histadrut is a combination of union movement, co-operative movement, workers' education movement, comprehensive health service, mutual aid society and social insurance work, land pioneering in rural settlements of various kinds, industrial development, and colonization and absorption of immigrants. Such a combination is unknown in any other country. In England for instance the Trade Union movement, the co-operative movement, the workers' education movement and the mutual aid societies all developed separate organizations, while the Health Service and social insurance are run by the State.

The Histadrut has its own publishing house, two daily news-papers, several periodicals, its own Trade Union College, its own vocational training centres and trade schools and a very large chain of public libraries.

In the field of health and social insurance the Histadrut developed a gigantic network of institutions and funds of various kinds such as funds for building workers, for agricultural workers, compensation funds, assistance fund, work fund and invalid fund. However, the most outstanding is the service of Kuppat Cholim, the health service with its comprehensive network of dispensaries, hospitals, rest homes, convalescent homes and holiday centres.

The co-operative settlements, such as Kibbutzim and Moshavim which produce two-thirds of Israel's agricultural output, form an integral part of the Histadrut.

Half of the basic heavy industry and 22 per cent of the total industrial output of Israel is produced by the Histadrut combine.

The total contribution of the Histadrut co-operatives of all kinds in farming, industry, transport and other services amounts to about a quarter of national output and a quarter of the total labour force in the country.

The functions of the Histadrut are so multifarious and of such a great variety that the Histadrut is bound to be an unwieldy omnibus which labours heavily and overshadows its purely Trade Union activities. The functions are difficult to combine and often are in opposition to each other.

As for purely Trade Union activities, the Histadrut has 30 National Unions of varying status, independence and strength. The highest status with a measure of independence is accorded to so-called Federations (Histadruiot), and there are six of these: of building workers, technical workers, engineers, clerical workers, teachers, academic staff in the faculties of art. The industrial workers have separate unions, sections and organizations with rather low status and little independence. These are in the process of re-organization according to the resolution of the last (Tenth) Convention of the Histadrut, which intends to group all industrial workers into three major federations to give them higher status and independence. The biggest single union is the Federation of Clerical Workers with 90,000 members (1964), next are the union of farming labourers with 70,000, the Federation of building workers with 45,000, the union of State employees with 40,000.

The union organization is sometimes based on craft, such as compositors in printing or on professions such as teachers, actors, physicians, engineers, painters and sculptors. Sometimes it is based on a single industry, such as building and sometimes on employment by one employer such as the union of workers in Histadrut-owned industry or those who work for the army in munition factories or those working for the Government in manual or clerical capacities. Unions are still in the process of formation and there is an element of instability and experimentation.

The union structure has three levels: in every plant or establishment there is the Workers' Committee organizing all workers in the establishment; the local union; and the national union. The Workers' Committees and the local unions are subject to dual supervision and control, for local matters by the local labour council, for national matters by the national union. The national union is subject to supervision and control of the executive committee of the Histadrut.

(ii) *Politization*

The Histadrut is an essentially political body with many similarities to the structure of the State, governed by similar electoral laws and a similar power system. All its organs are elected by rigid proportional representation by a ballot in which the political parties present their list of candidates in a national forum. Most national parties take part in the election, which is called the Little Election, with lists for the entire country treated as a single constituency. The Histadrut member votes for the national representatives of his party whom he sends to the Convention, not for his local union representatives whom he knows. Both the highest authority vested in the Convention and the most humble Labour Council in a town or village are elected according to a political key based on principles of proportional representation. Hence the party holds the power over the elected representative, as his chances of election depend not on his standing with the members of his union but on his standing in the party which assigns him a place on the list. He can be assured of his election according to his place on the list as much as a candidate for the Knesset election.

The political character of the Histadrut can be seen more clearly in all the debates in its institutions, such as the Convention or Council or Executive Committee. One speaker after another puts forward his view not in a personal capacity but as a representative of his Party. The reports quoting the name of the speaker also give his party allegiance. Discussion rarely takes place among members of the same party but between parties.

The main legislative body is the National Convention elected every four years. It meets once every four years. Between Conventions the General Council, elected by the Convention and assembling every four months, acts as the highest authority of the Histadrut. Next comes the Executive Committee, elected by the General Council, meeting once a fortnight and acting as the highest executive body of the Histadrut. The Executive Committee appoints a smaller body from its own membership to serve as the Executive Bureau and elects its General Secretary. All the governing bodies mentioned above are small replicas of the National Convention, i.e., composed of representatives of parties in proportion to their voting strength at the elections once every four years. This means that all minority groups are represented in these executive organs according to their voting strength.

The Histadrut is not a protest organization like Trade Unions in many countries; on the contrary it is part of the Establishment. Any clash with the Government is excluded by virtue of the fact that the same parties which are in power in the State govern also the Histadrut. At present the Alignment (a confederation between Mapai and Ahtud Avoda called the Unity of Israel's Worker) formed in 1965 is leading the coalition government, having polled 36·7 per cent of the votes cast in the election for the 6th Knesset, and at the same time is at the helm of the Histadrut, having polled 50·9 per cent of the votes cast for the tenth National Convention. The new united Israeli Labour Party (the merger of Mapai, Ahdut Avoda and Rafi in January 1968) will have a 64 per cent majority in the Histadrut and a near majority in the Knesset (54 seats out of 120). So both Histadrut and the Government will be in the same hands as they always have been since the inception of the State.

Histadrut wields great power in the State but not independent power. The power rests with the political parties, not with the organization as such or with membership. A member cannot reach the top of the pyramid of the Histadrut hierarchy by exerting himself in the organization. He can do so only outside the Histadrut by reaching the top of the political party or parties which drive the power motor of this vast and unwieldy omnibus.

The political structure of the Histadrut is at once its strength and its weakness. Its strength stems from the overwhelming power of the political parties in control of the Histadrut. If the Histadrut hierarchy decides or claims something, there is no effective power to oppose it. It has overwhelming superiority over its counterpart in labour relations, the Manufacturers Association, as the political power can always overrule the purely economic power. If, as sometimes happens, the business world cannot support the claims of the Histadrut, the State intervenes with subsidies or other means to make the claims viable. The Histadrut by its overwhelming concentrated political power can crush its opponents if it wants to. On the other hand the same parties which are responsible for the Histadrut are also responsible for the State, so they can easily overreach themselves by causing a general collapse. Therefore, the Histadrut must be careful in its policy to follow national interests instead of sectional interests. By its universality and generality, embracing all sections of the population, it is bound to pursue the wide, general interests of Israeli society as a whole, as seen by the political parties and their pressure groups. As a confederation of political parties the Histadrut must also be very careful in its actions not to strain the loyalty of the opposition parties and to avoid divisions and splits. Freedom of action is limited and space for manoeuvring is very restricted by the huge mass of its membership with contradictory interests and by the number of parties with opposing ideologies.

The main weakness of the predominantly political structure lies in the disenchantment, distrust and alienation of the members of the Histadrut. They feel that their interests, i.e., group, trade or vocational interests, are disregarded, as the Histadrut only echoes and duplicates the decisions and resolutions of the State apparatus. Who takes the initiative in a decision is of little importance. Sometimes the Government makes the decision and the Histadrut follows, at other times it is the reverse. But conflict between the two is essentially out of the question, as both are in the same hands, except if both sides want, for tactical reasons, to appear to be in conflict. Hence illegal strikes and the general lack of organizational discipline. The Histadrut decides one way, and the members organized by strong Workers' Committees, representing their interests in their work places, go the other way.

(iii) *Centralization*

The principle of 'democratic centralism' claimed by the Communist State is the governing rule of the Histadrut organization. The Histadrut styles itself as a Federation. However, the term Federation as used in Anglo-American practice is hardly applicable to Israel. The Histadrut is not a federation of labour unions; it is a monolithic structure. The usual historical process in other countries—first labour unions and then their confederations or federations or a congress as a superstructure—was completely reversed in the case of the Histadrut; here first came the Federation (or All-National Congress) and then the unions. At the time of its foundation in 1920 labour unions hardly existed on a national scale, except for a few small local unions, like that of printing workers or Jewish railway workers or in agriculture and building. On the national scale there was only one union, that of clerical men founded in 1919. All other national unions came into existence later, in most cases twenty-five years later. Most national unions started after the Sixth General Convention of 1945 on the basis of its general resolutions which called for the establishment of such unions. A very large percentage of these labour unions were called into existence by and through the efforts of the Histadrut itself and this process is far from completed. We must remember that when the Histadrut started there were only a handful of industrial enterprises with a few thousand workers. The membership of the Histadrut grew from 4,433 in 1920 to 900,000 in 1965.

The body of the Histadrut presents a highly integrated and centralized structure with strong central organs which can over-rule all others. The Executive Committee (*Vaad Hapoel*) has the decisive overruling power over all other organs in all fields, including the activities of labour unions. In the localities the same power is vested in the (at present seventy) local Labour Councils, elected in the same poll as the General Convention. The local Labour Councils are very strong bodies which are the instruments of the central Executive Committee with full powers over all matters of local interest. They have also the power of control of local labour unions and workers' committees and can overrule them.

Trade Unions are subordinated to the Histadrut central organ-ization. While one cannot become a member of a trade union without first joining the Histadrut, there are Histadrut members who do not belong to any trade union or who belong to more than one union. The member of a union does not pay his dues to the union, he pays them to the Histadrut. The unions have no financial independence, in most cases they have no budget of their own; the expenses of the union are paid from the general funds of the Histadrut. Most unions have no legal existence in the sense that they cannot acquire property or enter into contracts. The collective agreements are signed by the Histadrut itself jointly with the respective trade unions. The appointment of the Secretary of the local union or the election of the workers' committee must be confirmed by the local Labour Council, and the appointment of the secretaries of national unions must be confirmed by the Executive Committee of the Histadrut. Their salaries are paid from general funds of the Histadrut. All major decisions, including strike actions, must be confirmed by the general bodies of the Histadrut. A number of unions are entirely run by officers appointed by Histadrut authorities.

Only a few unions have statutes and by-laws of their own. In many cases the unions function within the general statutes of the Histadrut. However, there are unions with greater authority, mainly those which were formed independently and outside the Histadrut and which joined it later on, already fully developed. This is especially true of the six Federations which were mentioned previously.

The preponderance of the central bodies of the Histadrut over its labour unions poses many questions of principle and policy. It presents a source of strength, as far as responsibility and general control is concerned. It is very convenient for the purpose of economic planning and development. It assures the preponderance of national interests over sectional interests. The accent is not on narrow professional or class interests, but on the need for pioneering, on development of rural and border settlements, on the absorption of immigrants and on developing the country at large.

But on the other hand the members feel out-manoeuvred, deprived of real protection of their professional interests. They complain about bureaucracy which is invariably linked with excessive centralism. The unions complain about lack of independence, as everything is arranged for them. Hence the lack of discipline which expresses itself in illegal strikes and illegal workers' committees which assume great *de facto* power in defiance of the Histadrut higher bodies.

(iv) *The Universality of Membership*

The membership of the Histadrut is extremely heterogeneous, comprising diverse elements of very different character. The Histadrut represents (according to the figures of the Yearbook of the Histadrut for 1964), 78·4 per cent of all wage and salary earners and together with the members of two separate labour movements which participate in the trade union activities of the

Histadrut (Hapoel Hamizrachi and Poalei Agudat Israel) 87·5 per cent. Among the salary earners, professional managers up to the highest ranks can belong to the Histadrut provided they are not owners of the plant.

Apart from wage and salary earners there are also other classes of membership, as follows:

(a) Housewives who are full members of the Histadrut and have both active and passive votes to all institutions. At the end of 1961 they formed 30·9 per cent of all members of the Histadrut. The inclusion of housewives underlines the high status of women in the Israeli society.

(b) Members of rural settlements such as Kibbutzim and Moshavim, who are independent earners. At the end of 1963 they formed 10·2 per cent of all membership. Their percentage fell steadily over a longer period (from 18 per cent in 1947). But the actual weight of their membership in the counsels of the Histadrut is very much greater, as they form a strongly organized block of politically conscious and educated men. The Kibbutzim themselves employ workmen in their industrial enterprises and building, who belong to the Histadrut alongside their own members.

(c) Self-employed men such as independent professional men, independent artisans and craftsmen who employ up to three apprentices or learners, and members of private co-operatives, even if they employ others, provided they accept the conditions of employment as set out by the Histadrut. According to the by-laws of the Histadrut only 'workers who live by the sweat of their brow without exploiting other peoples' work' can join its ranks.

(d) Students of universities and colleges and adolescents in training, work or school. There is a special federation of youth at work or at school which organizes youth from fourteen up to eighteen. From the age of seventeen a youth becomes a candidate for membership and from the age of eighteen a full member.

Now a few words about the Arab members of the Histadrut. From the very start the Histadrut has been fully aware of the threat which the Arab question and the national division of the Histadrut movement posed to its democratic structure and its social and economic policy. At practically every convention and in every council the question of Arab workers came up for discussion with severe criticism from the Left Wing parties which demanded full and unqualified membership for Arab workers. This was granted in 1958. Up to that time the Arab workers appeared in a special Arab section of the Histadrut known as Alliance of Israeli Workers (Brith Poalei Israel). They were not full members with voting rights in the general body of the Histadrut, which was the Federation of Jewish Labour only. However, they always had full rights in the Trade Union section and in the Workers' Committees. Since the Arab members were admitted to full membership, the name of the Histadrut has been changed by the Tenth Convention from General Federation of Jewish Labour to General Federation of Labour in Israel. Since that time the number of Arab members has risen from a few thousand to 40,000 in 1965. It is reckoned that the 'Histadrut population' among the Arab minority rose from 11·9 per cent in 1958 to 26 per cent in 1965. The Histadrut has created a special fund for the development of Arab villages which has given rise to a number of co-operative enterprises operating with the financial assistance of the State.

There is one more class of membership worth mentioning, namely those who are members only of the Trade Unions and the Sick Fund (Kupat Cholim), i.e., those who participate in Trade Union activities and pay dues to the Health Service but are not members of the Histadrut itself and have no voting rights. That applies to the members of two labour movements of religious parties mentioned previously.

We see from this review, the enormous diversity of membership, including the employers themselves. This poses many fundamental questions: Can the Histadrut represent fairly all these diversified, often opposing interests, the interests of farmers and urban consumers, the interest of co-operative enterprises and their employees, the interest of manual workers and of professional men. The Histadrut often has to oppose one group within its body as against the other, at times turning all its power heavily against one section of membership which emerges from the contest defeated and full of resentment. But on the other hand, by its very comprehensiveness and many-sidedness the Histadrut can preserve a certain balance between those divergent interests, keeping them in line with broader national interests. The battle of interests is waged inside the Histadrut, instead of outside.

(v) *The Combination of the Status of the Employer and Employees' Representative*

This combination presents perhaps the greatest dilemma and the greatest paradox of the Histadrut existence. The Histadrut itself is the greatest single employer of labour in the country. 37 per cent of all its members are employed or occupied in the economy of the Histadrut and if we exclude the members of co-operatives about one-quarter of the Histadrut members are employed by the Histadrut itself. In industry 22 per cent of all labour are employed by Histadrut. Here the Histadrut appears in its double capacity, as an employer and as a representative of its own employees. The Histadrut is 'defending' its employees against itself. This is a situation which has its parallel in Soviet Russia, where the dialectical relationship between the employer and the worker has been obliterated and the workers are constantly reminded that there are no two sides in industry, there is only one side and they are working for themselves. Here the Histadrut finds itself in a constant inner conflict. Collective agreements in the Histadrut industry are not concluded, only memoranda as there are not two contracting parties, only one. In private industry the collective agreements are signed on behalf of the workers by the Histadrut as such in addition to the Trade Union but in the Histadrut industry the Histadrut cannot sign an agreement with itself. Here again we find a similarity to the Soviet practice, where no collective agreements were signed for a long time and when signed had a specific character within the frame of the Five Year Plans, with workers and management pledging to fulfil and over-fulfil the quotas determined by the Plan. Likewise the Histadrut entreats its workers to increase their efforts in its establishments, and generally speaking preaches the gospel of productivity in industry at large.

I have often asked the workers whether, in the Histadrut establishments, the Workers' Committee has a stronger or a weaker position *vis-à-vis* the management. The answer was: In some respects stronger, in some respects weaker. Stronger, because the Histadrut is eager to please them and their manager is also a member of the Histadrut. Weaker, because in the case of real conflict, it is difficult for them to prevail, as the arbiters in the conflict are the organs of the Histadrut which are bound by the general Histadrut policy.

When I asked a high-ranking Histadrut official, whether the workers in Histadrut industry have the right to strike he was indignant, answering, 'Why should they strike? We offer them the best conditions and terms. We give them the best we have, better conditions than anyone else. The problem is not how to protect the worker in our establishments, because we have nobody against whom we can protect them, we could protect them only against ourselves. The problem is reversed: how to protect Histadrut industry against excessive unjustified claims. Is there not the same problem in nationalized industries in Britain?' As a matter of fact in principle the workers in Histadrut establishments have the right to strike, provided they get the permission of the Local Labour Council or in some cases of the Executive Committee of the Histadrut, but actually only illegal or wild cat strikes are possible and not a few of them took place in recent years.

The workers are not very happy with this dual relationship of the Histadrut. They expected much more, a sort of syndicalist regime and full partnership. In fact the management is not elected but appointed from above without consultation with the workers. The channels of consultation and communication are the same as in any other establishment of the same size in private industry. Both sides eagerly seek ways out of this impass. The management says that the workers are not very interested in management or in assuming responsibility for the establishment, and the workers say that the management is not really interested in the workers participation in management. However, plans are being prepared for workers-management partnership on a new institutional basis, and partnership institutions abroad are being studied to learn from their experience.

(vi) *The Grass-Roots in the Workers' Committees*

The founders of the Histadrut hoped to underpin and underprop its structure by all-embracing and strong Workers' Committees. These were planned as grass-roots of the movement, as basic

cells of the Histadrut body and as such they are described in the
by-laws. They are very rarely found in other countries outside
the Communist Block in a such integrated, coherent and all-
embracing form with so many functions *vis-à-vis* the employer,
the higher bodies of the Trade Union Movement and the workers
themselves. They assumed power and authority far beyond anything experienced in Western countries, often taking on functions
which are normally reserved for personnel management. In some
places they run the personnel management service. They have
their own budget and funds made up of contributions by all
members of the staff, whether they belong to the Histadrut or
not. Accordingly the active right to vote in the election for the
Workers' Committee is granted to all permanent wage and salary
earners, whether organized or not. Individual candidates and not
party lists are submitted to the voters and those who receive the
majority vote are elected. This is the only instance of election by
majority vote. In all other Histadrut institutions the election is
based on proportional representation by party lists. However
candidates are usually chosen on a party basis in and most cases
are arranged in co-operation with the local Labour Council. But
this need not be so. The voter can select names from more than
one list.

Practically every establishment, even a very small one employing five or six workers, has a Workers' Committee. The small
establishments usually have one such Committee, medium-scale
establishments may have two and the largest establishments may
have even three, one for the clerical staff, one for the technical
staff and another for manual workers. However, there are some
very large establishments which have only one Committee, as it
should be according to the by-laws of the Histadrut. The Committees usually co-operate very closely, with the Committee of
Manual Workers in the lead. The clerical and technical staff prefer
separate committees, arguing that within one committee their
interests are not sufficiently safeguarded as they are often out-
voted on main issues.

The committees are elected once every two years. They meet
according to needs, usually once a week or once a fortnight but
not less than once a month. Each committee has at least one
secretary but large-scale firms often have three to five; the job
of at least one secretary in a large establishment is fulltime.

The most important function of the committees is bargaining with the firm, not only for collective agreements but also dealing with day-to-day execution of agreement, with complaints and grievances. Regrading and promotion is often done by the management, once a year, in co-operation with the committee. Frictions and small conflicts between workers themselves present another field of action. Israeli workers are very sensitive, very dignity conscious, jealous of their principles. Coming as they do from so many ethnical cultural backgrounds, workers often misjudge one another's intention. Hence there are many petty squabbles and every committee has its court of honour as the final authority for internal quarrels.

The committee assumes very important functions in the field of education and culture; it arranges lectures, discussion groups and training courses and often runs a lending library, arranges for collective buying of books and periodicals, and subscriptions to concerts and theatres.

In welfare services the committee runs a number of Funds such as the Sick Benefit Fund, Holiday Fund, Loan Fund, Fund for Mutual Assistance and Savings Fund. A secretary of the committee is a workers' factotum. He deals with all sorts of personal problems. Workers who used to turn to a Rabbi for advice, guidance or mediation, now turn to the secretary.

The committee is subject to double supervision by the Histadrut authorities, from the craft or industrial union and from local Labour Council. The latter is incomparably stronger than the former. According to Histadrut by-laws the committee cannot do much without the approval of the Labour Council. The secretary of the Labour Council or one of its officials visits the factory about once a week or fortnight, dealing with the problems of the Workers' Committee in all important matters. He supervises the election to the Committee and gives his final assent to the results. The committee is legally constituted only when it has the Labour Council's confirmation and the Labour Council has the right to dissolve the committee. In fact there is a constant tension between the Workers' Committees and the general body of the Histadrut, a latent tug-of-war.

The Workers' Committees were meant as the foundation of the power and strength of the Histadrut but in real life they have become the main source of internal weakness, dissention and lack of discipline. They are the main sources for dissent and protest of the members of the Histadrut against its policy. They are the organizers of illegal strikes, which form the big majority of all strikes in Israel. They are the real representatives of the sectional, professional interests of the workers. They have assumed a syndicalist flavour and threaten the unity of the movement.

The structure of the Histadrut is far from stable; on the contrary it is full of strains and stresses. There is a constant conflict between national and sectional interests, between politization and professionalism, between centralization and autonomy, between autocracy and democracy, between multi-functionalism and specialization, finally between the by-laws of the Histadrut and their implementation. There is a large gap between the law and the practice: the by-laws say one thing, the actual practice is very different. The strains are derived from the gigantic proportions of this immense apparatus, whose bureaucracy often takes over and pursues its own momentum. The Histadrut comes under heavy fire from many quarters which ask for reform and adjustment to the new conditions. The fact is that the Histadrut has not yet adapted itself to the new economic and social forces which have emerged in the State of Israel, and to the power of the State itself. The image of the Histadrut in the public eye has lost much of its pristine beauty and freshness. The general call is for basic reforms. The reforms called for are for greater democracy, decentralization, depolitization, specialization of functions and more independent but self-disciplined Trade Unions.

However, one must admit that in the situation of Israel as a beleaguered camp, the Histadrut basically fulfils the overriding requirements of Israeli society in its need for high work morale, work discipline and work productivity.

6.

The Devolution of Israeli Socialism

THE ATTRACTION of socialism for Israeli Jews is in itself an interesting sociological study. Why should one of the most individualistic and non-conformist people subscribe to a most anti-individualistic and conformist social system? Where does the source of attraction lie? In the lure of opposites? In the prophetic message of Judaism, regarded as the spiritual forerunner of socialist ideas? In the lore of the Land and the Star of Redemption? The elliptic model of the social psychology of the 'mino-majority' with two axes, one inherited from the Diaspora, the other developed in Israel, could be used as part of the explanation of this curious phenomenon. But the phenomenon itself is much more complex, because Israeli socialism was partly imported from Eastern Europe and partly developed in Israel.

Now, some reservations about the nature and degree of Israeli attachment to socialism.

Firstly the attachment is more to socialist ideas than to socialist practice. Socialist ideas, i.e., 'the verbal appropriation of the principles of under-privileged classes'[1] are more widely spoken of in Israel than its principles put into practice. A great deal of social rhetoric is heard but there is nothing very egalitarian about the policies adopted by the Israeli Labour Governments which have been in power since the inception of the State.

Israeli society is perhaps a little more egalitarian than many other established societies in the West but that is the outcome of spontaneous development and its poverty-stricken origin. Who were those who came to Israel to settle? At first the lower middle classes from the East European Ghettos, then those squeezed out or persecuted inmates of the concentration camps, finally those expelled from the Moslem Ghettos, all on the whole people of little means. The nascent society was egalitarian in character,

[1] Stanislav Ossowski, *Class Structure in the Social Consciousness*, p. 187. Routledge and Kegan Paul. London 1963.

because its members were all poor. But with the development of the country and with the rise of affluence class distinction became very much more pronounced and the distance between poor and rich became wider. And the co-efficient of inequality of income, as quoted elsewhere in the book, is not very much below the indices of Britain or Sweden (see Part I Ch. 2).

The craving for status distinctions is very pronounced and can be seen even in the Histadrut owned industries, in the civil service, and at the universities. The ladder of grading is being extended all the time. Privileges granted by the successive Labour Governments, especially in regard to land purchases, housing estates, credits, premiums and quotas, have considerably widened the social stratification. A new large bureaucratic stratum arose with a status of their own. The Oriental lower income group is turning more and more into a separate social class. Even the members of the Kibbutzim have assumed in the course of time a distinguishable status of their own, playing the role of landed nobility, staffing the highest positions in governments, the officer corps and the Histadrut.

Secondly, the attraction of socialism has been stronger among the intelligentsia than among the masses. The Israeli masses, when they vote for Mapai, vote for the government party, because it has proved its worth in conducting the affairs of the State for twenty years, is moderate, more national than socialist, and keeps the balance between conflicting social forces. Very little genuine mass support for socialism came from the German, Hungarian, Austrian, Yugoslav, British, American and the whole Oriental Jewry. Popular support for socialism was strong only from the Polish-Russian Jewry. Socialism was brought to Israel by the Jews from Poland and Russia, where racial and religious perse-cution joined hands with class exploitation, producing a syndrome of abject poverty and degradation exploding in a revolutionary upheaval. To the East European Jews socialism appeared prim-arily as a movement of total protest, in which they could launch their own specific protest, as a discriminated minority. Israeli socialism had a definite East European stamp with its revolution-ary vocabulary and phraseology. It took the Israeli socialists a long time to divest themselves of their East European origin; gradually under the impact of British rule their socialism became more infused with elements of Western socialism and the main stream of Israeli socialism (Mapai) came nearer in character to the British Labour Party. But this process is far from complete and a large section of the Israeli Labour Movement, such as Mapam, still bears a full imprint of its origin.

Thirdly, Israeli attraction to socialism must be more specifically related to its origin or rather continuation in an under-developed country. Israeli socialism is organically linked with a specific stage in the social and economic development of early Palestine. It was a bare country, deprived of an economic infra-structure; practically everything, even the soil and water resources and skilled manpower had to be created. The country presented a mixture of desert and unsanitary swamps, utterly neglected and lacking in security. The resources for building up the country were not available within the country and they were not available either among the immigrants, themselves poor. The country presented an enormous challenge. It was a challenge of a virtually virgin Jewish society in the making which could have been built up on rational and equitable lines without antagonistic privileged classes. The country was open to both the physical and economic planning, and the society was an ideal object for socialist engineering. Conditions in early Palestine did not lend themselves to private investment. There was no prospect of profit, no security of investment, no ready manpower for carrying out the tasks. Even if the pioneers had been completely deprived of socialist ideology, there would have been no alternative to the development of the country on collectivistic or co-operative lines. In fact the choice was not open to them.

And so socialist ideology was induced, strengthened and enforced by the conditions of early Palestine. Israeli experience in early Palestine seems to confirm the thesis that an under-developed country in its initial stage, where infra-structure is lacking, and no home capital and no skilled manpower is available, presents a strong case for socialist planning, both physical and economic.

However, the conditions of Palestine gradually changed and in the course of time Israel moved out of the stage of under-development into the present stage of an almost developed country. It started to attract private capital which can now see the prospect of profit, although the security terms are still questionable. As the economy developed and became stronger, generating capital resources of its own, Israel became less dependent on socialistic schemes and leaned more and more towards individualistic and capitalistic forms. The whole development of Israel's economy and Israel's Labour Movement can be viewed as a devolution of socialist thought and action. Socialism was of prime necessity at first but lost more and more ground as the country developed.

The incessant flow of donations, benefactions, development grants from abroad, and later German reparations, helped this development. Private capitalism can grow on private capital but not on public funds or funds donated to the State or to society at large. Contributions from abroad were converted into public investments, in the investments of the State, Histadrut, Jewish Agency, Kibbutzim and other public or semi-public undertakings. They contributed to the formation of a truly mixed economy, in which half of the national income is produced by public investment, including many semi-public institutions which are so characteristic of Israeli society. True, a certain percentage of public funds found its way by foul means or fair into private channels, producing a sector of parasitic capitalism. Another sector grew up which could be called parasitic socialism, a sector of socialist economy which lived on socialization of losses absorbed by public funds and on privileges granted by the State.

Again with economic development and the rise of affluence, conditions changed. The flow of benefactions and donations from abroad has lost its relative weight in Israel's economy. A large part of invested capital is found now either at home from capital resources accumulated in the process of development or abroad on a normal financial capitalistic basis. Also in this respect the original impetus of socialism fed by contributions from abroad lost its momentum.

The Israeli socialist can never forget the fact that his socialism was founded and nourished by foreign capitalism and it is still sustained by it. Its source was not revolution, nor the hammer and sickle, but a stretched out hand filled with donated dollars. This makes Israeli socialism a little shaky and insecure in itself. It has also influenced its development in another way. If socialism is built on donations, if the whole State is built up by benefactions, why should not all who need support and assistance receive the same benefit? This idea linked up closely with the basic conception of 'good works' in Judaism as acts of charity. In this way Israeli socialism was transformed in charity socialism. It means that everyone, every institution and every establishment, plants and weeds alike have a right to live. Inefficient, badly organized firms and establishments must be supported and they all deserve help and subsidy. After all, everyone has the right to make a living. A great deal of parasitic capitalism and parasitic socialism grew in this way.

Israeli socialism is a peculiar variety of its own. It combines various elements of great diversity.

First, it belongs to a pre-Marxian, what is called Utopian, variety of socialism. It is more linked with idealistic than materialistic philosophy. This characteristic has been frequently reported already of Jewish socialism in Eastern Europe.

'Lev Martov' (pen name for Juli Osipovitch Zederbaum), a Jewish socialist in the 1890's in Vilna, and himself an Orthodox Marxist, gives in his memoirs the following description of Socialistic Jewish Youth at that time:

> We were surprised to learn that the whole trend of their social mind was directed on idealistic lines, that their socialism bears the imprint of abstract utopianism, and that the idea of class struggle was absolutely alien to them. Whilst we looked at them as men who had to move the whole working class, as a tool in the hands of the revolutionary organization, they considered themselves as individuals who have outgrown the masses and created a new cultural milieu.[1]

Mutatis mutandis, the same may be said of Israeli socialism.

Israeli socialism has also a religious flavour derived directly from the Hebrew prophets. Jewish socialists, even of the left wing Mapam, study with great devotion the Hebrew Bible, the greatest Israeli treasure. Their socialism can be described as Marx plus the Prophets, perhaps Prophets more than Marx. There is particular religious socialism in Poalei Hamizrachi, with its own Kibbutzim, but all branches of Israeli socialism have a religious substratum. The influx of the Oriental population, which now makes up half of the Israeli inhabitants, contributed also to the strengthening of the religious elements in Israeli socialism. The immigrants from Asia and North Africa who now form the

[1] F. Zweig, *The Israeli Worker*, p. 276. New York 1959.

majority of manual workers in agriculture, building, industry and transport, joined the Histadrut and for the most part also the socialist parties. But in fact socialism is new to them and they think of it in an unorthodox way. They are traditionally religious and have a world view coloured basically by the Bible. In their view there is nothing worth while which either contradicts the precepts of the Bible or is not included in it. Socialism means for them simply justice and charity, as practised among Jews. Class war, class envy, class jealousy, do they not violate the tenth commandment which says explicitly: 'Thou shalt not covet thy neighbours house . . .'? Socialism is all right, but as preached by the prophets. This is the basic interpretation of socialism among the Oriental section of the population.

Israeli socialism is also much more individualistic, non-conformist, one could say libertarian than socialist movements in other countries. The Jew is a typical non-conformist and Israeli society is a permissive society *par excellence*. Israeli socialism turns against *Gleichschaltung*, the levelling down to the lowest denominator. It abhorrs the conformity of the Communist creed, from which it was additionally alienated by the rise of anti-Semitic tendencies in Moscow. It reasserts the right of the individual to opt out. It is an iconoclastic socialism. Even the most authoritarian branch of socialism in the very small Communist Parties of Israel is not free from non-conformism. A year ago there were four Labour Parties, apart from two Communist Parties, and although the split of the Labour Parties has been recently partially healed, there is a wide range of sects and factions within the parties.

Israeli socialism is not only non-conformist, but it has also a touch of anarcho-syndicalism, which has a strong tradition in the Diaspora. The ideas of control and ownership of means of production by workers themselves in each enterprise are very popular. The Workers' Committees often behave in a syndicalist fashion, and often subscribe to the principles of direct action. They often repudiate the directives of the Histadrut and feel free to act as they like. The Jew never takes for granted the necessity for government; for him society is prior to the State, superior to the State and of greater permanence. Not a few would like to get rid of the paraphernalia of the powerful, militaristic and restrictive State, encroaching more and more on the individual and to return to the old-fashioned principles of individual responsibility by which people can run their own affairs by mutual agreement.

Israeli socialism is also a much more middle class socialism than socialist movements in many other countries. It is a socialism of a man with middle class mentality and aspirations, not of a proletarian who is ready to stay proletarian his whole lifetime. The veterans who came to Israel were not proletarians and had no proletarian class consciousness. They did not want to hire themselves out as wage earners to swell other peoples' profits. They wanted to combine their socialistic aspirations with economic independence. The middle class aspiration of an independent merchant, industrialist or a professional man determined the specific Israeli road to socialism. The outcome was the formation of a chain of co-operatives of various kinds, in which a member is not a proletarian but the owner of the means of production. A Kibbutz member is not a hireling; he works for himself. The programme of Israeli socialism may be described as a programme for a property owning true democracy. Under the Israeli Labour Governments ownership of property became the norm and assumed proportions hardly known in any other country. About two-thirds of Israeli householders are owner-occupiers of their house or apartment. About two-thirds of Jewish mixed farming, half of the building industry, one-fourth of manufacturing and the largest part of transport, merchant marine, etc., all in all one-fourth of the national income is produced by Histadrut co-operatives. Israeli socialism emerged as a model of co-operative socialism, centred around strong co-operatives. State socialism is not the aim. It is not planned to turn workers into wage and salary earners of the State but to make them independent worker owners. This co-operative socialism can be regarded as typically Jewish, because it accorded well with the general craving of the Jew to be independent, to be his own boss. It is not the State which ought to replace the private employer. Besides the State was always a foreign entity in the eyes of the Jew. What was essential in the eyes of the Israeli socialism was the destruction of the whole employer-employee relationship. Everybody should be his own employer.

Of course this crystal clear gospel was far from simple. The co-operatives grew in time to sizeable enterprises and assumed more and more the atmosphere and ways of capitalistic ventures, with an army of wage and salary earners who fell into the usual pattern of employer-employee relationship. This was another factor in the weakening of socialism in Israel. The workers in Histadrut-owned co-operatives became disillusioned with their socialist 'property' as much as the workers in nationalized industry in Britain are. The co-operative sector of the economy has lost much of its dynamic impulse. Many Histadrut enterprises have been unable to stand the test of competition with private industry.

It is not enough to say that Israeli socialism is a sort of co-operative socialism. We must consider more specifically the impact of the Kibbutz model. We can hardly exaggerate the role of the Kibbutz in moulding the socialist movement. The Kibbutz became the spearhead and the nucleus of the whole movement. In the Kibbutz experience there is one aspect which is perhaps the most important in its impact on socialist thinking: an existence without money. The Kibbutz member achieved perfect security without money, he has no need of money, he repudiates and rejects it. This is an absolute negation of the Jewish bourgeois style of life. The Jewish bourgeois thought a great deal about money, perhaps no more and no less than any other bourgeois in the world, but the Kibbutz is certainly a living protest against him. This aspect of the Kibbutz experience is the source of the attack by Israeli socialism on the bourgeois culture and ethos. What is attacked is the style and way of life of the bourgeoisie, what is called in Hebrew *baalebatiut*, the sense of possessiveness. Not so much capitalism itself is being attacked, as the greed and lust for money, the desire to accumulate, the love of possession. This onslaught on the spirit of the bourgeoisie went very well with the Zionist concern for the moral regeneration of the Jewish nation. In this way Israeli socialism became Kibbutz socialism, a movement concerned more with ethical regeneration of the Jewish nation than with anything else.

However, we can further observe the devolution of Israeli socialism parallel with the contraction of the Kibbutzim in the Israeli economy. The decline in the status of the Kibbutzim is simultaneous with the general rise of affluence and *embourgeoisement* of society. In the last decade the Kibbutz has been on the defensive and with it the whole structure of Israeli socialism.

In Israeli socialism there is one more characteristic feature which needs strong emphasis; its national, if not nationalistic character. This feature was already strongly developed in Eastern Europe but it grew enormously in Israel. The veterans who came to early Palestine were not only socialists but also Zionists. If one would have asked them what was more important for them and more enduring, socialism or Zionism, they would not have known what to answer, and probably they would have said both, as both were linked organically in the programme of redemption of the Land and the people. They came with good intentions, as true international socialists, to extend their hand to their Arab comrades exploited by the Arab overlords, but the hand was declined and as the ensuing hostility grew stronger, Jewish socialism became an exclusively ethnical socialism.

Socialism means internationalism, based on international brotherhood and solidarity. Actually this aspect forms the main line of division between true socialism and other, more nationalistic forms of socialist movements. This has been recognized very strongly, particularly by Jewish socialists, who always stressed their belief in international solidarity and brotherhood rooted in the visions of the Hebrew prophets. But the weight of circumstances considerably weakened this international aspect of Israeli socialism. The general rise of Jewish nationalism in Israeli society, the constant warfare with the Arabs, the position of Jewish society as a dominant majority *vis-à-vis* hostile minority, all contributed greatly to the growth of the national character of Jewish socialism. The same collapse of international solidarity and brotherhood witnessed by international socialism on the world scene, was witnessed on the internal front by Jewish socialism at home.

We see what a cauldron of conflicting ideas and tendencies Israeli socialism is. It is a paradox, as all Jewish life is. Aspirations and realities clash, good intentions and crass necessity. The forces operating in Israeli socialism pull in opposite directions: internationalism and nationalism, the sword and the harp, Marx and the Prophets, Americanism and Israelism, East and West, the ethos of the New State and nonconformism. Although the Israeli socialists tried to organize so many conflicting ideas, tendencies and situations into some kind of synthesis, it is still most difficult to present it as a coherent organic system. It has

been overwhelmed by the flow of events and a swirl of contradictions, coming from outside and inside. The general pattern
which emerged from its original state, conveys the ferment of
Israeli society in the making, a society embattled from outside
and insecure in itself, not knowing exactly the way ahead. It also
reflects the fears of a small nascent society without great resources
of their own, overwhelmed by American donations. It reflects
the characteristic features of Jewish heritage of non-conformity,
diversity and individualism. It reflects also the deeper religious
aspirations of Judaism.

Israeli socialism still clings to the values of pioneer puritanism
in its opposition to the bourgeois, but it has had to come to
terms with the spirit of affluence and the rising tide of embourgeoisement. It still clings to its origin as agrarian socialism exemplified by the Kibbutz but it has moved a long way towards
a more urban and industrial socialism. It still clings to its internationalism but it has to face squarely the internal Arab-Jewish
hostility.

The devolution of Israeli socialism proves again that no
intellectually consistent system can do justice to the needs of
society. If a system is adopted, it becomes deflected in real life to
such an extent that only an outward package remains, a label to
which lip-service is paid. And the greater the deflection, the
greater the inroad in its principles and its coherence, the greater
also becomes the anxiety of the leadership of the movement and
more ardent becomes also the lip-service paid in its rhetoric.
Genuine devotion to a system and the attempt to observe its
principles may become a great encumberance and, in extreme
cases, a straight-jacket. Although the Jews are reputed to indulge
in *Principienreiterei*, no one can say that the Israelis have burdened
themselves excessively by the shackles of systems in the real
practice of successive Labour Governments. The principles are
set aside as soon as they became inexpedient.

The future of Israeli socialism, as everything else in Israel,
depends primarily on the future of Jewish-Arab conflict. If the
economy under the continuous and rising Arab threat assumes
the character of a siege economy, the restrictive character of
Israeli socialism may grow and develop into a sort of war
socialism. If the warfare continues and sharpens, the general rise
of nationalism is bound to affect the character of Israeli socialism

which will grow into a socialism *de la patrie*. On the other hand if the threats of Arab-Jewish warfare subside and the rise of affluence is allowed to continue, the general embourgeoisement of society will further deflect Israeli socialism from its previous course and the economy will gradually move into capitalistic channels. The public sector of the economy may not shrink in absolute terms, but its growth in relative terms may not follow the general spontaneous growth of the national economy based on the rebirth of private enterprise, up to now hampered by the vagaries of the vacillating policy of Labour Governments.

7.

The Process of Orientalization

RUDYARD KIPLING'S saying: 'East is East and West is West and never the twain shall meet' certainly does not apply to Israel. The twain meet and live side by side. But the problem arises: do they live happily and at ease with each other and how will the balance between them change in course of time?

Compared with its neighbours, Israel is definitely Western, but compared with Western countries Israel is still Eastern. Technically, scientifically and industrially, the Westernization of Israel has been a great success marked by Israel's superior warfare with the neighbouring countries. There is little doubt that the Israeli élite would like to mould the State in the traditional image of Western society, with Western industrial, scientific and technical standards. But in so far as the Western tradition means a secular and open society of a non-nationalistic brand with equal rights of citizenship, irrespective of creed, race or nationality, then the issue is not so clear. The religious basis of Israeli society is a great hindrance to the full acceptance of the Western model. Hebrew society based on the myths of the return of the tribes identified on religious basis cannot by its nature be a Western society, as understood and practised in the West.

The return of the Jewish tribes to their ancient Land can be viewed as a process of Orientalization of the tribes as far as the European elements are concerned. The Jewish people who originated in the Orient returned to their oriental location; they are now governed by ancient myths which originated in the Orient, and also by the landscape and climate of the Orient, by the new unmastered physical environment. They left the temperate zone for the semi-arid expanses of the desert. They are now becoming again the people of the desert.

They left the relative security and orderliness of the Western world for the insecure life of the frontier beset with tribal feuds.

They are following now the ancient call of their warrior ancestors. The life of wars, punitive raids and incursions, of alarms and ambushes has bred in them a spirit of intolerance, which is in itself a characteristic of the Orient. They left societies where nationalism has passed its peak and is dying fast for an area with highly inflamed, vociferous, newly awakened nationalism. They are both bearers and victims of their own nationalism and those around them.

They left old-established states to live in and among newly founded states conscious of recently won independence. They themselves are post-colonials and surrounded by post-colonials. They left highly developed industrial societies for an under-developed area, where ignorance, poverty and disease are rampant. They are surrounded by what is called external proletariat and semi-proletariat confronted with a rapid break-up of existing ways of life and decay of social forms. All around them peoples are in turmoil with devastating social economic problems in a quasi-revolutionary state.

They left the swiftly flowing stream of Christian civilization and entered the stagnant waters of the more static Islam civilization, placing themselves in the midst of the Arab dominions, spanning some 4,000 miles in Africa and Asia and comprising 100,000,000 people.

They left areas of relative stability of population for areas of high pressure of population. The population explosion of the East is constantly encroaching upon them, and sooner or later they will have to adjust their own rate of fertility to that of the area, if they are to withstand the pressure of the Arab masses around them.

Certainly the pioneers did not choose an easy path. The area itself, which was not chosen but historically conditioned, was the least favoured by nature or man and full of enormous hazards and uncertainties. They plunged head on into a sea of troubles. And yet they swam through at a good speed and in spite of all the factors which made for Orientalization, they achieved a high degree of outward Westernization.

It must be remembered that the pioneers themselves and the Europeans who followed them were not strictly speaking Westerners. They were East Europeans who viewed Western civilization and culture through the eyes of East Europe. The

Western model of the European Jews was impregnated not only with Jewish values but also with East European values partly derived from the Orient.

The establishment of Israel brought in its wake the disruption of whole centres of Jewish life in Arab countries and soon the mass immigration of Afro-Asian Jews into Israel followed. They and their descendants today make up half the population of Israel and their influence is growing fast. Their fertility rates are roughly speaking twice that of the families of European origin and in ten to twenty years' time they will form the overwhelming majority of the Israeli population. They brought with them the values and standards of the Orient, of the Islamic civilization in which they were immersed for many centuries. They had been much less mobile than their European co-religionists and had remained in their countries of origin for long periods of time without break. They were therefore much more assimilated to the ways of their country of origin than the East European Jews had ever been. They are the true indigenous population of the Orient, deeply rooted in the region.

They are learning now the values and standards of the European Jews who form the governing élite; they are very eager apprentices and very quick in adopting the new ways, but the outward signs of the Western world are more easily adopted than the deeper values which are less accessible. However, the process of learning and teaching of new values and standards is in itself a matter of give and take. In art and design, in food and clothing as well as in manners, the Oriental influence is marked.

Before cultural parity is reached between the two sections of the population, the influence of the Oriental population with its rapidly rising birth rate is bound to increase. In both sections the Oriental and European values are increasingly intermingled, and the offshoot may be a hybrid of the two civilizations with the balance in favour of the Oriental element.

In addition there is the constant influence of Arab civilization. The Arabs in Israel have one of the highest fertility rates in the world, even higher than that of India. The non-Jewish population in Israel increased from 156,000 at the end of 1948 to about 300,000 in 1966. Although the Arabs form a separate entity which mingles only in the market place, when buying and selling goods and services—the Israeli society is a 'plural society' in the strictest sense[1]—they have all the same a powerful psychological effect on the Jewish population. The Jewish-Arab conflict itself has a most powerful impact on the Jewish mentality, as one side imposes on the other some of its standards and values. In the close embrace of a life and death struggle one side imparts to the other its very life blood.

The complexity of the Israeli society arises not only from inter-mingling of Western and Oriental values but also from the parallel change of values in both sections of the population. Many of the values of both sections are rooted in ancient myths of the Orient revived in the contact with the new land and many new values are required as a response to the conditions encountered in the land. The impact of the new climate, geography and history, on both sections of the population tends to diminish somewhat the value distance between the two sections. There is also the impact of the awareness that Israel must come to terms with the Arab civilization around her. The question arises, although it is rarely articulated, as to what kinds of changes in the mental and spiritual climate and in the cultural style of Israeli society would be most conducive to bridging the gap between the Arabs and the Israelis.

In the heated discussion of Arab hopes for the slow strangula-tion of Israel, the historical simile of the Latin Kingdom of Jerusalem is often invoked by the Arabs. Referring to the Arab boycott of Israel, a prominent Arab writer gives the following account of the Arabs' 'profound hope that in the course of time their refusal to have anything to do with Israel will cause the isolated state to wilt and perish. . . . They remember that the Latin Kingdom of Jerusalem came to an end after enduring a hundred years. To them Israel is another such artificial creation— a forced plant that has no place in the Arab world. . . .'[2]

---

[1] The 'plural society' was defined by J. S. Furnival in his *Colonial Policy and Practice* (Cambridge University Press, 1948, p. 304), as follows: 'In Burma as in Java, probably the first thing that strikes the visitor is the medley of peoples—Europeans, Chinese, Indians and natives. It is in the strictest sense a medley, for they mix but do not combine. Each group holds by its own religion, its own culture and language, its own ideas and ways. As individuals they meet but only in the market place, in buying and selling. There is a plural society, with different sections of the community living side by side, but separately within the same political unit. Even in the economic sphere there is a division along racial lines.'

[2] Edward Atiyah, *The Arabs*, p. 238. Pelican Book. London 1955.

Arabs' hopes in this respect are as unfounded as the comparison with the Latin Kingdom of Jerusalem is invalid. The Kingdom of Jerusalem was not settled in mass by people of Latin descent of all classes from highest to lowest. It was a military venture, an autocratic creation made up of the upper crust, a head without a body, and the settlers were a minority entirely alien to the region. By contrast Jewish society embraces all classes and all social layers and comprises a large majority in the country. More than half the population, namely the Oriental Jews coming from the Arab countries, is indigenous to the region. They are in fact Arabic Jews, who were squeezed out of Arab countries in spasms of anti-Jewish hostility. In another twenty years' time they will probably form two-thirds of the country's population. At present the architects and state builders of Israel are of European origin but the supremacy of the European élite will not last very long, as the demographic basis is constantly shifting in favour of the Jews from Arab countries. In half a century Israel will demographically conform to the indigenous population of the Middle East. The Orientalization of Israel in this sense is an elemental process which cannot be halted. Maybe then Israeli-Arab co-operation will be more easily achieved.

The contrast between West and East is sometimes presented as the contrast between the materialism of the West and the spirituality of the East. Does the Orientalization of Israel mean also her spiritualization, the growth of spiritual awareness and spiritual unrest? Will it mean claiming the old spiritual heritage of the ancestral East? Anyway, in due time the Oriental wing of the World Jewry will be represented almost entirely by the Israeli society, and the dialogue between Israel and the Diaspora will more distinctly echo the dialogue between West and East.

Part III

two mystiques

1.

The Mystique of Violence

NATIONS and men who have arrived are peaceful and peace-loving. The underdog is not so peaceful, and not as obliging as he should be. Fighting exploitation or oppression implies violence riots, rebellion or revolution. Nations, races and social classes in their quest for redress or justice embrace the mystique of violence.

The mystique of violence is often presented as part of the lore of freedom. Throughout long stretches of history the symbol of the free man was his sword or his rifle, and the mark of the free man was his courage and his determination in defending his rights. Conversely the symbol of the serf was his utter defenceless-ness, and his mark was servility and docility. His defencelessness invited exploitation and oppression. Was not the proverbial defencelessness of the Jew a standing invitation to trample on his rights and to mock him?

Throughout long stretches of history, the Jews were not only defenceless but also meek and docile. They were the easiest and most profitable target of violence both organized and unorgan-ized, official and unofficial, by governments and mobs. And yet the idea of rebellion or even organized disobedience never crossed the mind of the Jew. He accepted his fate, as God ordained it and even gave it a spiritual meaning. 'The favourite mythical symbol to represent the divine mission of the Jewish Dispersion was Deutero-Isaiah: the graphic image of the Suffering Servant.'[1] All churches are peace-loving and help policemen to keep order and peace, and the Jewish ecclesia was not an exception. It helped enormously to keep the Jew in his place and to keep him quiet. It was, therefore, not surprising that 'almost all the movements springing from Jewish nationalism, whether Zionist or Diaspora

[1] Ben Halpern, *The Idea of the Jewish State*, p. 99. Harvard University Press 1961.

nationalist, were largely unconcerned with religion, and in a great measure hostile to it'.[1]

All national liberation movements, movements for racial equality and left wing radical movements have embraced the mystique of violence as part of the process of vindication and redress. The gospel of Marxism merged with the gospel of nationalism, providing a most powerful powder box which tore asunder the old order both in internal and international relations.

The same applies to the process of national liberation as implied in the conquest of the Land of Israel by the Jewish Tribes. The myths of Israel present the resettlement of the land as a process of Return, but the process has not been peaceful and could not have been peaceful. It has been compared to the Crusades as forming the last and most successful Crusade by the West, or to the process of colonization by white settlers in colonial countries. 'The Jews in Israel are in the ambiguous situation of the last of the white settlers in Asia, after the European imperialists and colonizers have made their exit from the two Continents'—writes J. L. Talmon, Professor of History at the Hebrew University of Jerusalem.[2]

The Jews in ancient Judea were a warrior nation, very daring and restless, always on the brink of uprising, challenging the greatest power of the ancient world. It is interesting to note that, returning to the land after 1,900 years, they acquired some of the former warlike qualities of their race, shedding the docility and meekness of the Diaspora Jews jointly with the old traditional values of Diaspora Judaism. Is this coincidence, or simply the logic of history and the situation?

The Sabra, when soldiering, fashions himself not on the image of the professional soldier—soldiering is nothing to be proud of and even the professional soldier of highest rank soon returns to a civilian calling.[3] He styles himself rather on the image of a warrior who combines soldiering with idealism, and discipline with initiative, enterprise and responsibility. He is not a cog in

[1] Jack J. Cohen, *The Case for Religious Naturalism*, p. 169. The Reconstructionist Press. New York 1958.

[2] J. L. Talmon, *The Unique and the Universal*, p. 267. Secker and Warburg. 1965.

[3] The Colonels in the Israeli Army went back to their cowsheds in the Kibbutz after the war.

an all-embracing soulless war machine. He reserves the right to think and act for himself. The Israeli army, the greatest Israeli experiment after the Kibbutz and the Histadrut, is a model unique in itself. It has a unique system in the mobilization procedures for the reservists, and a unique system in the integration of all three services under one single command. The emphasis is on a high standard of quality, training, intelligence and initiative, and on leadership by example. It is a people's army resembling at heart a revolutionary force of civilians.

The mystique of violence has not been openly part of the mystique of Zionism, but just the contrary. Hess, Herzl and Weizmann entertained great hopes for the Jewish State as a peace-loving force bringing benefits to the world at large. Herzl wrote in his *Judenstaat*, 'We shall live at last as free men on our own soil and die peacefully in our own homes'. But on the same page Herzl writes, 'And what glory awaits those who will fight unselfishly in our cause! Therefore, I believe that a wonderous generation of Jews will spring into existence. The Maccabeans will rise again.' The myths of the Maccabeans and Bar Kochba and later, Massada, were implied in the programme of national liberation, like a built-in mechanism waiting to be released the moment the programme ran into violent opposition from other quarters. The dialectic of liberation had to be the dialectic of violence. The mystique of violence as a liberating force and a force of renewal in Judaism had been brought over by veteran pioneers from Russia and Poland, and the use of force marked the watershed between the meek, docile and bent Jew of the Diaspora and the proud, free and upright rebellious Israeli. The model of the veteran pioneer was not only the settler who tills the soil with love, but also the *Shomer* (the guard) with his rifle, and this picture of the sunburnt young boy staunchly standing guard still adorns the pages of the primers which have to instil the pioneering ideology of the Founding Fathers. This ideology of pioneering implied an aggressive leadership and mobilization for action, both in defence and as a deterrent against hostile outbursts from an environment which included the Mandatory Power, at one time hostile to the aspirations of the Palestinian Jews.

There is no denying that in the process of the liberation of Israel violence played a large part, not only in the constant fighting with the Arabs but also in terrorism and underground fighting against the Mandatory Power. The terrorists of the *Irgun Zvi Leumi* and the *Stern gang* were at first disowned by official opinion in Jewish society. 'However much Ben Gurion may have wished to extricate the Haganah and the Jewish Agency from the contamination of terrorists, it was hard to do it now.'[1] Later on the terrorists were rehabilitated and completely reinstated in public esteem—in 1966 in Tel-Aviv, official tribute was paid to them—as freedom fighters, as those who made their contribution to Israeli independence by laying down their lives. The fruits of violence depend very much on the response of the other side. Violence which fails is, in most cases, condemned by all sides, violence which succeeds has altogether a different reception. Even if the fruits of violence, as in the case of Israel, cannot be disentangled from the fruits of patient diplomacy and the force of events, the claims of violence cannot be refuted altogether. The spirit of violence was linked with a passionate love for freedom and independence, and produced the 'heroic myths' of Israel (to use George Sorel's phrase), a lore rich in romantic and heroic exploits. And this spirit is still in demand in the never-ending national emergency.

Young Israeli children, when they play little games with guns in mock battles, are fighting against Arabs, not cowboys or Indians. Certainly they are not taught to hate, for a campaign of hate is absent in Israel, but still the residuum that remains from childish pranks and games, and from newspaper reports of the constant battling with the Arabs and of mutual accusations of atrocities, is enough to provide ample material for the lore of violence. To quote Professor Talmon again, 'Some Zionists were so self-centred and self-righteous, that Arab resistance appeared to them as nothing but perversion and wickedness, and Arab guerillas as bandits and assassins. Many consciously or unconsciously sought to ease their conscience by attributing to the Arabs a greater dose of original sin than that possessed by any ordinary people.'[2]

Such outbursts of hostility against the Arab population as occurred in Ramle and Natania in 1965 in the form of riots by bands of Jewish youths was very disturbing to public opinion and

[1] Christopher Sykes, *Cross Roads to Israel*, p. 418. Collins. London 1965.
[2] *Op. cit.*, p. 256.

strongly condemned by the government. But still, this is an inescapably tragic result of the situation in which Israel finds herself.

The mystique of violence in Israel has similar roots to those found in any other national or revolutionary movement. It reflects a deeply pessimistic view of the human condition. Rights, justice, freedom, independence can be won not by arguments, however noble, just and rational they are, but only by counter force and countervailing power. Try as you may to convince the powerful and the mighty that they should not exploit the weak and the powerless, preach Christianity for 2,000 years about love, charity and justice, and you will not abolish exploitation and oppression. It is difficult to answer the question: who has done more for the poor and exploited, Jesus preaching charity and love, or Marx preaching the gospel of resistance and rebellion? Jesus tried to mollify the mighty and powerful with the spirit of charity and mercy, and undoubtedly helped those who could not rise and help themselves. Marx tried to raise the poor and exploited by their own efforts and to infuse in them a spirit of resistance and self-defence by organizing them into a countervailing power opposed to exploitation. The human condition and the state of the world is so conceived that the weak and powerless invite a great deal of exploitation and a small dose of charity. And who wants charity in any case?

Is not a State an organized and authorized system of violence, and has any State in the past or present been formed otherwise than by violence in one form or another? The Soviet Union, which tried to condemn the Israeli 'aggression' of 1967 in the UN Assembly has herself been born of and grown on violence. She preaches the Leninist-Marxist doctrine of class war, the idea of a violent redress by the working classes and by under-developed countries.

This is the background philosophy of the mystique of violence, which is a pessimistic, one could say, despairing reflection on the human condition, in which the love of freedom and justice is organically entwined with violence and hate, in which even the noblest manifestations of the human heart and mind such as religion have been closely linked with violence and persecution.

Has the emergency passed for the Jewish people at large, and more specifically has the emergency passed for the Jews in Israel?

Gideon Hausner, the chief prosecutor in Eichmann's trial in
Jerusalem writes in his book presenting the case:[1] 'Were the
shattering events the last convulsion of a horrible past or the
forerunner of an even more disastrous future . . . antisemitism is
still a powerful and dangerous evil.'

And Menachem Begin, the leader of the Herut (freedom) party,
and at present a member of the Israeli Government,[2] expresses
the same concern for the future:

> We are a small nation which has laid the foundation for its freedom.
> Our enemies are many; our friends are very few. Who knows, what
> the morrow holds for us, whether there will not be new attempts
> to subjugate us. The history of the Revolt and the fact of its victory
> will guide us in the unknown future. They will teach us never to
> despair even in conditions of enslavement. For a nation, enslaved,
> dispersed, beaten, decimated, on the brink of utter destruction,
> can yet arise to rebel against its fate and so come to life again. . . .
> This is the lore of revolt. . . . It is needed above all by our people. If
> we learn and remember, we shall overcome all our enemies. They
> will never succeed in enslaving us again.

The mystique of violence has often undertones of despair, and
is sometimes tinged with a suicidal mood. Freud would say that
it is marked with the instinct of Thanatos. The motto, 'Fight and
fight again, even unto death', was often used to mean that the
Jew must be prepared to fight, if he has to, even alone against
the world. In one of her speeches[3] in 1956 Golda Meir, the then
Foreign Minister of Israel, contended that it is nothing new for
Jewry to find itself in a struggle for survival against the entire
world. In the past, the Jews have faced the hostility of the whole
world and have survived.

Facing the Arab threat in 1967, the Israeli Jews had no illusions
that, if the war went against them, no nation would have moved
to save them from annihilation. Many nations might have felt
very guilty allowing a new Holocaust to occur. Perhaps a remnant
might have been saved, but only a remnant. And the awareness
of this position is what the Israelis call their secret weapon,
phrasing it *Ein Breira* (we have no choice)—win or perish.

[1] Gideon Hausner, *Justice in Jerusalem*, p. 448. London 1967.
[2] Menachem Begin, *The Revolt*, p. 380. Allen. London 1951.
[3] Before the National Press Club in Washington D.C., 11 December 1956
and in an N.B.C. Television Programme, 2 December 1956.

This feeling is actually the result of the cataclysmic experience of the Holocaust. In the judgement against Eichmann Judge Halevi stated, 'Israel cannot be cut off from its roots which also lie deep in the catastrophe of European Jewry' and this is also true with regard to the mystique of violence, which has its roots in the camps of Europe.

The mystique of violence found perhaps its best expression in the dramatic staging of the Eichmann trial, and the commando raid on foreign soil which culminated in Eichmann's abduction on an El Al plane. The trial and its circumstances were not only an expression of the mystique of violence, but also considerably strengthened it. Many misgivings about this trial were felt among Diaspora Jews,[1] and also among official representatives of world Zionist organizations and of the World Jewish Congress, such as its President, Dr Nahum Goldman, who called upon Ben Gurion to set up an International Court in Jerusalem with judges for each of the countries that had suffered under Nazi occupation. Many outstanding non-Jewish friends of Israel such as Guy Mollet, former Prime Minister of France, made a similar plea. The misgivings concerned more the circumstances preceding the trial than the trial itself. The organization of a commando raid on Eichmann, the abduction of a drugged man on an Israeli aircraft, and the obtaining of his consent in writing to his abduction and trial in Israel had some undignified features which can be traced directly to the mystique of violence. What was the purpose of this elaborate and difficult and not altogether legitimate operation which involved Israel in an international conflict with the Argentine which had to be settled finally before the Security Council?

The capture of Eichmann and his subsequent trial was designed by Ben Gurion as an act of historical justice; but even more, his purpose was to instruct the world in the facts, the circumstances and the reasons of the holocaust. During the days of the trial he said repeatedly, 'We must teach the youth what happened'.[2]

[1] See Hanna Arendt's angry book, *Eichmann in Jerusalem*. New York 1961 and the pamphlet of Victor Gollancz, *The Case of Adolph Eichmann*. London 1961. Martin Buber called the trial and the execution 'a mistake of historical dimensions'.

[2] Maurice Edelman, *Ben Gurion, a Political Biography*, p. 190. Hodder and Stoughton. London 1964.

Gideon Hausner also underlines this aspect of the teaching qualities of the trial, hoping to instruct by the proceedings 'our people at home', 'the teenagers of Israel' and 'the world at large'.

The new Israelis, deeply steeped in the mystique of violence, simply could not believe that 6,000,000 Jews (there are only two and a quarter million Israelis) could let themselves be slaughtered without any attempt at organized resistance. The trial had to show why this was possible, so that the New Israelis could believe it and not show contempt for meek and docile creatures so unlike themselves, the 'relics of the Diaspora'.

> The reaction of the youth who followed the trial with great interest, was summed up in a phrase that recurred in many letters and school essays 'Our eyes have been opened'. The trial thus proved to be a strong educational factor in strengthening Jewish consciousness.... Important also was the realization that the only reason it was possible to hold the trial at all was that there is now a Jewish State on the map.... Now it was the Jews themselves who could decide what was best for their condition, they could do so because they had their own machinery of justice, their own prosecutors and their own policemen.... The trial thus brought home to everyone in Israel the basic facts and lessons of our time, but even more significant was the feeling of self-assurance and confidence that swept the nation.[1]

The spirit of violence affected also the religious life in Israel. Nowhere is Jewish orthodoxy so militant and fanatical as in Israel. And similarly the Left is nowhere else so hostile and uncompromising to religion as in Israel. Tempers on both sides are fiery and pugnacious, leading to riots, demonstrations and counter demonstrations.

The spirit of violence is felt throughout the Land as a liberating force, as a discharge of pent-up energy, a release from the unbearable pressure of servitude, as an affranchisement, a kind of redemption. Psychologists would say that violence is felt as an inverted love, the compulsion to win love from others by force. The 'nobody loves me' complex of the Diaspora Jew has turned into a compulsory desire to win love, if by no other means, than by sheer force.

The mystique of violence is not without its own backhanded religiosity, linked by a sense of personal mission and dedication.

[1] Hausner, *op. cit.*, pp. 453–4.

At times it has assumed an almost Messianic flavour, arising out of a peculiar single-mindedness of purpose and dream of greatness. Gheula Cohen, who took part in terrorist activities in 1943–8, writes in her memoirs[1] of the Messianic longings of the Freedom Fighters, longings for the 'realization of the Jewish dream', the Redemption, the evolution of an integral Jewish consciousness and the establishment of a boundless field for the release of Jewish creative energy.

The mystique of violence has also its own code of morality centred on the new Nation which assumes the status of the Sanctum. Gheula Cohen formulates it in the following way:[2] 'Whatever benefits the nation, even if it brings harm to many individuals, is morally desirable. Whatever brings harm to the nation, even if it proves a blessing to many individuals, is morally undesirable.' This code allows for a ruthless and unqualified use of force, and absolves the use of terrorism, and more specifically of border terrorism. This policy demands the use of retaliation in force against border incursions by the Arabs, by applying to them the same weapon of border terrorism destroying life and property on the other side. It applies the principle of collective responsibility in which the innocent suffer with the guilty. It is meant as an object lesson, instilling fear in the other side and respect for a violent and strong arm. This is supposed to act as a deterrent against further incursions and eventually to bring peace to the area.

Sometimes the deterrent is used against a party which was not directly involved, as for instance in the frontier raid against Jordan in November 1966, in which forty houses were blown up in a border village in the South Hebron Hills, involving the death of innocent villagers (although it was announced that most of the villages were first evacuated), while the reprisal was actually intended against Syria, meant as a warning to the Syrian Government. Israeli opinion is deeply divided on this issue of retaliatory raids, their justification and their effectiveness, which, up to now, have not been shown by events. They involve the principle of collective responsibility, well known in Jewish history as a method in anti-Jewish pogroms.

[1] Gheula Cohen, *The Woman of Violence. The memoirs of a young terrorist 1943–48*. Translated from Hebrew. Rupert Hart Davis. London 1966.
[2] *Ibid.*, p. 55.

The ethical problem of the conflict between righteous ends and evil means has been the subject of agelong discussions in Judaism, and Jewish people have always sided against the justification of evil means. The delicate balance between ends and means in Israeli practice is—to say the least—very disturbing. What seems to be the effective means of bolstering the Israeli cause is accepted as right, even if the means are foul. The justification of collective responsibility, which has been a traditional anathema to the Diaspora, is a very disturbing feature.

The mystique of violence has deep roots in Israel, having been conceived as a rebellion against the Jewish situation in the Diaspora, but it is far from being a dominating element in Israeli society. It undergoes strong fluctuations according to the outward and inner resistances encountered by the society. It was very strong at the time of the struggle against the Mandatory Power, and gains momentum in times of border raids and wars against the Arabs. It was on the ebb during the period of affluence in an atmosphere of relative peace in the decade between the first and second Suez Campaigns. In the book quoted, Gheula Cohen notes the impression of her former comrades in the terrorist movement concerning the experience of living a relatively peaceful, prosperous and free life:

> 'I can't understand it, I simply can't,' I was recently told by a friend who had been involved in some business dealings with an ex-Lechite (freedom fighter), I had known in the old days. He used to be willing to sacrifice everything he had, even his own life. Nowadays he'd slit your throat for a penny.[1]

If peace were firmly established the mystique of violence would lose greatly in intensity and scope. In a situation in which Israel finds herself a beleaguered camp, it has, up to a point, a functional value as part of the fighting spirit needed in a battle of survival.

The dysfunctional value consists in the growth of crimes of violence. Murder, physical assault, and rape are practically unknown among Diaspora Jews, but their incidence is rising in Israel. In the period 1949–64, the annual absolute figures for murder ranged, in Israel, between 23 and 61, for attempted

[1] *Ibid.*, p. 71.

murder between 32 and 109, for manslaughter and causing death by carelessness between 35 and 191, for assault and bodily harm between 1,334 and 8,740, for robbery and attempted robbery between 67 and 201.[1] An enquiry was recently suggested, and is actually being carried out, to find out why murders among Israeli Jews are so much more frequent than among Diaspora Jews. The answer is of course obvious after what has been said.

A much more serious dysfunctional value of the mystique of violence is its distortion of the character of Judaism and Jewry. The mystique of violence becomes a danger to the cherished, deeper spiritual values of Judaism, not only in Israel. Of course one cannot have it both ways, and rebirth implies death. The question arises, how much of the Jew has to die to make room for the Israeli and what is the balance in terms of gain and loss of quality. No sociologist would dare to answer this question which brings us into the realm of values.

The problem for Israel is how to combine the two requirements, that of defence which fosters the cultivation of an ideology of militancy, with that of humanity, tolerance and the spirit of human solidarity, which are the heritage of Judaism. If peace were to come to Israel, this balance would be easy to attain. But in the situation in which Israel finds herself, she needs a very strong injection of spiritual values to counteract the mounting forces of militant nationalism and to keep the necessary balance.

The mystique of violence in Israel is a deep reflection of the tragedy of the human condition, in which the Jews are more deeply involved than any other people. Is not violence a built-in mechanism of human life, and can one escape from its effects in the conflict of opposing forces, whether individual, national, racial or social?

No-one has better expressed the dilemma and the tragedy involved in the situation of Israel than the late Moshe Sharett, former Prime Minister of Israel, in his soul searching mood after the Sinai Campaign, and in his speech (reproduced in a Hebrew quarterly)[2] in Beit Berl in November 1957:

> There is of course great value in Israel being a strong country with an international reputation as a small but powerful State, a tough

---

[1] *Statistical Abstract of Israel*, p. 625. 1965.
[2] *Ot* No. I. A Quarterly published by the Alignment in Israel.

nut to crack (I do not present this as my own opinion, but it is one which may exist). There is undoubtedly great value in Israel gaining glory as a land of heroes, but someone may well ask: Is it to your advantage or disadvantage for Israel to earn a reputation of a country of this sort? Is that an asset or not? It could be argued that it was of no importance; that it is preferable for Israel not to fence herself in behind the legacy of prophecy, the vision of justice, righteousness and truth. But if Israel upholds these virtues, she owes something to their observance, even if this means a sacrifice. If not, she is manoeuvering herself into a position from which there is no way out, morally or, in the long run, politically either.

2.

The Mystique of Redemption

THE MYSTIQUE of violence in Israel is the experience of the tragic, dark and tense side of the Israeli life in its fight for survival, but this is only one side—there is another side, brighter and more joyful, full of hope and faith. This is expressed in the mystique of redemption as derived directly from the possession of the Holy Land. Actually both the mystique of violence and the mystique of redemption are closely linked with the Land of Israel. The holy wars of ancient Israel, the holy wars of the Crusades, the recent holy wars for the possession of the Holy Land, are the forerunners of more holy and unholy wars to come.

The Holy Land has known in abundance both violence and the most sublime flowering of the life of the spirit; the Land has bred both the most appalling feats of cruelty and inhumanity and the most divine messages of peace and good will. And both aspects were closely linked with each other. The prophets of Israel foretold gloom and disaster and out of this gloom and disaster they presented a vast vista of hope and good tidings. In the darkness they reached out for the light and professed their message of faith. This ever crisis-ridden Land has given birth to immortal tides of faith, this most embattled land to ideas of peace; this most violent land to ideas of divine justice.

Was this a coincidence or was it the logic of history which moves by contraries? The three great religions were born of violence and grew on violence. The Old Testament describes the conquest of the promised land, and the fratricidal wars, feuds, battles and feats of cruelty and savagery preceding and following the conquest. The New Testament gives a message of resurrection following on the most violent and cruel death of the founder of the new religion. The Koran was also proclaimed by fire and sword. Fear and faith, anxiety and confidence, despair and hope, physical helplessness and spiritual strength are linked by their tail (to use the phrase of Socrates), and this can be nowhere seen more clearly than in Israel.

When one walks on the bare rocks of the Judean hills, or in the forbidding wilderness of the Negev, one often has in mind this enigmatic question: why was the Word sounded here, why did the waters of faith flow out of this land and no other? And one seems to find the answer. Out of the wilderness resounds the small voice, out of the barren rocks flow the water, out of suffering, Joy, out of anxiety, faith ('God is my shepherd, I shall not want', Ps. 23), out of fear, hope ('In my distress I cried out unto the Lord and He heard me', Ps. 115). The spiritual dialectic of helplessness and strength, of despair and hope is very well symbolized by the rocks of the Judean hills and the Negev Desert, awe-inspiring, powerful and fantastic. Every rock seems to have a meaning, a language of its own, as it stands out chiselled by sand, wind and storms, as if arguing, threatening or promising something.

There is little doubt but that the Land has a personality of its own which radiates far beyond its own confines. It exerts a magic spell which is often felt by those who come into contact with it, even fleetingly. One can feel a certain emotional intensity, a sort of magnetic attraction coming from the deep recesses of the Land. One feels strongly moved to do something for the Land, to immortalize oneself by taking part in the life of the Land. Of course the force which is emanating affects only those who have a sense for it, who develop a specific awareness. The Jews, by their belief in the sanctity of the Land, have acquired this sense, strengthening and developing it even further. This is the explanation of their unique achievements. The Land grows and develops with the men who took it over. The Land has become for them a spiritual experience. For Christianity and Islam there are only holy places in the Land, but for the Israelis the whole Land is a sanctum, a sanctum which has its meaning and all-pervading force, applying only to those who are attuned to it. They believe that the soul of the Land can be revealed only to them because it is identical with the soul of the People. The possession of the Land is a constant source of happiness, it generates a pronounced sense of spiritual joy and uplift. Therein lies the source of the vigour of the new nation. Arnold Toynbee, in his *Study of History*, called the Jews a fossil, but this fossil seems to have retained its original state with a strong hidden life in it. How deeply surprised must Arnold Toynbee be that he misjudged the dynamism, the life-giving and life-emanating qualities of this 'fossil'. The re-awakening of this fossil must be partly due to its being restored to its native soil.

The great religious thinker of the last generation, Rav Kook, spoke about the spiritual rebellion which he expected to arise from the contact of the Jewish people with the Land: 'It has come down to us that there will be a spiritual rebellion in the Land of Israel and in Israel in the period in which the beginning of National re-birth takes place'.[1]

Martin Buber speaks about three levels on which the contact with the Land expresses itself: the levels of existence, creativity and redemption (holiness). The secular and the sacred are fused into one. The Land is a safeguard against sterile conventionality and mediocracy, it infuses both creativity and a feeling of sacred-ness. It is the means of liberating the spirit of Judaism, and of fulfilling its dream of greatness, which is the real meaning of the process of redemption.

> The significance of the regaining of the Land of Israel by the people of Israel is to be understood on three levels, each of which, however, only reveals its full meaning in connection with the other two. On the first level it is acknowledged that the people can only in the land achieve its existence again; on the second, that it is only there that it will rediscover its own work, the free creative function of its spirit; on the third, that it needs the Land in order to regain its holiness.[2]

The mystique of redemption often implies a suggestion of a new revelation coming through contact with the Land. A. D. Gordon, the poet of the dignity of labour in the new Land, speaks about a voice coming from the deep roots of the Jewish tribes in the Land: 'It is not we, it is our Land that speaks to the people. We have much to express and intimate to words spoken by the Land. . . .'[3]

A new revelation is also implied in the prophetic vision that

[1] Quoted by Martin Buber, *Israel and Palestine. The History of an Idea*, p. 151. East and West Library. London 1952.

[2] *Ibid.*, p. 147.

[3] Quoted by Buber. *Ibid.*, p. 161.

'out of Zion will come forth the word'. Chaim Weizmann writes, 'The prophetic vision that out of Zion comes forth the word of the Lord is not a legacy of the past but is the commandment of the present and the hope of the future'.[1]

Similarly Ben Gurion said, 'the vision encompasses the fulfilment of the aspiration of our prophets and teachers for the restoration of Jewish national life on its own soil and for the establishment there of a model society which will become "A light unto the nations" '. [2]

The mystique of redemption is closely intertwined with the deeply ingrained and widely shared belief in miracles, which is nourished from many other sources. Is not the return of the Tribes a miracle? Is not Israel's survival against the greatest odds a miracle in itself? Miracles form a specific revelation, they speak their own language telling us about providential design, they are interpreted as part of the mystique of redemption. The recent war like the previous wars has considerably strengthened the Israelis' belief in miracles. Who has heard of a Six Day War fought simultaneously against three countries? Was the victory due entirely to the qualities of the Israeli clerks and shopkeepers turned soldiers? The Arabs believed that the Anglo-American Powers took part in the war against them because they could not imagine that the Israelis could have achieved all that by themselves in so short a time. Not a few Israelis also believed that they were not alone in the battle for survival, that there was an intervention. Maybe believing in miracles produces miracles.

The strange transformation, which the Jewish people are undergoing in their Land, is inexplicable to the Israelis themselves. They feel that they are caught in a whirlwind, that they are immersed in a process far transcending their own judgement. Therefore they are very eager to hear what other people think about this process, unique in itself. First of all, they would like to know what theories can be offered for this strange transformation of Jewish society which is going on in the ancient Land. Is there any coherent theory offered which stretches far into the Jewish past and reaches out into the distant future? Has the

---

[1] Quoted by Maurice Samuel in 'The Road from Motol'. *Chaim Weizmann. A Biography by Several Hands.* Dial Press. New York 1944.

[2] *Ben Gurion Looks Back in Talks With Moshe Perlman,* p. 230. Weidenfeld and Nicolson. London 1965.

restoration something to do with the Divine Prophecy, and will the Prophecy come true all along the line? Is the ingathering of the exiles an end in itself, or is it a starting point of a much larger and more fundamental process of renewal in which not only the Jews are involved? Has the resurrection of Israel something to do not only with the Holocaust in Europe but with the threat of a Holocaust for the entire human race? Most Israelis are convinced that, if by any chance a second Holocaust should afflict Israel, this would be the forerunner of a third and total Holocaust involving the whole human race.

In the mystique of redemption large fragments of the mystique of violence are embedded. The mystique itself has a spectrum of violence and self-assertion. Somehow the quest for redemption and the quest for national independence have been intertwined, and as we know the latter has been strewn with victims of the fierce, protracted and never-ending struggle. The mystique of redemption was not a hindrance to the Jewish fighting spirit. On the contrary, the courage and bravery of the Jewish fighters were inspired and enhanced by this myth. One could say that Israeli soldiers carry in their knapsack not the proverbial Field-marshal's baton but rather the staff of the prophet. How they danced and wept from their hearts around the Wailing Wall in ecstasy and rapture in a way not unlike ancient prophets of Israel and the dancing of King David. No other army ever danced and wept around a Wailing Wall in a blissful transport, expressing the release of the same old powder box of violence and ecstasy. One could easily harness this enthusiasm for works of greater import both for the Region and the world at large.

The mystique of redemption may be open to a narrow nationalistic interpretation with a very great proportion of arrogance and violence, or else to a universalistic interpretation with a great proportion of humanity and a sense of human brotherhood. Which interpretation will win in Israel? On this answer will depend the fate of Israeli society and its future course.

Memories of a stormy past mingled with a heartache of nostalgia for homes left behind, strong fear of an uncertain and threatening future mixed with hopes for the millenium, warlike urges combined with the deepest and strongest longings for peace, the mystique of force and the mystique of love, produce a unique atmosphere heavily laden with great, unrelieved tension which can break out in great works or in great upheavals. Jewish history is marked by discontinuity, cataclysms, upheavals, leaps forwards and backwards. Israel today, a great symbol of the leap forwards, is still marked by the same characteristics.

3.

The Figure of Jesus on the Israeli Horizon

THE FIGURE of Jesus, the Jew from Nazareth, looms large on the Israeli horizon, although not much is said about him openly and most Jews cautiously refrain from mentioning his name in public. Still he is very much in the mind of the Israeli Jews, more now than ever, and the awareness of his shadow in Israel is constantly growing.

In the Galilee, the most beautiful and inspiring part of Israel, he is the dominating figure. Every site of antiquity and every beauty spot in Galilee bears his footprints. He is still 'walking by the sea of Galilee' (Matthew IV, 18), 'on the Sabbath day he enters into the synagogue in Capernaum' (Kfar Nahum) (Mark I, 21), in Tabgha close to Capernaum he performs the miracle of the loaves and fishes (Luke XI, 17). On the Mount of Beatitudes which overlooks the waters of the Lake, he utters his immortal Sermon on the Mount. Of course, Nazareth is the centre of his life, and Jerusalem the scene of his last ministry. Much of the charm and magnetism of the holy land is due, not only to echoes of the Bible, but also to the echoes of Jesus' life.

Being confronted with Jesus in this way is a new experience to the Jew. In the Diaspora Jesus looked alien to the Jew, an outsider, an interloper. But in Israel he is seen as the Jew from Nazareth, a native of this country, a Sabra, with claims to the land as strong as any. He cannot be brushed aside as a foreign influence.

How to deal with him? Of course he is a valuable asset to his country. He is a big 'dollar earner', as a first-class tourist attraction. The tourist posters of the Israeli government, of El Al[1] and of all Israeli shipping lines proclaim, 'Come to the Holy Land, see

[1] The El Al advertisements in the British Press read: 'Come to Israel to see the Room of the Last Supper, Via Dolorosa, Bethlehem and Nazareth, where Jesus spent his boyhood and his youth, the Kfar Cana of the Gospels where Jesus performed his first miracles', etc.

all the Holy Places', meaning not only those holy for Jews but also for Christians. The tourist guides are full of descriptions of sites venerated by Christians.

When the Jews left their land two thousand years ago, the land was holy for them alone; when they returned, the land was holy also to more than half of the world. The land had become sanctified in the meantime to millions and millions of non-Jews. The same applies to the Bible which had been a book holy to the Jews alone and which has become a holy book for millions of non-Jews. Both the Book and the Land have become sanctified to the world and this was not the work of the Diaspora Jews who, in spite of the injunction, did not become 'a light to the Gentiles', but was the work rather of a single Jew and his band of Jewish followers, all of them Sabras. They were all born and bred in the Land, which is in this sense the most fruitful land on earth.

Shall the Israelis disclaim and brush aside this work with an allegation that it was all heresy, an allegation which sounds hollow to a secular Jew in the twentieth century (and most European Jews in Israel are secular Jews), or shall they claim back their natural inheritance, the fruit of the Land to which they have returned?

The Israelis cannot forget that in a way Jesus was also instrumental in their return to the Holy Land. Have they reconquered the Land all by themselves? Were they not helped by the British at first, then by the Americans and the United Nations? Were they not assisted by all the Christian Zionists, including Churchill, Roosevelt, Truman? Was not the vision of the Holy Land, restored to the People of the Holy Book, instrumental in obtaining this help? The wish to fulfil the Divine Promise and the Holy Prophecy for an ingathering of the scattered Tribes, and for the resurrection of the Dry Bones of Israel, was consciously and even more sub-consciously a driving power towards the assistance which has been forthcoming from the Christian countries under many forms, such as political support in the United Nations, armaments and finance. Suffice to say that, without Jesus, the Holy Book would have remained for the non-Jew an obscure Book, and the Holy Land an exotic small country with no greater significance than Tripoli or Sudan. Actually the Jewish re-conquest of the Holy Land may be considered as an heir to the Crusades, strange as this may sound. One could class the re-conquest of the Holy Land by the Jews as the last and the most successful Crusade, undertaken this time by the Jews but not without considerable help, especially initial help, from the Christian powers, without which the Crusade could not have started and gained its initial impetus.

When the Jews returned to Israel, they had to re-define their historical identity, which is now centred and pivoted on the Land of Israel, and they had to make a long journey backwards in time, in fact two thousand years back. The Third Commonwealth, the present-day Israel, had to be linked with the end of the Second Commonwealth. And that was the time of Jesus' ministry. The exile from the Land coincided in time with the spread of Jesus' message. And when the Israeli Jew starts to ponder over the annals of the end of the Second Commonwealth, he has first of all to ask the fateful question: Were his forefathers right in rejecting Jesus? Why is it that more than half of the world have accepted Jesus as God (Christians), or as a Prophet (Moslems), or as The Ideal Man (Humanists), while the Jews of his own kith and kin have rejected him? And his answer must be that after all and in spite of everything, from the point of view of the preservation of a distinct body of Jewry, the ancestors were right in rejecting Jesus, when they lost their Land and began their pilgrimage. They had really no alternative but to reject this universalistic interpretation of the Jewish Faith if they wanted to preserve a distinct body of Jewish people, once they had lost their Land, their State and their language. If the Jews had accepted Jesus, the Jews would have been dissolved in the sea of Christianity and that would have been the end of their road. Diaspora Jewry was forced to close its ranks, erecting the Ritual Law which enclosed the Jewish community of the Ghetto. Any universalistic interpretation of the Judaic creed was out of the question if the Jews wanted to survive as Jews.

But how is it now? Do the Jews who have returned to their Land need the props of the Ritual Law to retain their identity, now that they have their own Land, State, language and culture? What is the reason now for rejecting Jesus who was the fulfilment of Jewish dreams for greatness and importance in the world, the fulfilment of their dreams to be a light unto the nations? Can Jesus the Jew be taken back to the fold where he belongs, can he be incorporated in the body of Judaism, as a genuine Israeli product?

Of course one does not refer here to the doctrines of Christianity which grew on and from Jesus' teaching, which in essence are and must remain foreign to the Jew, here one refers only to the teaching of and personality of Jesus the Jew, as presented by his Jewish disciples in the Synoptic Gospels. They show Jesus as a Prophet in Israel, a major product, an heir of Isaiah and Jeremiah.

Was he then a prophet in Israel? Secular Jews are often inclined to answer this question in the affirmative, and religious Jews answer of course in the negative. The main argument against Jesus' status as a prophet in Israel is based on the contention that he, in his message, lacked a national and political awareness or a concern about the fate of Israel. This view is for instance expressed by Joseph Klausner, the author of *Jesus of Nazareth*, who writes that 'he lacks the prophet's political perception and the prophet's spirit of national consolation in the political-national sense'.[1] Such a view seems to be devoid of both meaning and substance. Firstly, because the prophet's spiritual and religious perception was always superior to his national and political perception, and secondly, because Jesus' message was highly relevant to the political and national issues of his time. His injunction 'Love thine enemy' was not only the greatest and noblest of personal messages but also had highly significant nationalpolitical implications. It had a great functional value in the time directly preceding the destruction of the Second Temple, and might have saved Jerusalem and the Temple from total destruction, had the Jews followed the precepts and attempted to 'love' the Romans, or at least to be friendly with them and understand their point of view, understand the great values of the GreekRoman civilization without imitating or following them. After all Rome and Athens were great centres of civilization and culture. Jesus sensed the coming disaster, the greatest disaster in the history of the Second Commonwealth, which sealed its fate. Hence his messages: 'Resist no evil' and 'Render unto Caesar what is Caesar's', which if followed could have saved Israel from the impending disaster.

Martin Buber has interpreted the message of Jesus: 'Resist no

[1] *Jesus of Nazareth*, p. 144. Jerusalem 1922.

evil' in a not dissimilar way, linking it directly with the age-long teaching of Judaism, writing *inter alia*:

> The other message of Jesus: 'Resist no evil' means: resist the evil by doing good, do not attack directly The Realm of Evil, but join forces to attain the Kingdom of Goodness—then the time will come, when the Evil will not be able to harm you, not because you have overcome it, but because you have redeemed it. Jesus wanted to build out of Jewry a Temple of True Community, which could bring down by its mere appearance the walls of the state governed by force. However, the future generations have not understood him in this way.[1]

The controversy about Jesus as a prophet in Israel has had new light thrown upon it unexpectedly by the discovery of the Dead Sea Scrolls. The coincidence of this discovery with the emergence of the New State of Israel is a fact remarkable in itself, as if the Scrolls had been waiting for two thousand years to be brought to light just at this very moment. The first Dead Sea Scrolls were found in the caves of Qumran in the spring of 1947, and were first deciphered in 1948-9, when the Jews were fighting for the New State. Afterwards, further explorations of the caves were made and hundreds of additional fragments of ancient manuscripts were found. Also the ruins of an ancient Jewish retreat inhabited by the Jewish sect of Essenes in the Qumran neighbourhood were unearthed, and they have thrown additional light on the life and teaching of the sect. These discoveries and explorations threw a startling new light on the background of Jesus the Jew. They prove once more that the ethics and ideas of Jesus were a product of an organic growth spread at least over two centuries in the midst of Judaism. It was not a product of the one man Jesus, or of Jesus and John the Baptist, or of Jesus and a handful of his Jewish disciples, but it was the creation of several generations of holy men who had given up all their possessions, had lived without women and money, had preached the word of God and worked for salvation under the Teacher of Righteousness. It proves that the teaching of Jesus was a further elaboration of the doctrine of the Essenes who, although they disagreed with the priests in Jerusalem, were a completely Jewish sect, probably

[1] Martin Buber. *Der Heilige Weg. Ein Wort an dir Juden and an die Volker*, p. 44. Frankfurt 1920.

numbering tens of thousands of men. Their Manual of Discipline reveals to us a monastic community, in a way a forerunner of the modern Kibbutzim. Many of the passages of the Manual are written in the spirit and style of the Gospels. Many Gospel rites, including baptism or the holy feasts, were already practised by the Essenes. The Messianic idea, first presented by Deutero-Isaiah, of the voluntary martyrdom of the Annointed, is applied to the Teacher of Righteousness in the ideas of the Essenes, and it looks quite probable that Jesus, an Essene or a disciple of the Essenes, conceived his life and his ministry as that of the Teacher of Righteousness and shaped it accordingly. It is probable that he consciously or sub-consciously willed his martyrdom in fulfil-ment of the prophecy, and in fulfilment of his basic role as the Teacher of Righteousness as conceived by the Sect. As the Manual of Discipline proclaims, the Teacher of Righteousness 'meant to give his life as a ransom for many' in fulfilment of the Old Testament prophecy.

Millar Burrows, Professor of Biblical Theology at Yale University writes, 'Dupont-Sommer, after reading the Habakkuk Commentary, declared that Jesus now seemed "an astonishing reincarnation of the teacher of righteousness". Like Jesus, he said, the teacher of righteousness was believed by his disciples to be God's Elect, the Messiah, the redeemer of the world. Both the teacher of righteousness and Jesus were opposed by the priestly party, the Sadducees; both were condemned and put to death; both proclaimed judgement on Jerusalem; both established com-munities whose members expected them to return and judge the world.'[1]

Professor Burrows himself passes the following considered judgement:

> The doctrines and practices of the covenanters substantially enrich our knowledge of Judaism at the time just before and during the origin and early growth of Christianity. It is now abundantly clear that we cannot understand the Judaism of the Roman period simply in terms of the Pharisees and Sadducees. The tree whose trunk was the Old Testament had then many branches which later were lopped off or withered away.[2]

It is accepted that the Qumran community was not an isolated

[1] *The Dead Sea Scrolls*, p. 330. The Viking Press. New York 1955.
[2] *Ibid.*, p. 345.

outpost of Jewish non-conformity in Roman times. Matthew Black[1] of St Mary's College, St Andrew's University, expresses his conviction that:

> the movement may have been as great and as influential as that of the Pharisees themselves. It was a peripheral sect only in this sense that it was pursuing an unworldly life, but not in the extent of its influence on the religion of the period. . . . There is a credible patristic evidence for the existence in pre-70 Palestine of a widespread movement of Jewish or para-Jewish 'non-conformity', characterized by its ascetic or puritanical tendencies and manner of life, and by its baptizing cult, holding a different canon of Scripture and different customs from the orthodoxy (or orthopraxis) of the Pharisees. The Qumran Essenes were one branch of this movement.

The Scrolls are a disturbing document not only to Christians but also to Jews. Writing about the Scrolls, Edmund Wilson notes:

> I was already beginning to realize the explosive possibilities of the subject. . . . It had already been made very clear to me at the Hebrew University that the sect had 'grown up inside Judaism, but had nothing to do with Judaism', and I had seemed to note also, on the Christian side, a certain reluctance to recognize that the characteristic doctrines of Christianity must have been developed gradually and naturally, in the course of a couple of hundred years, out of a dissident branch of Judaism.[2]

Disturbing as they may be, the new Scrolls are living documents to be studied by the Israelis in their search for spiritual renewal. They show Jesus in a new light as the heir to the spirit of the Jewish prophecy. They show Jesus as a genuine product of the Land, a native growth of the Second Commonwealth. If Israel is the heir to the Second Commonwealth, is she not heir also to the most significant spiritual message of that Commonwealth? Rabbinical Judaism was the Judaism of the Diaspora. What is the Judaism of the Third Commonwealth to be? Should it not incorporate the most important message of the preceding Commonwealth?

The mystery of this simple Jew from Nazareth, who managed

[1] *The Scroll and Christian Origins*, pp. 165–6. Thomas Nelson. New York 1961.
[2] *The Scrolls From the Dead Sea*, pp. 106–7. W. H. Allen. London 1955.

to conquer almost the whole world and whose spiritual power was stronger than that of the whole of Jewry is simply puzzling the Israeli Jew. Who was he? Where lies the secret and mystery of his power? How did this Jew manage to attract the immense love and adoration of the world, while the Jews attracted only hatred and contempt? How did he manage to fulfil the task set in the Bible for the Jews to serve as 'a light unto nations', while Jewry failed? Why was it that only he managed to shape and mould the world, while the Jews played a losing game, rolling in the dust? Why has the genius of Jesus never been repeated within the Jewish gates? And will it ever be repeated?

A hope is often expressed in many quarters, both Jewish and non-Jewish, that the Third Commonwealth will bring forth a new felicitious and forceful message, a good tiding similar to the message brought forth by the Second Commonwealth. Louis Finkelstein, chancellor of the Jewish theological seminary in the United States, speaking about Israel as a spiritual force, expressed this hope in the following way: 'It may seem arrogant to suggest that the State of Israel, recognizing the severe limitations of the temporal world, and associating itself with Jewry in other lands, may yet beget such an idea, a concept so forceful that it may itself redeem mankind; yet the world's need for such an idea can scarcely be questioned.'[1] He seems to have forgotten that the most forceful and significant idea begotten by the Second Commonwealth still remains rejected up to the present and is left outside the gates of the Third Commonwealth. How can the Third Commonwealth beget 'a new forceful and significant idea', if the forceful and significant idea of the Second Commonwealth is expelled from its precincts?

A similar hope was expressed by the greatest Israeli poet, Chaim Nachman Bialik:

Not in vain has the hand of God led this people through the straits of Hell, only to restore it to its home for the third time. The book of Chronicles, last in the Canon, is not the final record of Israel's career. To its two sections shall be added a third. If the beginning of Chronicles is 'Adam, Seth, Enosh', and its end the Cyrus Proclamation which after six hundred years resulted in tidings of salvation for the ancient pagans, so shall the beginning of its third

[1] Moshe Davis, *Israel: Its Role in Civilization*, p. 14. Harper Bros. New York 1956.

division be the Balfour Declaration and its end—the new tidings of salvation for humanity.[1] . . . Israel gathers in its land for the third time. Why cannot the miracle occur again?[2]

Other Israeli poets, novelists and writers have speculated also on the same theme of Jesus and new tidings, such as the novelist A. A. Kabak and the poet Avigdor Ha'Meiri. The great Israeli writer Y. C. H. Brenner said,

> The same importance which I recognize in the Bible in remnants of memories from distant days and in the development of the spirit of our people and the humanistic spirit within us over many generations and ages—such importance I also feel in the books of the New Testament. . . . The New Testament is also our book, bone of our bone and flesh of our flesh.[3]

The American Rabbi, David Polish, writes about Israel interest in Jesus:[4]

> Ever since the new Yishuv began, a special interest in Jesus has been manifested. This does not indicate, as some theologians have wishfully stated, a turning toward Christianity. It does, however, show that in the free atmosphere of Israel, a new approach towards Jesus, removed from the realm of polemics or vituperation common to medieval Judaism, is taking place. It is to be expected that in the land where Jesus lived and from which the Christian message went forth, a deep interest should be stirred among Jews.

And Rabbi Polish expresses again the same hope and expectation as that quoted earlier,

> The view of the State as an instrument of higher purpose is very old in Judaism, but it can be given a special and an urgently needed application now. The reconstruction of the Jewish Commonwealth was only a road towards a messianic goal. It was to be the source from which the universal concepts of peace and world unity were to emanate. Unless Israel addresses itself to this task, even now, amidst its travail and its jeopardy, it will fail in its chief justification.[5]

---

[1] Bialik, *Devarim Sheb'al Peh*, p. 55, Vol. I. Tel Aviv 1935.

[2] *Op. cit.*, p. 54.

[3] Brenner, *Kol Kitve, Ha-Poel Ha-Mizrachi*, pp. 103–4, Vol. VI. Dvir. Tel Aviv 1927.

[4] David Polish, *The Internal Dissent. A Search for Meaning in Jewish History*, p. 207. Abelard-Schuman. New York.

[5] *Op. cit.*, p. 210.

We can find a very strong contrast to those millenial hopes and expectations in the present moral and religious atmosphere of Israel, which can be best described as one of alienation from its deeper self. I believe it was Hegel who first coined this term: The alienation of society from its deeper self. This term has nowhere fuller application than in Israel. It is a new society but with very old values which are rapidly being totally discarded, while equivalent new values are not forthcoming, hence the general feeling of a spiritual vacuum. The tragedy of Israel is that the old religion, practised only by the orthodox, is ritualistic, petrified and ossified, and deprived of its vivifying, life-enhancing and tender forces, while the rest of society, the majority, is atheistic, agnostic or religiously indifferent, disinterested or unconcerned. So religion in Israel is hardly alive in any direction. This situation was tolerable so long as socialism and social humanism were the living creeds of the élite. The pioneers in Israel were either socialists or Humanists, who believed in man and his progress, and substituted Man for the Godhead. This creed no longer holds the allegiance of the élite, let alone the masses of Israel. Consequently we are witnessing a very general aridity of the spirit. Generally speaking ideals are at present out of fashion everywhere, not only in Israel, and Israel is not unique in this situation. But it is worse for these reasons:

Firstly, the Jews are a spiritual nation with spiritual needs and aspirations. The Jew needs a creed for his very existence as much as anyone else needs air and water; secondly, Israel is a new society which has to be built on new foundations, and these must have roots in spiritual values of a more permanent nature. Thirdly, Israel is ingathering her Tribes which need a common creed as a cementing factor.

Emile Durkheim, himself a son of a French Rabbi, in a lecture to the International Congress of philosophy at Bologna in 1911, speaking about value judgements and judgements of reality, referred to spells of collective enthusiasm and creative synthesis which take place at crucial moments of historical development. 'At such moments this higher form of life is lived with such intensity and exclusiveness that it monopolizes all minds to the more or less complete exclusion of egoism and the commonplace.'[1] Such a creative synthesis, and such higher forms of life

[1] Durkheim's *Sociology and Philosophy*, p. 93. Cohen and West. London 1953.

have not occurred in Israel up to now. The creation of the State of Israel, a unique historical moment, has not been accompanied by a supreme and unique creative intensity of social and spiritual life, out of which great symbols or great ideals could emerge to provide a frame for social integration, identification and aspiration, for the society as a whole. The supreme creative synthesis which should have accompanied the supreme event in Jewish history, really the two supreme events, the Holocaust on one hand and the creation of the Jewish State on the other, has up to now failed to materialize. The culminating point in the development of the Jewish identity has not been accompanied by the creation of a culminating creed or renewal of creed or the emergence of an ideal-synthesis of Jewish existence. There is no 'purified reflection of the unique historical moment' to use Durkheim's phrase, there is no all embracing dynamic ideal to act as a catalyst of emotion, as a focus of national communal interest, as a spur for a dynamic drive towards the fulfilment of the age-long aspirations of Jewry.

The Jewish religion seems to be at present to the large mass of Israeli Jews uninspiring and uninspired. Could it be that Jesus could give it a new lease of life? Could a new, Israeli stage of Jewish religion, escape from the Ghetto wall made up of 613 bricks, and instead incorporate the personality and message of Jesus, the Jew from Nazareth, as a major prophet for Israel, of course excluding all Christianized stylization of Jesus as Christ? These are perhaps the most exciting, the most portentious questions, most pregnant with potentialities, affecting not only the people of Israel, but also those of the world at large. The Tribes of Israel parted with what the world regards as the best and the finest they have produced so far when they left the Ancient Land, no doubt for good reasons, if one looks back from the vantage point of history. But now, coming back to their Land, will they be able to claim back also their spiritual inheritance which was nurtured in their Land, the child of their spirit and body? Accepting this inheritance and nourishing it in their own spirit, reinterpreting it in the spirit of Judaism, might make all the difference in the fight for survival by the Israeli Jews, in their development as a nation, and as a spiritual force in the world, as well as in the peaceful settlement of their conflict with the Arab nations.

Part IV

encounters and dialogues

1.

The Arab-Israeli Conflict

THE ORIGINS of the Arab-Jewish encounter lie deep in history. The ancient Israelites were probably part of the inhabitants of Arabia. Both terms, Hebrew and Arab, seem to stem from roots denoting in both languages, Nomads. Both were peoples of the desert, and the desert is still in their blood. Both languages are close to each other, having many common roots, as for instance the name of the Godhead, El, Elohim and Allah, or the common greeting, *shalom* and *salam*. They both belonged to what is called the Semitic race, claiming their common descent from Shem, the son of Noah. They have both been great traders, carriers of great civilizations and founders of great cultures. Both have had periods of pristine theocracy. Both have had the same problems in keeping frontiers around their people in ethnic and religious terms.

Their religions are very close, Islam being the upshot of Judaism with an admixture of Christian lore. Muhammad waited for the Jews to join him, and regarded his revelations as a restoration of the original faith of Abraham. Abraham, Moses and the prophets are regarded as Divine Messengers in Islam, the Old Testament is venerated as a Holy Book, and there are holy places common to both. The Mosque resembles closely the synagogue. Fasting and pilgrimage,[1] dietary laws (the eating of pork is prohibited in both religions), and circumcision play an important role in both religions. The representation of animals and human figures in art is banned in both religions, hence the abstract design of Muslim art.

They are both more productive towards other civilizations than on their own home ground; they are synthesizers, binders and joiners of cultural values. The Arabs created a marvellous civilization in Spain, which they occupied for 800 years (and in which Jews played a prominent and distinguished part, as previously in

[1] Alfred Guillaume, *Islam*, pp. 68–70. Pelican Books. London 1954.

the Caliphate of Baghdad), far exceeding the civilization in their own country. The same could be said about the Jews.

They have many common characteristics. They are both difficult people to lead. As far back as the fourteenth century, the great Arab historian and philosopher Ibn Khaldun, whose work was described by Arnold Toynbee as 'undoubtedly the greatest work of its kind that has ever been created by any mind in any time or place', wrote about the Arabs,

> Every Arab regards himself as worthy to rule, and it is rare to find one of them submitting willingly to another, be it his father or his brother or the head of his clan, but only grudgingly.[1]

The same can be said of the Jews.

Lawrence of Arabia wrote about the Semitic-Arabic races,

> They were a people of spasms, of upheavals, of ideas, the race of the individual genius. . . . Arabs could be swung on an idea as on a cord; for the unpledged allegiance of their minds made them obedient servants. . . . They were incorrigibly children of the idea, feckless and colour blind. . . . They were a people of starts, for whom the abstract was the strongest motive. . . .[2]

The same can be said about Jews who are people of the idea and the abstract.

Mr E. C. Hodgkin writes about the Arabs, 'It was to the family that an Arab's first loyalty was due. . . . For most Arabs the State remains an impersonal and faintly hostile concept. . . .' In another context the same author refers to the 'Islamic suspicion of the outside world', and, speaking about radio propaganda, writes, 'Their love of language made them willing to appreciate speeches and commentaries of vast length'.[3] The same is more or less true of the Jews.

Apart from the early wars with the Arabic Jews in the times of the Prophet Muhammad, Jews and Arabs have lived peacefully side by side for long stretches of time. The Arab rulers were on the whole tolerant towards the Jews, anyway more tolerant than

---

[1] Quoted in Edward Atiyah, *The Arabs*, p. 46. Pelican Books. London 1953.

[2] T. E. Lawrence, *Seven Pillars of Wisdom*, pp. 37 and 41. Jonathan Cape. London 1926.

[3] E. C. Hodgkin, *The Arabs*, pp. 21, 115 and 83. Oxford University Press. 1966.

the Christian rulers in the middle ages. The Crusaders killed in Jerusalem and in Safad every Jew they could lay hands on, and the Arabs often took revenge on them for those acts. Jews persecuted in Europe often found refuge under Moslem rulers. Arabic was the vehicle of Jewish thought in the Middle Ages. The greatest sages of this period, such as the second Moses, Maimonides, Saadia, or Al-Harizi, and the greatest poets, Jehuda Halevi, and Ibn Gabirol, and the philosophers, Bahya, Nathaniel Ibn Al-Fayumi, author of the *Garden of Wisdom*, or Tibbonides, wrote in Arabic.

It was a tragic coincidence that after the long lethargy of both peoples, their modern nationalisms started at the same time. Both Jewish and Arab nationalism started at the end of the last century and grew rapidly during the First World War and immediately afterwards. The Balfour Declaration, which greatly strengthened the cause of Jewish nationalism, was issued at the same time as Lawrence of Arabia was leading the insurgent Arabs, and greatly contributing to the strengthening of Arab nationalism. The British contributed greatly to both nationalisms, making promises to both. Lawrence of Arabia was the channel through which flowed British subsidies to Arab insurgents, and he kept in close touch with King Hussein's son, Feisal, who led the Arab Revolt in the field, as an ally of the British forces. On 3 January 1918, Feisal signed an agreement with Weizmann, endorsing the Balfour Declaration, parts of which reads as follows:

Article I. The Arab State and Palestine in all their relations and undertakings will be controlled with the most cordial goodwill and understanding and to this end Arab and Jewish duly accredited agents shall be established in their respective territories.

Article III. In the establishment of the constitution of Palestine all such measures shall be adopted as will offer the fullest guarantee for carrying into effect the British Government's Declaration of 2nd November, 1917.

Article IV. All necessary measures shall be taken to encourage and stimulate immigration of Jews into Palestine on a large scale and as quickly as possible to settle the Jewish immigrants on the land through close settlement and intensive cultivation of the soil. In taking such measures the Arab peasants and tenant farmers shall be protected in their rights and shall be assisted in forwarding their economic development.[1]

Two days before signing this agreement Feisal wrote in his Memorandum to the Peace Conference *inter alia*:

In Palestine the enormous majority of the people are Arabs. The Jews are very close to the Arabs in blood, and there is no conflict of character between the two races. In principle we are absolutely at one. Nevertheless the Arabs cannot risk their responsibility of holding level the scales in the clash of races and religions that have, in this one province, so often involved the world in difficulties. They would wish for the effective super imposition of a great Trustee, so long as a representative administration commended itself by actively promoting the material prosperity of the country.[2]

Those hopeful prognostications, and the agreement itself, were soon abandoned and forgotten. The Arab *Effendim* were ready to sell their land to the Jews at inflated prices, but the Arab multitude was hostile. Already before the First World War, Arab-Jewish clashes were a common occurrence but they were usually of the nature of frontier feuds forming individual and tribal acts of violence. They had also an economic background in the elimination of the Arab labourers from Jewish estates, enforced by the pioneers in what was called the 'Conquest of Work' (*Kibbush Avoda*). A new phase was reached in 1920, a phase of a growing and deepening, bitter struggle, when the Third Arab Conference was convened, which appointed an Executive Committee to represent the Arabs of Palestine and demanded the establishment then of an exclusively Arab Government. Soon afterwards, in 1921, the Arabs struck and rioted, and then on a bigger scale in 1929 with the Wailing Wall outbreak. A large-scale Arab rebellion broke out in 1936, and the struggle was extended far beyond the frontiers of Palestine, when committees for the defence of Palestine were formed in Baghdad, Amman, Beyrut and Damascus, and volunteers from neighbouring Arab countries joined the guerillas. The War of Independence did not

[1] George Antonius, *The Arab Awakening*, pp. 43-9. Appendix F. Hamish Hamilton. London 1938.
[2] J. C. Hurewitz, *Diplomacy in the Near and Middle East*, Volume II, pp. 38-9. Princeton 1956.

mark the end of the Arab-Israeli warfare. The Armistice agreements were conceived by the Arabs as a cessation of hostilities only, and the War of Independence as a first round only.

After the War of Independence there was a short period when the Arabs were inclined to come to terms with Israel, but at that time Israel did not take up the challenge seriously enough. Soon afterwards the Arab position hardened and, since Nasser's coup in 1952, it has become more and more directed towards the total elimination of Israel. With guerilla raids and Israeli retaliation in border reprisals, Arab hatred had been mounting progressively, reaching an almost pathological intensity and compulsion.

The Sinai campaign of 1956, undertaken on British-French initiative, further fanned Arab hatred, providing them with an argument for their thesis that Israel is a tool of Western Imperialism. The necessity and wisdom of Israel in breaking the armistice in the Sinai Campaign is open to debate. In all other campaigns Israel was basically on the defensive, or struck only as a response to aggression. The Sinai campaign has not improved the position of Israel in her ultimate quest for a peace settlement. It brought her considerable gains, mainly by opening the Straits of Tiran to Israeli shipping, and by the liquidation of the terrorist Fadayan units which operated from the Gaza Strip. However, the campaign brought in its wake a great emergency and its aftermath in the Six Day War, when the gains of the Suez Campaign were contested by the withdrawal of the United Nations forces from Gaza and Sharm el Sheikh, accompanied by Nasser's avowed and publicly stated intention to 'destroy Israel'.

All this is almost forty years of war since the first Arab uprisings, and it still drags on relentlessly through its various phases of uprisings, wars, raids and reprisals. Both sides seem to be resigned to the necessity of war, continuing indefinitely.

The constant and unprecedented triumph of Jewish arms is in itself a major theme for sociological investigation. It is agreed that the major source of Jewish preponderance has been Jewish superiority in terms of intelligence, organization, planning and technique but not in terms of quantity or quality of equipment. The main factor has been the superiority of a technical and scientific civilization as represented by the Jews to the less advanced civilization of the Arab countries. But the Israeli cause has been superior also in terms of the morale of their combatants. While the Arabs are fighting for their rights, rights of ownership and possession, the Jews fight for sheer survival. This has given them their dogged determination, singleness of purpose and tenacity. The genius of history often favours superior causes of this kind.

Strangely enough the Israeli is a much tougher fighter than the Arab. Israeli youth have acquired some of the fighting spirit of their great ancestors, while the Arabs, who have been a subject race for the last few centuries, have not yet recovered the fighting spirit of their forefathers.

The unbroken chain of their disastrous defeats in their wars against Israel, have produced in them a complex of national shame and humiliation, a blot on the good name of heroic Arab exploits from the past. This complex demands compensation in the continuation of the struggle; it is perhaps the greatest single hindrance to Israel-Arab reconciliation. It produces two side effects: the fear of Israeli aggrandisement on the one hand, and a vision of glorious revenge on the other. It would need a great and courageous Arab leader to break this complex by facing the realities of the situation.

This complex has been aggravated by several factors. First, by the problem of the Arab refugees, whose place in Israel has been taken over by Jewish refugees not only from Europe but also from the Arab countries themselves, in more or less equal numbers. Secondly, it has been aggravated by the arrested economic and social development of the Arab States, which has been shown up drastically by the Jewish development of Israel. Thirdly, it has been aggravated by Arab disunity, in which the issue of Israel is used as a banner of unity and a trump card in the contest for Arab leadership. Finally, it has been aggravated by the rivalry of the great powers, who exploit the Palestine issue in their own power game.

The effects of the various campaigns have given Israel spectacular gains, some of them unexpected, not even hoped for. One can say that Israel became expansionist against her own will. The Israelis were ready to accept the 1937 partition plan, in principle but the Arabs refused it. Again the Israelis were ready to accept the UNO Partition Plan, but the Arabs refused it. The Israelis were ready to convert the armistice agreements of 1949 into a permanent peace settlement, but the Arabs stubbornly refused to do so. In June 1967, a similar situation arose with the impassioned appeal by the Prime Minister Eshkol for peace which was disdainfully rejected by Nasser.

The Six Day War completely transformed the situation of Israel, both in the region and internationally. Internationally, because the U.N. General Assembly refused to condemn Israel or to demand her withdrawal to pre-June frontiers. The emergency session called for by the Soviet Union in July 1967 ended without a resolution being adopted. Israel regained full control of the old capital of Palestine, and pronounced it an integral part of Israel. The Arabs, having blockaded, boycotted, threatened and attacked Israel since her inception, find themselves on the defensive and in disarray. It will be some time before they will be able to challenge Israel on the battlefield, and again to seek 'a military solution to the Palestine problem'. The communication lines of Israel are no longer threatened, as Israeli defence forces guard both the Straits of Tiran and the Border of the Suez Canal. Instead of being an encircled nation under siege, Israel has become a dominant power in the Middle East with strategic frontiers removed from the main centres of her population. Instead of being an underdog threatened with annihilation, Israel has turned into the master of wide territories populated by more than one million Arabs.[1] Instead of being able to argue only about Arab refugees, Israel is now in the position of being able to do something constructive about the lot of refugees taken over from Jordan and Gaza. Instead of being a purely Jewish State, Israel has become a *de facto* bi-national state, simply by the weight of demographic realities, which, in the long run, are more threatening than anything else, not only to the Jewish majority rule, but also to the occupational structure of the Jewish population. (The Arab birthrate in the State of Israel (51·4 per 1,000 in 1964) is the highest in the Arab world, and is more than double the Jewish birthrate (22·4 in 1964).)

If the Arabs refuse to negotiate peace in direct talks with Israel the present armistice lines may become fossilized for a long time to come, and may even turn into the permanent frontiers of Israel, in which case 2,365,000 Jews will face 1,367,000 Arabs,

[1] According to the Israeli census of the occupied territories, 600,000 Arabs live on the West Bank, 350,000 in the Gaza Strip, 33,000 in Sinai, 14,000 on the Syrian Heights and 70,000 in East Jerusalem which is now recognized as part of Israel.

i.e., the Arabs of the new territories plus the 300,000 Arabs of the pre-June Israel.

If the claims of Israel were accepted to East Jerusalem, the Gaza Strip and the Heights of Golan, the Arab population in the new Israel would amount to about 25 per cent of the total population (350,000 in the Gaza Strip, 70,000 in East Jerusalem, 15,000 in the Golan Heights plus 300,000 in pre-June Israel). It would not be very long before the swift tide of Arab fertility gave the Arabs a clear majority in the State. In such a State, the occupational structure of the Jewish population would also be strongly disturbed, as the Jewish population would revert to administrative, professional, technical and commercial work, while the Arabs would provide for agricultural, building and manual work at large.

The enormity of the problems facing the Jewish leadership in Israel is simply staggering. There are great challenges and opportunities but also great threats and dangers. It is not the first time that a victorious state can be devastated by the fruits of its own victory which are delicious to taste but very hard to digest. Israel is exhilarated by the triumphs of her arms, she is in a mood of uplift and thankfulness, but all the same apprehensive.

No one wishes to prophesy, no one can predict the future. Will the Arabs face realities and accept Israel's offer for direct negotiations and the recognition of her existence? Will the thirteen members of the Arab League, or rather their most active members, at present divided between the 'revolutionaries'— Algeria and Syria, the 'progressives'—Egypt and Iraq, and the 'conservatives'—Jordan and Saudi Arabia, be able to resolve their bitter rivalries which are a hindrance towards their facing realities? Will the Israelis show moderation and long-range foresight, accepting not the standards prevailing in the region, but the standards and values pioneered by world Jewry in their long historical record? Will they be able to win the goodwill of the Arabs who are under their control? Will they be able to solve the problem of the refugees without waiting for a peace settlement, by bold constructive initiatives within the areas under their control?[1] Will the great powers come together and agree on a

[1] At present about 570,000 Arab refugees of the 1948 War live under Israeli rule, namely 300,000 on the West Bank and 270,000 in the Gaza Strip. New refugees from the West Bank and Golan Heights are estimated to be of

solution which could be imposed on the contesting parties? These are the main questions, behind which also looms the prospect of future nuclear power, which can be, in ten years' time, in the hands of Israel as well as Egypt—in which case, war would turn into a mutual suicide pact, with a danger of triggering off a world nuclear war.

The Arab-Jewish conflict is a tragic one because there is no way out for the two sides except to come to terms and accept the realities of life: for the Arabs to accept the political, economic and strategic realities, and for the Israelis to accept the demographic realities of the region. They are set like a small island in an Arab sea, and nothing can alter this fact, which no amount of power can remedy in the long run. The life of a nation, its interests, must be viewed not in terms of years or even decades. For the next decade Israel's existence is safe, but who can guarantee her existence in twenty or fifty years' time? The Arabs resembling the elemental force of a sea can afford to lose a hundred battles, but Israel cannot afford to lose even one. Both sides have to face realities, realities of a different order but equally compelling.

For Jews of the Diaspora, there are two most important issues in this conflict, both of primordial interest. One is the security of Israel, the guarantee of her peaceful existence and development, which would enable her to fulfil her task and the role for which she was designed. But equally important is the issue of finding a solution to the conflict which will not jeopardize values and standards pioneered by world Jewry, so that Jewry should not lose its sense of justice and righteousness by imposing on the other side something which could be regarded as unjust and as a violation of natural rights. The Diaspora which always had

---

the order of 250,000. There are also 300,000 'old' refugees settled in Transjordan and 100,000 in Lebanon. Some refugees settled also in Syria, Saudi Arabia, Iraq, Kuwait and Egypt.

Israel could start a plan of her own for the compensation, restitution and resettlement of refugees under her own control, using the experience she gained in the resettlement of her own immigrants from the Arab countries. This would be an important step towards Arab-Israel reconciliation, an act of plain justice and an act of penance for the wrong committed, though involuntarily.

an intense preoccupation with moral issues is interested that justice should not only be done but be seen to be done. Israel must not only be at peace with her neighbours, but also at peace with herself.

This requirement is the most difficult of all to fulfil for a young nation threatened by enemies all around her, as their intransigence forces Israel to apply 'a hard line'. The bitter and hateful hostility of one party infects the other in a deadly embrace: it demands a natural response of the same order. No one can expect the Israelis to be saintlike in the face of threats, abuse and terror.

Israel cannot escape the historical law to which all nascent states, present and past, have been subjected. No state was ever born otherwise than by war and revolution, by conquest, invasion, rebellion, and generally speaking by violence and struggle. The ancient State of Israel, although 'guided by Jehova' could not escape this law in its conquest of the Land of Canaan. The genius of history is far from being an angel of peace. If it is true that God reveals himself in history, He reveals himself in upheavals and storms, in fear and trembling.

The founders of Zionism were all men of peace and goodwill, and it did not occur to them that the Jewish State would come to be tested by forty years of bitter warfare. They wanted the Jews to escape from the hatred around them, but they did not realize that their own scheme would produce an even more powerful and concentrated hatred in the new land. If they had been able to envisage such a situation, it is doubtful whether they would have unfolded the flag of Zionism. They were convinced that Israel would bring peace and prosperity to the Middle East, and that the Arabs would gain considerably in economic and cultural terms from Jewish settlement, and would accept them with open arms, the more so as they were 'cousins' racially, and the vast expanses of the desert would be turned to productive use. 'And whatever we attempt there to accomplish for our own welfare, we will react powerfully and beneficially for the good of humanity', wrote Herzl in his *Judenstaat*.

Only one French writer, Ernest Laharanne, an early forerunner of Gentile Zionism, foresaw what was coming, writing in the aftermath of the Crimean War in a booklet published in 1860, *La nouvelle Question d'Orient* (with sub-titles: 'Empire d'Egypt et d'Arabie; Reconstitution de la nationalité juive'). Envisaging the

ultimate dissolution of the Ottoman Empire he proposed the
formation of three strong viable Middle Eastern States: Egypt;
Arabia to embrace all Arab territories in Asia; and the reconstitution of ancient Judea in a Jewish Palestine enlarged to include
the Sinai Peninsula. Addressing himself to Jews all over the world
he made the following appeal:

> What an example, what a race! . . . We bow our heads before you
> strong men. Because you were strong throughout your ancient
> history, you were strong even after the drama of Jerusalem. . . .
> During eighteen centuries you had to suffer enormous tribulation
> . . . but the remnant could rise again and rebuild the gates of
> Jerusalem. . . . March forward, you sons of the martyrs! The riches
> of experience which you have accumulated during your long exile,
> will help to bring again to Israel the splendour of Davidic days. . . .
> Oh, how the Orient will tremble on the day of your arrival.

In fact the Orient did tremble. The human condition is such
that power, if unopposed, is abused, and a victorious nation
behaves differently from a defeated one—this at least is a historical
fact which is exemplified once more in the case of Israel. One
can easily imagine what would have happened if the Arabs had
been victorious. The fear that Israeli would treat the Arabs in
the same way that the Arabs would treat the Jews, if the victory
were theirs, has not been an insignificant element in the flight of
Arab refugees. But there is no denying that the military occupation of territories exclusively populated by Arabs, creates dismay,
hatred and an ominous situation. There is also no denying the
fact that the fate of the Arab refugees presents a crisis of conscience for the victors. They themselves have been refugees for
many centuries, and now their tragedy is that they have caused
others to suffer a similar lot. However, they can contend that
once the two sides resorted to war, the issue can no longer be
viewed in terms of ethics. The effects of a war in terms of those
killed, maimed and made homeless can hardly be judged by the
criteria of morality, once nations have resorted to a 'tragic
choice'. And tragedy 'elicits admiration as well as pity because it
combines nobility with guilt'—to use Reinhold Niebuhr's phrase.
I quote now the whole passage which has a very apt application
to Israel's predicament:

> The tragic element in a human situation is constituted of conscious

choices of evil for the sake of good. If man or nations do evil in a good cause, if they cover themselves with guilt in order to fulfil some high responsibility or if they sacrifice some high value for the sake of a higher or equal one, they make a tragic choice. . . . Tragedy elicits admiration as well as pity because it combines nobility with guilt.[1]

This is the tragic element in Israel's situation. One can regret the tragic choice, but one cannot help admiring the noble faith of Israeli youth which has moved mountains, and the extraordinary heroism of the Jewish fighters, the ready self-sacrifice of young life (for instance in storming the impregnable fortifications on the Syrian heights of Golan) in the defence of their land. And so there is nobility with guilt!

The Jewish people have been for centuries an underdog and had of course the high morality which befits an underdog. In Israel the Jews have become for the first time a topdog, and they are perplexed and bewildered by this new situation which gives ample opportunities for the abuse of power. Many Israelis are conscious of this predicament and they very much regret that from time to time some of them yield to the temptation to abuse power.

There is no denying that there is a large element of hypocrisy in the presentation of the Jewish case, in the self-righteous claims for the exclusive justice of their cause. Such a conflict as the Arab-Jewish one does not lend itself to a clearcut indictment as to who is guilty and who is not, as there is no possibility of 'doing justice to both sides'. Chaim Weizmann, the first President of Israel, declared so quite openly. 'In his memorable evidence before the United Palestine Committee Weizmann defined the position as he saw it in a way all his own. This was a problem which you could only solve along the lines of least injustice. Equal justice to both was impossible.'[2]

The position is quite clear. The Arabs have a natural claim as the established inhabitants of the land for centuries. The Jews have a historical and religious claim, recognized by the United Nations since the Peace Treaty of Versailles. They also have a

[1] Niebuhr, *The Irony of American History*, Vols. IX–X. James Nisbet. London 1952.

[2] Quoted by J. L. Talmon, *The Unique and the Universal*. Secker and Warburg. London 1965.

natural claim, having been squeezed out of Europe, as well as from Arab countries themselves (the refugee problem can be presented as a forcible exchange of population on both sides). They also have a claim consisting in their genuine deep love and reverence for the Land which they have reclaimed and sanctified by their toil and blood.

But how is it possible to weigh up these controversial claims? Even if justice were on the side of the Arabs, can any Jew say: '*Fiat iustitia, pereat mundus Judaicus*'? Even if justice were on the side of the Jew, can any Arab say: '*Fiat iustitia, pereat Palestina Arabiensis*'?

If the Israeli feels that full justice cannot be done without disastrous effects for his own people, or if the Arab would feel the same were victory on his side, what can either do to be at peace with himself? He can only openly assume full responsibility for the situation, remedy whatever it is in his power to remedy, and also openly accept his guilt. By accepting his guilt he would satisfy his integrity, his sense of justice and his deeper moral self. This is what is actually required of Israel. She has to accept responsibility for the effects of her actions, for the displacement of refugees, and for turning the Arab majority into a minority. She has to remedy what it is in her power to remedy, namely to solve the problem of the refugees and to redress genuine Arab grievances.

She has also openly to accept her guilt for the disastrous effects of her actions on the Arabs, in spite of her good intentions and her conviction that she was acting in an awareness of the fulfilment of historical necessities, or in theological language as 'fulfilling God's ordinance'. Spinoza, the rationalist mystic, called 'everything that happened according to natural law . . . in so far as it directs human life through external and unexpected means', 'The ordinance of God'.[1] And that is how Israel came into existence 'by external and unexpected means' and 'according to natural law' or the laws of history.

The Arab-Israeli encounter is a most fateful encounter, and is the key to the future of Israel. What Martin Buber declared in his testimony before the Anglo-American Commission in 1947 is still true today:

[1] *A Theological-Political Treatise*. Chapter Three, 'Of the Vocation of the Hebrews'.

A regenerated Jewish people in Palestine has not only to aim at living peacefully together with Arab people but also at a comprehensive co-operation with it in opening and developing the country. Such co-operation is an indispensible condition for the lasting success of the great work, of the redemption of their land.[1]

Also basically true is what Magnes and Buber declared to this Commission concerning Jewish policy in this field:

Jewish-Arab co-operation has never been made the chief objective of major policy. Sporadic and at times serious attempts have been made in this direction. But whenever such attempts encountered difficulties, as they were bound to, they were all too lightly abandoned.[2]

There is no alternative to persevering with patience and determination in a policy of peace by acts of peace, by doing justice and letting it be seen that justice is being done.

The Jew who came to Israel under the Zionist flag wanted to live his own life apart from others, without sharing his living space. The paradoxical outcome of the Six Day War was that he was thrust by his victory again into co-existence with Arabs in a *de facto* bi-national state. The irony of this development, springing from the unprecedented victory of his arms, carries also a lesson for him. The moral is that willy nilly he has to share his living space with others.

Dr Edmund Leach, Provost of King's College, Cambridge, in his Reith Lecture (17 December 1967) described nationalism, 'the lamentable delusion that only the separate can be free', as 'the contemporary disaster'. 'We can never be separate. We live in an evolving society as part of nature. In nature species do not evolve in isolation but in combination. . . . To be fit to survive you must be content to share your living space with other living things. . . .'

This is the moral of the great Israeli victory of arms.

The solution to the Arab complex of national humiliation and shame may be found on the psychological, ideological and religious plane. It is not easy but it is possible to win over a

[1] 'Arab-Jewish Unity.' Testimony Before the Anglo-American Commission by Ihud (Unity) Association by Judah Magnes and Martin Buber, p. 46. Jerusalem 1947.
[2] *Ibid.*, p. 11.

former, even an implacable enemy. This has been done many times in history, and it is being done in Europe at the present time. But one must address oneself to this task with determination and perseverance, with magnanimity, truth, singleness of heart and humility. The Jew of Nazareth said, 'Love thy enemy' and this injunction should not be treated as a precept of nobility but as sheer common sense, as the only means to break out of the vicious circle of war without end and to put an end to the perpetuation of bitterness and hatred.

The Israelis have regained some of the valiant spirit of their warrior ancestors in the Land of Israel, and perhaps they should try to recover some of the prophetic spirit of their ancestors. The warriors must turn to their prophets in order to try to win the soul of the Arabs, by developing a new ethos, a new spiritual and missionary atmosphere. The warriors have been adequate for defence, but they cannot attain nor safeguard peace. Peace will come only when the prophetic element among the Israelis can come forward and take over the leadership of the country, and if they do so with a strong enough voice to penetrate to neighbouring countries. The situation itself compels Israel to engender universalistic movements which can overcome both Israeli and Arab nationalism alike. The two nationalisms are at loggerheads with each other like two ferocious dogs. Only if both nationalisms are overcome can peace return to the Holy Land and make it really holy, that is, fit to be the habitat for the three greatest religions of the world.

2.

The Israeli-British Encounter

THE BRITISH rule in Palestine (1917–48) left indelible marks in many fields of Israeli life, not only in administration, the armed forces, legislation, court proceedings, education and sportsmanship, but also in the mental make-up of the new nation. British rule was a deep and lasting emotional experience which can be compared to childhood experience in the life of an individual. It was the time of the youth of a new nation when all its impressions were strong and vivid and formed a nucleus of its new character.

The Taggart police forts are prominent symbols of the British rule. The British Criminal Law is still in use as far as procedure and precedents are concerned. In Knesset British political usages are often quoted as examples to follow. Mapai styled itself on the British Labour Party and is close in spirit to the party. One could say that the East European socialist pioneers became gradually Anglicized as time went on and shed a great many of the blinkers acquired in the Polish-Russian Ghetto. The Israeli welfare state follows the pattern of the British welfare state. Both owe their origin to the same ethos of middle class socialism. The best streets in Israeli towns were named after Allenby, Balfour and Orde Wingate.

Britain was the focus of Jewish-Christian encounter in the land of Israel, one of the basic and most crucial encounters for the new society. In this encounter, fears, suspicions and prejudices inherited from the Christian world on one side and the Jewish world on the other, played their full part in mutual relationships. The load of history cannot be so easily disposed of, even with goodwill on both sides. No one can claim that those who carried out the tasks of British administration and army were unprejudiced towards the Jews, and vice versa, which of course hampered the smooth working of the British apparatus.

Britain was the focus of great love and great hopes in the

beginning, disenchantment and disappointment in the middle years of the British rule and hate at its very end. British soldiers under Allenby, when they arrived in 1917 were greeted as deliverers, but when they left in 1948 they were booed with scorn and derision. The Balfour Declaration of 1917 was hailed by the national poet Bialik as the Cyrus Declaration of modern times, similar to the declaration which ingathered the ancient Israelis into the Promised Land from Babylonia, while the end of the Mandate was marked by anti-British terrorism, commando raids on British stations, kidnapping of British soldiers and officers, murders and violence. Britain was the nation which was loved, admired and trusted among all the other Powers, but at the end Britain was the only power, against which the instrument of political assassination (Lord Moyne the Minister of State in Cairo) and fanatical terrorism (such as the hanging of kidnapped British soldiers as a reprisal for hanging terrorists), was ever used by Jews in their entire history.

There is no other nation to which Israel owes a greater debt than Britain. It was Britain which put Zionism on the map, hallmarking Zionism in its initial stages and turning Zionism from a vision and dream into a practical, realistic political movement. It was Britain under whose protective wings the Jewish national home grew from its tiny seed up to a fully grown, well-established tree. The Jews learned from the British how to rule the country; they also learned from them the art of war. The nucleus of the Haganah and unofficial Irgun Zwi Leumi were British-trained units. When the Jews attacked British outposts, they attacked with British arms and British-trained skill. It was also Britain which in the Peel Commission (1937) first uttered the startling term, 'The Independent Jewish State', and made it an internationally valid conception.

Now let us review the salient features in consecutive stages of this unique Israeli-British encounter, which was crucial for the establishment of the State of Israel.

The first stage may be called the pre-Zionist stage of British interest in Jewish Palestine. After the abortive attempt at cooperation with Imperial Germany made by Herzl, the Zionist movement orientated itself on Britain, hoping to come under

Britain's wings and protection. There was in Britain a tradition of a revivalist movement of old standing with its belief in the Second Coming, to which the prerequisite conditions would be Jews' conversion to Christianity and their return to the Holy Land. The Earl of Shaftsbury, in a political debate in the House of Lords following the Damascus Affair in 1840 (ritual murder charge by a Franciscan Monastery), advocated settling Jews in Palestine and Disraeli expressed similar ideas. The English mystic Laurence Oliphant went to Constantinople to try to persuade the Sultan to invite Jews to settle in Palestine and to offer them self-rule in a strip of desert land in the Sinai Peninsular.

Very early the British Foreign Office showed its interest and sympathy for the Jewish cause in Palestine. As far back as 1848, long before the Zionist movement was born, when Palmerston established a British Consulate in Jerusalem, he instructed the Consul to take the Jewish communities in Palestine under his unofficial protection. The British Colonial Office, in the person of its Secretary, Joseph Chamberlain, was involved in discussions with Herzl as far back as 1902. Soon afterwards came the Uganda offer, a concession in British East Africa, with a measure of self-rule for the Jewish Colonial Trust, accepted by Herzl but eventually turned down by the Zionist Congress in 1903. This put the Zionist cause on the map of British Foreign Policy. When the Balfour Declaration came out in 1917, it was a logical development from its early tentative soundings. Both Balfour (under whose premiership the Uganda offer was made) and Lloyd George (who as a solicitor drew up the text of the Uganda Charter) under whose premiership the Balfour Declaration was made, were already conversant with and sympathetic to the Zionist cause. They were also well aware of the problem which the Exodus of Russian Jews escaping from the Tsarist persecution was likely to produce in Britain, and Balfour himself was the author of the Aliens Act meant primarily as restriction against the immigration of Russian Jews.

With the Balfour Declaration[1] we reach the next stage of official

[1] The Balfour Declaration stated unequivocally that, 'H.M. Government view with favour the establishment in Palestine of a national home for the Jewish People and will use their best endeavours to facilitate the achievement of this object, it being clearly understood that nothing shall be done to prejudice the civil and religious rights of other non-Jewish communities in

Zionist-British co-operation. The Balfour Declaration was the outcome of a unique historical situation: the war situation and the need to strengthen the Allied Cause through the support of the American Jews and America at large; the coming defeat of Turkey and the opportunity to gain another foothold in the Middle East; the need to do something constructive with the waste land under Turkish control, which could use Jewish capital and skill; finally the plight of the Eastern Jews, whose constant exodus was felt also in Britain. It was a blend of British idealism (the Baptist Revivalism of Lloyd George) and practical Imperialism of Foreign and Colonial Offices. It killed many birds with one stone. It appealed to the deeper mystique of the British Empire, it caught the imagination of British leaders, brought up on the Bible, always fascinated by the East and its vast possibilities. Disraeli would have been proud of his Party for intending to complete the work which he began in the Suez Canal and in his exploration of the Orient.

The Balfour Declaration was embodied in the British Mandate for Palestine, entrusted by the Allied Powers' Supreme Council at San Remo in 1920. It was granted by the League of Nations (1922) for the specific purpose of 'the establishment in Palestine of A National Home for the Jewish People'. In this way Zionism became not only British endorsed but also an international affair backed by the community of nations. Britain assumed certain international obligations, not only towards the Zionist movement but also towards the League of Nations, to whose Permanent Mandates Commission she had to report.

The Mandate, which was drafted by the British Government in co-operation with the Zionist Organization, was a sort of contract between three parties. The League of Nations was a sleeping partner who had to be informed, and also had the right of control and advice, although it rarely exercised its rights except at the very end of the Mandate. The Zionist Organization was a junior partner, primarily interested in seeing that the terms of the contract were kept, but with no executive power. A special body known as the Palestine Zionist Executive was formed to act as a link between the British administration and Zionist interests.

Palestine, or the rights and political status enjoyed by Jews in any other country'.

However, the main responsibility and the full executive power was vested with the British Government.

The two principal partners did not speak the same language, had two different conceptions of the task in hand and pursued two different objectives. The objective of the Zionist Organization was clear and simple, the establishment of the Jewish National Home, while the objective of the British Government was primarily to treat Palestine as part of its Imperial Middle Eastern Policy, and within this framework to promote the Jewish National Home. At first it looked as if the two objectives could be reconciled. The appointment in 1920 of Sir Herbert Samuel (later Lord Samuel), a Zionist Jew, with an administrative staff, in which many prominent English Jews held first rank, was an expression of this belief and a symbol of the status of the Zionist Organization, treated at this stage still as a partner. But very soon the political scene in Palestine and the Middle East at large underwent a substantial transformation. The awakening of Arab Nationalism and the growing Arab pressure both inside and outside Palestine as well as the growing weight of Middle Eastern oil interests shifted almost dramatically the parallelogram of forces determining British policy. The creation of the Kingdom of Iraq and the Amirate of Transjordan under British Mandatory protection marked the beginning of the new British policy which linked Imperial British interests with Arab nationalist aspirations. In Palestine itself serious Arab rioting broke out in May 1921, directed against the Jewish National Home.

1922 is the year which starts the gradual withdrawal from the Balfour Declaration and the policy of increasing concern for placating and protecting Arab interests. The Balfour Declaration in its original form seemed incompatible with the new pro-Arab policy and a new version was presented in a White Paper of 1922 which can be called the Balfour Declaration in a minor key. This was the beginning of a growing and deepening conflict between Zionism and Britain, growing estrangement and growing embarrassment of Britain by Zionism which came to be regarded finally as a burden to be shed, a hindrance to the full fruition of Arab-British friendship.

The White Paper interpreted the Balfour Declaration as aiming only at 'a further development of the existing Jewish Community' in Palestine; it limited immigration to the volume of the country's economic capacity at the time and it denied to the Palestine Zionist Executive 'any share in the general administration of the country.'[1]

The year 1922 was the end of the Zionist-British honeymoon and the beginning of a more strained relationship. As the Arabs were not prepared to accept the Balfour Declaration, even in the White Paper's interpretation, the British attitude towards the Jews hardened and the administration of Palestine took more and more the form of an ordinary colonial type, under a new High Commissioner (1925), Lord Plumer, a British Army Commander in the First World War, who was succeeded in 1928 by Sir John Chancellor.

In 1929 came the Wailing Wall outbreak of Arab violence on a large scale, which resulted in the appointment of the Commission of Enquiry, headed by Sir Walter Shaw. Following the recommendation of this Commission, the subsequent White Paper, called the Passfield White Paper of 1930 accepted further limitation of Jewish immigration and restrictions on land sales to the Jews. It was strongly resented and condemned by the Zionist movement as contrary to the terms of the Mandate, and in fact was never put into operation. But it was clear from the tone of the White Paper and from the British Report to the Permanent Mandates Commission that the terms of the Mandate became an increasing burden and embarrassment to Britain which regarded them as unworkable.

Now we come to the Hitler period. Under the pressure of Nazi persecution the immigration to Palestine reached an unprecedented level, rising in 1933 to 30,327, in 1934 to 42,359, in 1935, 61,458. With large-scale immigration and capital influx came also prosperity. The Jewish national Home grew stronger and stronger under the wings of the Mandatory Power in spite of its misgivings and reluctance. But at the same pace grew also Arab nationalism, organized resistance and violence. The new British proposals for Legislative Council in Palestine, meant as a preparation for a bi-national State, triggered off the Arab Rebellion. In April 1936, the general Arab strike broke out under

[1] John Marlowe, *The Seat of Pilate. An Account of the Palestine Mandate*, pp. 62-3, Cresset Press. London 1959.

the organization of the Higher Committee, which announced that the strike would continue until the Jewish immigration stopped. Committees for co-operation with the Palestine Arabs were set up in all neighbouring countries. From then on the Palestine issue became the focal point of Arab nationalism. The Peel Commission appointed to investigate the underlying causes of disturbances marked a turning point in the history of the Mandate. Its Report of 1937 attributed the causes of the disturbances to the terms of the Mandate itself which was considered as a hindrance to the development of any self-government in Palestine and recommended the British Government to take the appropriate steps for the termination of the Mandate on the basis of the partition of Palestine into three parts: Jewish, Arab and those parts of religious or strategic importance to remain under the Mandate. In the meantime it also recommended fixing the ceiling of Jewish immigration in the interim period, in blatant contrast to the mounting and pressing Jewish need for immigration caused by the Nazi persecutions. The British Government announced its general agreement with those recommendations. The Arab leaders rejected the idea of partition, the Zionist Congress rejected the boundaries of the State which was equivalent to a Tel-Aviv State, while accepting the principle of partition. The League of Nations opposed the idea of the immediate creation of the new independent State but conceded that it was worthwhile to examine 'the advantages and disadvantages of the new territorial solution', as the old Mandate was unworkable.

In the meantime the Arab Rebellion raged all over the country with ever-rising momentum and mounting protestations against the Peel proposals. Those proposals were eventually withdrawn by the British Government and after the last and unsuccessful attempt by the British Government to reach Arab Jewish agreement in a specially convened London Conference in January 1939, came the final White Paper in May 1939.

H.M. Government now declare unequivocally that it is not part of their policy that Palestine should become a Jewish State. . . . It should be a State in which two peoples in Palestine, Arabs and Jews, share authority in Government in such a way that the essential interests of each are secured. . . . The object of H.M.G. is the establishment within ten years of an independent Palestine State in such Treaty relation with the U.K. as will provide satisfaction for all commercial and strategic interests of both countries. . . . Jewish immigration during the next five years will be at the rate which, if economic absorptive capacity permits, will bring the Jewish population up to approximately one third of the total population of the country . . . this would allow of the admission of some 75,000 immigrants over the next five years.[1]

In this way Zionism was officially discarded, the Jews were outraged, while the Arabs were not pleased with the prospect of the further immigration of 75,000 Jews. In the eyes of the Jews the White Paper finished the role of Britain in nursing Zion. The Mandatory administration outlived its functional role.

We enter now the stage of the Second World War. The Jews, although outraged by the White Paper, were the natural ally in the war against Hitler, which was the crucial factor overriding any other consideration. Ben Gurion's slogan was: 'We will fight the White Paper as though there were no war, and we will fight the common enemy as though there were no White Paper'. While the Arabs with their pro-Axis sympathies took practically no part in the war effort, the Jews were anxious to offer their services. By the end of 1940 there were 15,000 Jews in the Jewish Settlement Police which acted as a Home Guard. Jewish troops took part as commandos against the German invasion of Greece and Crete. Jewish pilots parachuted into occupied Europe. Wingate's force was composed of Palestine Jews. Forty-three members of the Haganah imprisoned in Acre were released in 1941 to lead a British unit through the mountain passes for the invasion of Syria. The Commander of the terrorist Irgun, David Raziel released from prison took part in the British Commando Operation in Iraq and was killed. In 1944 Churchill gave his permission for a separate Jewish Brigade consisting of 5,000 men and at the end of the war there were 26,000 Palestine Jews of both sexes serving in the British Army.

Immediately after the end of the war in Europe, namely in June 1945, the Jewish Agency submitted its request for 100,000 certificates for immigrants from the D.P. Camps in Europe, a request which was supported by the Truman Administration. The British answer was negative, insisting on the quota of 1,500 certificates a month, according to the White Paper formula of

[1] *Ibid.*, p. 156.

1939. That was the end of the Zionist-British co-operation, the end of the rule of law and the beginning of the Jewish rebellion. Palestine, to use Arthur Koestler's bon mot, 'became John Bull's other Ireland'. The period from June 1945 up to the end of the Mandate was the stage of Jewish rebellion, in which not only the Irgun Zwi Leumi and the Stern Gang took part but also the main body of the Haganah. An armada of illegal ships brought tens of thousands of immigrants to the shores of Palestine; the British Navy was busy patrolling the coast and when shiploads were caught, the immigrants were transferred to the internment camp in Cyprus, where the survivors of the concentration camps had another spell of life guarded this time by the British troops. Dramatic and tragic incidents occurred with loss of life among the immigrants, most famous being the unhappy wanderings of the ship *Exodus* which carried the immigrants back first to France, and finally right back to Germany. This incident more than anything else caused an outcry all over the world and compromised Bevin's policy. Clashes with the police and military forces in Palestine became a daily occurrence and the scale of violence increased to the proportions of a war. R.A.F. stations were attacked and aircraft wrecked, British camps assaulted, radio stations in Tel-Aviv dislocated, reprisals and kidnapping of British soldiers followed the arrests of the terrorists.

The British public was outraged by this unique spectacle and demanded the speedy end of the Mandate and evacuation, as no glory and no benefit could be expected from the muddle, confusion and mutual violence which marked the final stage of the British Mandate. In February 1947 the British Government announced its intention to refer the Palestine problem to the United Nations and in November 1947 came the UNO Assembly Partition Resolution, in which Britain abstained from voting. Soon afterwards the British Government announced its intention to end the Mandate on 15 May 1948, and the Jewish State was born.

In the ensuing War of Independence Britain backed the Arab States which invaded Palestine, hoping for Arab victory and reinstatement of British Rule to protect the doomed Jews under her own terms. Britain was factually at war with Israel through the Jordanian Arab Legion, which was financed, trained and officered by the British and commanded by Glubb Pasha, a British Brigadier. In the last stage of the War of Independence

British troops appeared at Aquabba to prevent the Israeli units from occupying the Jordanian port.

Britain's role in the War of Independence makes very sad reading not only for Israelis but also for the British themselves, because it was based not only on bad faith but also on bad judgement, bad information and orientation. That the Bevin-Attlee Government should entangle Britain in that way, was doubly painful for the Israelis as they believed in the Labour Government and had great hopes for future co-operation. (A Jew was at that time the Chairman of the Labour Party and there were 23 Jewish backbenchers among Labour M.Ps.) Still the Labour Government soon realized that they had backed the wrong horse, grossly underestimating the strength and resilience of the Israelis and overestimating the strength and cohesion of Arab nationalism. The whole policy of the Labour Government was severely censured by the British Parliament and not only by the opposition. Seven months after the Declaration of Independence the Government announced the *de facto* recognition of the New State which was already recognized by two Super Powers, the U.S.A. and the U.S.S.R.

Already in 1950 Britain joined the U.S.A. and France in the Tripartite Agreement in which they undertook to take immediate action within and outside the United Nations against any violation of frontiers and armistice lines in the Middle East, although later on the agreement was on the British side watered down to action through United Nations. In the Suez Canal Campaign Israel became a *de facto* ally of Britain with an important role assigned to her in the campaign; and after the campaign Britain supported strongly Israel's cause by upholding the principle of treating the Straits of Tiran as an international waterway. In the crisis leading to the Six Day War, British sympathy was overwhelmingly pro-Israeli, for which Britain paid the penalty of the Arab boycott. The old feuds seem well buried. Also the feelings of the Israeli public towards Britain are more than friendly. The British are actually the most popular among all the foreign nationals. The Israelis look up to Britain and everything British is regarded as the best. In their eyes the British are the most cultured, the most human and the most disciplined people and the Jews would like to emulate them. Of course there is also the other side of the coin which is expressed in the Israeli conception of British hypocrisy. When the time of British administration is recalled, the first terms to be used is 'Albion's perfidy'. However, the Israelis are well aware that the British manoeuvred themselves into an impossible situation, taking on a task which had an inherent contradiction in terms.

What the Israelis admire most in retrospect is the absence of British retaliation in the final phase of the Mandate, when the British soldiers were kidnapped and hanged by Israeli terrorists and Britain kept her nerve. The reaction of the British public was not the demand for revenge and retaliation against the Israeli Jews but retrenchment and withdrawal from the impossible task. That was the measure of British maturity and self-discipline.

The people of Israel in their struggle against the British administration also matured but in a different way. From a docile, subjugated, dependent, subject race at the mercy of the man with the gun, they became fierce fighters. They stopped believing in fine phrases and the power of appeals to humanity and reason and started believing in muscle and steel. The State was born in 'sweat, blood and tears' and that is how most States are born and most international issues settled. The War of Independence gave Israel a mystique of her own. The Jews returned to their ancient heritage but they paid for it a full price as any other nation does for its homeland.

The Jews in the Diaspora and the world at large watched the armed struggle against the British, not deprived of its romantic, almost Robin Hood trimmings, with amazement and wonder. A new Jew emerged, unknown to the nations and unknown to himself. Many stereotyped ideas about the Jews had to be discarded.

There is little doubt that the Diaspora Jews were proud of the Israeli record in this unequal struggle, although most of them did not approve of the fanatical and at times vicious acts of terrorism.

Among the British who stand out in the memories of the Israelis as their real and devoted friends, a special place is reserved for the late Major-General Orde Wingate who in 1937 was sent to Palestine as an Intelligence Officer. A deeply religious man he fell in love with the Palestinian Jews and considered himself as a Zionist. He not only, on his own initiative, trained the first units of the Haganah but also inspired them and gave them self-confidence.

> They knew he was giving them something more than military training. He was trusting them and respecting them, and preparing them with confidence against the day when would come their supreme test. . . . He proved to them over and over again that they had all the qualities needed for success on the field of battle. He banished for ever from their hearts and minds the spirit of the Ghetto engendered by centuries of persecution.[1]

Wingate, as a man of vision, who foresaw the victory of the Jewish cause, wanted to bring the Jewish Commonwealth into the British Commonwealth, an idea which was at that time looked upon with sympathy by Weizmann and Ben Gurion. But the genius of history knew better.

> Wilfred Thesiger once asked him (Orde Wingate) why he a non-Jew, should be so wholeheartedly with Zionism. He replied somewhat as follows: 'When I was at school I was looked down on, and made to feel that I was a failure and not wanted in the world. When I came to Palestine I found a whole people who had been treated like that through scores of generations, and yet at the end of it they were undefeated, were a great power in the world, building their country anew. I felt I belonged to such people.' But he gave a more illuminating account to Frederick Kish. In his earliest days, he said, he had received an injection of the Bible, but the effect only appeared many years later. Here we may remember again his occasional resemblance to the Puritans of Cromwell's day. Many of them became Zionists through much reading of the Holy Writ. It is sometimes forgotten that the famous Rabbi Manasseh ben Israel was invited to London from Holland largely through the pressure of Zionist-minded Puritans who believed that if Jews were settled in England the 'scattering' prophesied by Daniel would then be complete, so that the return of the people to Israel might be accomplished, a prophecy which, as no one seemed to notice, was actually fulfilled in 1917. But the fact was noticed in 1936 by this spritual descendant of Protectorate England.[2]

[1] Alice Ivy Hay, *There Was a Man of Genius. Letters to my Grandson Orde Jonathan Wingate*, p. 71. Neville Spearman. 1963.

[2] Christopher Sykes, *Orde Wingate*, p. 110. Collins. London 1959.

There are now many institutions in Israel and many sites which bear the name of Orde Wingate such as the Wingate Institute of Physical Education or Yemin Orde, the children's village south of Haifa devoted to the care of young orphans. Wingate is remembered with the greatest affection ever afforded to any non-Jew and regarded as one of the Founding Fathers of Israel.

3.

The Israeli-American Dialogue

AMERICAN-ISRAELI relations far transcend the relations of the Israeli and American Jewry. There is a strong affinity and attraction between the U.S.A. and Israel based on underlying common values and a certain similarity in their historical origin.

The Israeli is a frontier man like the American once was. Both had to fight against hostile indigenous population, although both came with good intentions. They were both colonizers, but not tools of foreign imperialism, they both came with an anti-imperialistic creed.

'The Pilgrim Fathers, we now are told, were simply representatives of the restless, upheaving middle classes; their ideas expressed the rising "Protestant ethic", which was the true prophet of modern capitalism.'[1] The Israeli Pilgrim Fathers also came from the restless upheaving middle classes, also with the ideas of puritan ethics of the Bible which was the true forerunner of modern socialism.

The Israeli came to his land in quest of freedom and independence, fleeing from oppression. In his inaugural address of January 1965, President Johnson made the following comment:

> Our destiny in the midst of change will rest on the unchanged character of our people and on their faith. They came here—the exile and the stranger, brave and frightened—to find a place where a man could be his own man. They made a covenant with this land. Conceived in justice, written in liberty, bound in union, it was meant to inspire the hopes of all mankind.

Both American and Israeli civilizations are what is called ideological civilizations. The American poet Robert Lowell comments on American ideological civilization:

[1] Daniel J. Boorstin, *The Image or What Happened to the American Dream* p. 52. Weidenfeld and Nicolson. London 1961.

261

We were founded on a Declaration, on the Constitution, on Principles and we've always had the idea of 'saving the world'. And that comes close to perhaps destroying the world. Suddenly it is as though this terrible nightmare has come true, that we are suddenly in a position where we may destroy the world, and that is very closely allied to saving it.

This comment *mutatis mutandis* could be applied to the Israeli civilization, if for 'the world' we substitute 'the Jewish world', the Diaspora, and instead of 'constitution' the Bible. The Israeli ideological civilization is based on a particular set of beliefs centred on the Bible and the central idea is the 'saving' of world Jewry. But this idea may come very near to the position of being able to destroy the Jewish world. Both ideas are closely akin.

The American sympathy for Zionism goes back a long way. In 1844 John Adams, President of the U.S.A., wrote to Mordecai Immanuel Noah, an American Jew, expressing sympathy for his plan to establish a Jewish State in Judea. After John Adams, interest in Jewish Palestine and Israel became traditional for American Presidents, including Woodrow Wilson, Franklin Roosevelt, Truman, Kennedy and Johnson. Enough to recall here some of the acts of President Truman such as: the demand for 100,000 certificates for Jewish immigrants in Palestine; restraining the hand of the British Government in fighting Jewish resistance movements; the backing of the UNO partition plan; immediate recognition of the State of Israel; the declaration of the so-called Truman doctrine of the defence of the Middle East frontiers which terminated in the Tripartite Agreement of 1950; and early American aid to Israel.

In 1956 after the Suez Campaign, although President Eisenhower turned against Israel's claims for keeping the Gaza Strip and Sharm el Sheikh under occupation, yet he endorsed and guaranteed her free use of the Straits of Tiran, declaring it an international waterway and initiating the presence of UNO forces in Gaza and Sharm el Sheikh.

In the emergency of 1967 the U.S.A. backed Israeli demands for the use of the Straits of Tiran, in the Six Day War adopted friendly neutrality towards Israel, and in the UNO Assembly Emergency Session strongly supported Israel's case.

In many other ways Israel is indebted to the U.S.A., with whose assistance in economic and financial terms she grew and developed. American loans are a very important contribution to various community campaigns conducted for Israel. Israel is well aware of her debts to the U.S.A. and of her organic, indispensable links with America, whose protection is now more necessary than ever as a counterbalance to Soviet encroachment in the area.

All the same Israel is not very happy to be regarded as part of the American camp, as an ally or even less as a satellite; she would be happier if she were able to declare herself as part of the Third World of the unaligned nations, which would be more in line with her natural position and interests. But the hostility of the U.S.S.R. pushes her unconditionally into the protective arms of America, even more so after the unfriendly acts of General de Gaulle after the Six Day War. Whether Israel will ever be able to join the Third World depends primarily on the attitude of the U.S.S.R., which holds the key to many prospects for the future.

Now, we come to the relations of Israel and American Jewry. In economic and financial terms Israel may be regarded as an outpost of American Jewry. She could not have been founded, she could not have survived, without the constant assistance given so liberally by American Jewry. Many Israeli institutions such as Universities, the Weizmann Institute, Technion, training schools, community centres, hospitals, and many afforestation and irrigation schemes, are directly supported by American benefactions. Many factories and workplaces were established by Americans. True, only a trickle of American Jews come to Israel and an even smaller number remain there but in all other respects the Jewish American support for Israel has been outstanding.

The American Jews were also instrumental in the formation of the State of Israel. As early as in May 1942 the American Zionist Conference adopted the Baltimore programme, demanding complete freedom for the Jewish Agency to develop Palestine as a Jewish Commonwealth 'integrated in the structure of the new democratic world'. This was the first outright and clear claim for Jewish Statehood in the whole of Palestine. When, in 1946, Ben Gurion was prepared to settle the Palestine issue on partition ('Peel plus Negev') which would mean giving up most of the present coast of Palestine, the American Zionists in the person of Rabbi Hillel Silver protested against 'sacrificing part of the sacred soil of Palestine'. When, in December 1946, at the 22nd Zionist Congress, Weizmann pleaded for moderation, ready to settle the Palestine issue on partition or to continue with Britain on a promise of freer immigration, he was dismissed from leadership by Ben Gurion's coalition with the American Zionists.[1] The two American Zionist leaders, Stephen Wise and Hillel Silver, developed an effective pressure group (having established good relationships with President Roosevelt and afterwards with President Truman) in the Congress as well as in political parties. During the final stages of the British Mandate and during the War of Independence the Israeli Foreign Office was unofficially in the hands of American Zionists, primarily Rabbi Hillel Silver.

So the Israelis are strongly indebted to the American Jews on many counts but this does not exclude serious dissensions in the Israeli-American-Jewish dialogue over many basic issues. The dialogue takes place on an ideological plane, each side putting forward its own idea for the Jewish future. The dialogue is complicated and at times overshadowed by the uneasy relationship of a beneficiary to a benefactor, of a borrower to a lender, of a newcomer to an old-established firm. Israel sees herself primarily as a working class country and American Jewry as capitalist *par excellence*. Acknowledging the benefactions, there is the natural resentment of a poor relation to his benefactor. The Israeli likes the dollar but he is afraid of it; he would say that the dollar is a good servant but a bad master. But even a good servant in time gains an ascendancy over his master, and so a great deal of Israeli life, not only in finance and economics but also in science, art and literature, in architecture, fashions, ways of expression and thinking can be directly attributed to American influence. University syllabuses, the style of university campuses, the style of the university President as the administrative head of the university are all American. The books which are on the bookstalls come from the U.S.A.; exchange of scientists, artists, writers, post-graduates are with the U.S.A. Cars, household goods, all the gadgets come from America. American English is the second language and the dollar the second currency.

The American influence in Israel fills the Israeli with dismay. The idea of the pioneers was a socialist society of worker-peasants

[1] Barnet Litvinoff, *Ben Gurion of Israel*, pp. 171–2. Weidenfeld and Nicolson. London 1954.

who would till the soil with love and devotion, free from the vices of the bourgeois middle class mentality. Now the veteran pioneer sees his ideals obliterated in wave of second-hand Americanism. This is the brand of capitalism which the pioneer rejects most decisively, and yet he is powerless to suppress it, as the wave is genuine, spontaneous and powerful and supported by the new trends of economic, technical, scientific and cultural development all over the world. The age of affluence, of auto-mation, nuclear energy, space flight, supermarkets and jazz, is the American age, to which the Israelis succumb as much, or perhaps even more than the others, as the links with America are very strong and cannot be severed.

The attitude of the American Jew to Israel is that of an older brother, more successful, more educated, more experienced and more resourceful. He wants to be proud of his younger brother, to show him off, to use him as a showpiece. He would like his younger brother to follow in his footsteps, as this is the way to success. He is resentful that his advice is often disregarded but all the same he has to support his younger brother, as this is his duty. The failure of Israel would be a calamity for Jews all over the world. Too much is at stake now, after Israel has been established, so it is not surprising that Zionists and non-Zionists alike are bound to support her.

The Israeli resents being treated as a younger brother but all the same he has to come to terms with Americanism as best he can. He knows that he is dependent and although the older brother would not abandon him whatever he does, he cannot alienate him too much. He cannot say openly, 'All we need from you now is money'.[1] So from time to time he makes a gesture of listening to his advice. And yet what the Israelis dread most is that Israel may become a 'little America'. That, they think, would be the end of Israel. It would rob Israel of her *raison d'etre*; for that Israel would not be needed.

Of course the Americans do not think in terms of turning Israel into a 'little America', but they would like to see a type of society, in which private enterprise and initiative are restored to

[1] Professor Selig Brodetsky in his Memoirs, *From Ghetto to Israel* (Weidenfeld and Nicolson, 1960), writes: 'The idea was that nothing more was wanted from Zionists except money. They thought the State of Israel would do everything else.' (p. 288.)

their rightful place with greater emphasis on fair and open competition instead of government privileges, grants, subsidies, credits and restrictions. They would also like to see a restored balance of power between the Histadrut and the private sector of the economy, primarily by a process of depolitization and decentralization of the Collosus, which overshadows everything else in Israel.

Even more important to the American Jew would be the development of an open society, free from fanaticism and intolerance, excessive nationalism and ethnic exclusivity, free also from religious manifestations in public life, a society which could fully subscribe to the Universal Declaration of Human Rights. The American Jewish Congress expresses deep concern whenever some coalescing of church and state takes place in the U.S.A., such as for instance using taxpayers' money in some of the states for parochial schools, so how could it approve of the close integration of the State of Israel with the Jewish ecclesia.

So this is the first subject for the Israeli-American dialogue: the nature of Israeli society. No less important are three other issues which are subjects of the Israeli-American dialogue: the nature of the Jewish identity; the meaning of the Holocaust; the place of Israel in the Jewish world.

The Problem of Jewish Identity

The 'National Home' of early Palestine was conceived as a home primarily for East European Jews. The Jews in the 'Pale' felt themselves to be not only a religious minority but a separate national identity of a sort. The American, the English, the French Jews felt no such separate identity. They left the ghetto two or three generations earlier, and felt completely at home in their own country. They were, by and large, not interested in setting up a 'national home'. When, under the pressure of East European Jews (Herzl was a Central European and both Weizmann and Sokolow were East Europeans), the British Government proclaimed its Balfour Declaration, the British Jewry made sure that 'no claim is or will be made that Jews constitute a separate political identity all over the world'.[1]

Slowly and progressively, and more so under the impact of the Jewish calamity in Europe, the Diaspora adopted Jewish

[1] *Sir Robert Waley Cohen*. A Biography by Robert Henriques.

Palestine and later on Israel as its own cause. Today the Diaspora Jews are almost to a man pro-Israeli (this has become very clear in the great emergency which led to the Six Day War) but that does not mean that they have been converted to Zionism. Louis Lipsky states this fact succinctly: 'World Jewry is almost unanimously pro-Israel without having become Zionist'.[1]

This is especially true of American Jews. What Marshall Sklare wrote in his Report presented at the Tercentenary Conference on American Jewish Sociology in November 1954 is still true today: 'We find that the answers to "How do you feel about the State of Israel?" indicate that almost unanimously both parents and teenagers possess positive feelings about the State of Israel. . . . Answers to the other important question: "Would you like to live in Israel?" (show that) almost 9 out of 10 respondents, both among the teenagers and the parents, answer in the negative.' American Jews identify themselves completely with American State and nationhood. Some would say that they are American first and then Jews, others that they are Americans and Jews *pari passu*. They interpret the nature of Jewish identity not as purely religious identity but also not as political national identity. They have developed a concept of their own, a sort of mid-way house between religion and nationhood, which they call by the name 'peoplehood'. 'However, in regarding religion as the basis of Jewish existence, he [the American Jew] does not negate Jewish peoplehood. Quite the opposite. The concept of Jewish peoplehood is an integral part of his religious belief.'[2]

Except for a very small group represented by the American Council for Judaism, the overwhelming majority of American Jews do not deny the *sui generis* ethnical character of Jewish identity, although rejecting the claim for a separate political national identity. Judaism is more conceived as a 'folk group' with an awareness of common origin and common cultural heritage and the will to live and cultivate this cultural heritage. This specific peoplehood is the peoplehood of American Jews as such and not Jews at large. Their culture is interwoven with American culture, giving and taking in a very close and intimate relationship.

[1] 'Portrait in action', *Chaim Weizmann. Portrait by Many Hands.*
[2] C. B. Sherman, *The Jew within American Society*, p. 223. Wayne State University Press. Detroit 1961.

This was best expressed as follows:

They [the American Jews] exist as a separate ethnic group and will remain so in the foreseeable future. . . . The difference between them and a caste or quasi-caste is the voluntarism with which they approach their separateness. If they were to retain their ethnic identity solely because the majority refuses to absorb them, then their existence would be marked by all the frustrations and bitterness that naturally accompany externally imposed separateness, and their spirit would bear the imprint of the entire misfortune of marginality. If, on the other hand, their group identity is founded on their will to live and to enrich America with whatever creative originality they possess—then they will be able to make of their exceptional status a joy to themselves and a blessing to the United States.[1]

The future of Judaism is viewed on the assumption that 'the dispersion of the Jews must henceforth be accepted as a permanent condition. As citizens of the country they live in, they cannot aspire to become a trans-national group of a political character or to function as a political unit.'[2] . . . 'Judaism can function only as a secondary civilization for its members, the primary one being the civilization of the country they live in.'[3]

The Israelis view this conception and this development with great dismay, scepticism and suspicion. The accepted theory in Israel is that the tree of American Judaism, as well as other Diaspora countries, is bound to wither away in the process of assimilation and mixed marriages which are multiplying in the air of freedom and tolerance. The greater acceptance of Jews within all walks of American life will eventually loosen the ties of Jewish tradition, exclusive education and community life. The increasingly secular mood of modern society will eventually do away with Judaism as a religious identity or mere 'peoplehood'. Therefore, they argue, the future of Jewry can be secured only by inspiring the Jews to separate national identity and their ingathering in the Land of Israel.

The American Jews view their future in a different light. 'Virtually all these groups affirm in the possibility of Jewish life

[1] Sherman, op. cit., p. 227.
[2] Mordechai M. Kaplan, The Greater Judaism in the Making, p. 452. New York 1960.
[3] Ibid., p. 453.

in the Diaspora. . . . Especially is the conviction strong that Jewish life will endure on the American scene.'[1]

The will for survival among the Jewish people has been the dominant factor in Jewish history. It shows itself in Soviet Russia after fifty years of Communist rule. In the U.S.A. it has not been weakened in the post-war development in spite of the growing percentage of mixed marriages. (A recent survey of Washington Jews has shown 10·2 per cent of mixed marriages for the first American-born generation, 17·9 per cent for the second generation and 37 per cent for the college educated.) A growing number of Gentiles who marry Jews convert to Judaism. In Los Angeles two schools of instruction for converts function continuously. 'The taste, ideas, cultural preferences and life-styles preferred by many Jews are coming to be shared by non-Jews' (Marshall Sklare). Jewishness became the popular theme of American literature as much as the Middle West and the South in their time, and Jewish names abound in American literature, developing the themes of Jewish life with Saul Bellow, Malamud, Salinger and Mailer to mention only a few.

All community surveys record a constant rise in the rate of affiliation to synagogues. The Reform Group trebled its membership from 1945–58. The Conservatives doubled their membership from 1948–58, the Orthodox also increased considerably their membership affiliation.[2] There is also a considerable growth in Jewish education with *Bar Mitzvah* (confirmation) of both sexes at the age of thirteen at the terminal point. The synagogue has been turned into an organized community centre, more important than ever before with social, cultural and educational functions.

This process is largely due to the Reform Movement as the most dynamic factor of social change in Jewish life in America. Since the time of the immigration of German Jews who streamed into the U.S.A. after 1848, America became the citadel of Reform Judaism with services attended by both sexes, often in English, with abbreviation and modernization of prayers, with organ music and mixed choirs. Apart from the Orthodox there are numerous wings of Judaism such as Reform, Conservative, Liberal and Constructionist and all of them are flourishing. It has been said that American life is constructed in such a way that

[1] Ira Eisenstein, *Judaism Under Freedom*. New York 1956.
[2] Sherman, *op. cit.*

an American Jew who wants to be a good American has also to be a good Jew and that means primarily supporting Jewish causes. 'The American Jewish Community became integrally part of American society; the American Jew is now in a position where he could establish his Jewishness not apart from, nor in spite of, his Americanness, but precisely through and by virtue of it. Judaism has achieved its status in the American Way of Life as one of the three "religions of democracy".'[1]

In the growing Reform Movement in America we see again a violent clash with the Israelis who, in their religious allegiance, are either orthodox or nothing. There are no Reform Movements in Israel, as Israel refuses to adapt the Jewish religion to modern times.

The other important division between Israeli and American religious life is the nature of secularization of religion. In both countries, Judaism is being increasingly secularized by the big majority of youth. Judaism assumes a secularized version practically without dogma and theology, almost without belief in supernaturalism. In Israel, as already pointed out in another context, the new secularized religion is centred around the Land and the Israeli nationhood, becoming a new 'religionality'. In the United States the secularized Judaism is centred around communal Jewish life, American-Jewish Way of Life. 'Yet it is only too evident that the religiousness characteristic of America today is very often a religiousness without religion, a religiousness with almost any kind of content or none, a way of sociability or "belonging" rather than a way reorienting life to God.'[2]

We see that the chasm between the American ways of Judaism and the Israeli ways is ever growing and in time to come it may become more difficult to bridge the gap between them. This is of real and great concern to Israel, which would like to keep the Jewish identity in the two greatest centres of Jewish life, reasonably close to enable them to find a common meeting ground. Israel hopes that this could be found in developing a common and unitary Jewish culture, but there is not, and never has been, such a thing as a common unitary Jewish culture. What is called Jewish culture is a culture of Jews in a certain region within a

[1] Will Herberg, *Protestant, Catholic, Jew. An Essay in American Religious Sociology*, p. 198. Anchor Books. 1960.

[2] *Ibid.*, p. 260.

certain pattern of civilization. There has been an outstanding Jewish culture in Eastern Europe, or Jewish culture in Germany, or there is a growing Jewish culture in America but there is no Jewish culture *per se* which embraces all the Diaspora countries in the West and in the East. And culture is a very dynamic phenomenon which follows its own laws of development. In Israel it is developing on its own lines hardly relevant to the development of Jewish culture in America. The Jewish culture in Israel is a Hebraic culture, inward looking, more or less closed, strongly national, centred around the Land, based on the environmental setting which is Oriental in character, while getting in fact very little nourishment from its natural cultural background in the Arab world. In opposition to this the American Jewish culture is open, outward looking, humanistic, Western in orientation, enjoying the fructifying vital spark of the symbiosis with the huge scientific and cultural collosus of America. The great historian of the last generation, Dubnov, envisaged a great future for Jewish culture, not in Palestine but in America—and it is true that Jewish education and culture flourish in the United States to a degree which in many ways overshadows Israel's achievement in this field. The American Jewry, almost 6,000,000 strong, has developed a rich and promising culture with a number of outstanding cultural and scientific organizations such as Jewish Theological Seminary, American Academy for Jewish Research, College of Jewish Studies, Hebrew Theological College, Dropsie College, Jewish Book Council, American Jewish Historical Society, Jewish Publication Society, Jewish Theatrical Guild and a hundred and one others both national, regional and local.

The Meaning of the Holocaust

The Holocaust is an experience which will take decades to digest, to contemplate and to interpret, not only as a gigantic, shattering event but also as a recurrent symbol of Jewish fate and destiny. The Holocaust is unique in its dimensions but not unique in its essence throughout Jewish history. One can discern a sort of cycle in its recurrence. Jewish history reveals a craggy vista of precipices, into which the Jews were plunged or into which they plunged themselves. Is it destiny and fate, or is it the system of beliefs and ideas for which the Jews stand that causes the crash?

Or is the cause a conflict of economic and class interests, or a clash of styles of life and patterns of behaviour? The full revelation of the meaning of the Holocaust has not yet been granted to us. However, all the Jewish movements, Zionists and non-Zionists, religious and secular, agree on one thing: we must try to make sure that this will not happen again. But how?

The Israeli answer is simple: by a mass exodus to Israel. Israel can in due time house all the Jewish Tribes from all the corners of the world, if the Jews will come. Israel can be developed in such a way that her absorptive capacity could be increased many times over to accommodate all who want to live 'a fuller Jewish life'. The meaning of the Holocaust according to the Israeli vision is clear. It shows the bankruptcy of the Diaspora, the failure of the Jewish symbiosis with other nations. The policy of adjustment does not secure the survival of the Jews, the 'protective colouring' is not a real protection, to be 'like others' does not save the Jews. Sooner or later a similar phenomenon may occur in other countries, when those will be faced with an emotional or historical crisis, as the Jews are the ideal scapegoat for emergencies.

The American Jews take the opposite view. They opt for the permanency of the Diaspora as the essence of the fate and destiny of Jewry. The Jews have always been and are to remain world people, not a separate little nation. The indestructibility of Jewry is secured by its dispersion. The value of Jewry consists in its symbiosis with other nations, as the value of all people is enhanced by intercourse. The Jews have developed this specific skill in bringing out their best and other people's best by an intimate relationship. An intimate relationship is not to be feared, even if it leads to losing a certain percentage of Jewish stock to other nations. Jewry is rich in talent and can afford this.

American Jewry sees the challenge of Holocaust primarily as a challenge of hate, cruelty and malice of a larger order, in which anti-Jewish hatred is only a special case. One cannot escape hatred simply by turning one's back on it, one has to engage it actively by fighting the ugly powers of all the 'anti-isms'. The Israeli Jews, who wanted to escape the anti-Jewish hatred in the Diaspora, did not succeed in escaping it, they changed only one hatred for another, no less fierce, no less virulent and dangerous. The danger of catastrophies in Jewish life is related to the intensity of hatred engendered against the Jews. Often the hate was engendered by the decaying society, by society in turmoil, burdened by a devastating heritage of the past against the background of social and economic oppression. In most cases the anti-Jewish hatred was only a part of a general atmosphere of hate, cruelty and illwill against everybody, in which the most defenceless groups paid the highest penalty. Sometimes the hatred has a more tangible and specific background of real clash of vital and irreconcilable interests such as that encountered in the Jewish-Arab conflict.

But hate is always like a firebrand. It rages and reverberates and consumes victims and incendiaries alike and many innocent bystanders besides. The Holocaust consumed not only Jews but also its incendiaries and many millions of non-Jewish victims in Europe.

The fight against hate, rancour and malice, against deep-rooted prejudices and 'scape-goatism' must not be regarded as hopeless, for which the only remedy is escape. It can be won by persistent social action, education, legislation and individual courage and determination. But it needs mobilization of efficient fire brigades, in concerted action, aggressive, counter-checking as well as preventive. The Jews have not only the right but also the duty to take an active part in this mobilization, not only for their own sake, but also for the sake of their fellow citizens, and not only in the struggle against manifestations directed against them but against all manifestations of 'anti-isms', anti-feelings and anti-attitudes, striking at the very roots of hatred.

This is the simple and clear philosophy, which is being developed in the Diaspora in response to the great challenge of the Holocaust. This philosophy entails also a persistent and long-term programme of re-education and reconstruction among Jewish masses themselves to mould their personality structure and their pattern of behaviour in a way which could support this philosophy and give it a full backing in everyday life. The aim is to mould the personality structure and pattern of behaviour in such a way that the Jew should inspire love instead of hate, sympathy instead of antipathy, understanding instead of resentment. He should be admired not for his possessions and money and not even for his talents, gifts and intellectual equipment, but primarily for what he is. He should be admired not for his power of adjustment but for being true to himself and his spiritual heritage. He should try to improve the image of the Jew which is current in most countries. It has been improved already in the last two decades but it can be further improved, not by propaganda and public relations but by working on oneself. The American Jews who spent large sums on Jewish causes have ample opportunities to conduct research into ways to emancipate the Jew fully to his new role in a free, progressive and tolerant society to make sure that the Jews will not be caught napping, while the forces of hatred rage freely around him. The American-Jewish society has developed a string of powerful national organizations such as American Jewish Congress, American Jewish Committee, Anti-Defamation League, National Community Relations and others, which are watchful.

The Place of Israel in the Jewish World

The Americans view Israel with affection and pride, regarding the new State as a supreme achievement of Jews in modern times. They give to Israel causes, as the saying goes, 'till it hurts', having contributed since 1948, $1\frac{1}{2}$ billion dollars. Still they resent Israel's claim for unconditional and uncritical admiration, reserving for themselves the right and duty to cast a critical and objective eye upon the Israeli scene. They view the role of Israel in international Jewry much more modestly than do the Israelis.

There are four basic conceptions of the relationship of Israel and the Diaspora.

First, we have the conception of the centrality of Israel and its primacy over the Diaspora. Israel is the first born, the fruit, the fulfilment, the hope, the future. The Diaspora exists primarily to give support to Israel, to give it impetus and strength in demographic as well as economic and political terms. It has no permanency of its own, it is bound to disintegrate and split into two halves: one to disappear in the process of assimilation, the other to be swallowed up as new immigrants by the State of Israel. The true 'remnant' (the conception of the 'remnant' is a unique Jewish conception, as Franz Rosenzweig once remarked) will be the people in the Land of Israel. It follows from this conception that the Diaspora should subordinate its needs to those of Israel, primarily by immigration, even at the expense of uprooting whole centres of Jewish life in other countries.

The second conception is the conception of the primacy of the Diaspora over Israel. The Diaspora, according to this conception, must be regarded as the lasting and permanent home decreed by providence or by historical forces, or, as Spinoza would put it, by 'election', namely by the chain of natural events in which the Jews themselves had little choice. Out of three to four thousand years of Jewish history, the sojourn in the Land of Israel, to say nothing of the duration of an independent State or Kingdom of Israel, is to be counted in hundreds of years, while the age of the Diaspora must be reckoned in thousands. The Diaspora did not emerge as popularly assumed, with the destruction of the Second Temple. It long antidates that event. Jewish history, as Franz Rosenzweig remarked, began with exile and exile is its dominant and permanent feature. The Diaspora will not come to an end with the firm establishment, growth in power and influence of the State of Israel. The majority of Jewry will always be dispersed among nations for reasons already stated two thousand years ago by Philo Judaeus. The State of Israel is not eternal, as no single State in history has been. In fact the Jewish people survived because of the Dispersion. If all Jews had remained in the Land of Israel, they would have disappeared as have all other nations of antiquity.

Moreover, not only the physical but also the spiritual destiny of the Jewish people is linked with the Diaspora. Their task as 'light unto the nations', as 'witness', as 'servant', as 'ferment' or simply the full development of all the potentialities, abilities and gifts deposited in the Jewish stock and the fulfilment of historical aspirations can be accomplished only through the sojourn of Jewry among nations and not by physical withdrawal and separation.

From this conception of the primacy of the Diaspora it follows that the State of Israel should subordinate its needs and requirements to that of the Diaspora, that it should do nothing to undermine its position, its influence, its range. Not only should the State of Israel not seek to liquidate or uproot whole centres of Jewish life in the Diaspora but on the contrary it should encourage and strengthen them. It should not try to nationalize the Jewish masses in the Diaspora and thus hamper their integration into the cultural and social life of their neighbours. It should limit itself to the engendering of a proud, self-respecting Jewish consciousness desirous of participating in the upbuilding in the new Jewish centre in the Land of Israel.

The third conception is the conception of full equality of all centres of Jewish life. This conception denies the validity of the idea of the Diaspora as such. The Jews are not dispersed in the homes of other nations and do not find themselves in exile. They have their homes in the countries that they sojourn in. The problem of Israel and the Diaspora does not exist in the sense envisaged by two previous conceptions, because there is no Diaspora. Actually the problem should read: Israel and other centres of Jewish life. Israel is a new centre of Jewish life, which ought to be compared with other centres, say the American. The valid problem is actually that of the relationship of different centres to each other: how should they live and co-operate with each other, keep their lines of communication open, strengthen each other and render mutual aid? Israel *per se* is no more important than the American or previously, the Polish centre. Her importance must be measured in terms of productiveness or fruitfulness, and her contribution to the whole.

From this conception it follows that one centre should never try to live at the expense of another. The surplus of strength and vitality of one centre should be diverted to other centres but no living and working centre should be allowed to vanish from the map. Young centres should be helped to grow and develop in their infancy, therefore Israel should be helped at present but eventually Israel should repay its debts by extending its help to other, perhaps still younger centres which may develop in the future. We know by bitter experience that centres grow, shift and move constantly in the collective body of Jewry. Old centres disappear, new centres are constantly being born. No centre stays put for ever. It does its work and when its historical role comes to an end, it declines and finally disappears from its social scene. The tree of Jewry is eternally young but it is heavily pruned and lopped.

The fourth conception is the conception of special relationship of Israel, but not of centrality. This conception does not deny the unique character and unique value of Israel as the breeding place of purely Jewish institutions, ideas, art and culture, as a laboratory for purely Jewish models which could be of value not only to Jewry as a whole but also to the world at large. It is the main locum for the renewal of the Jewish spirit, for the strengthening of the Jewish personality. The sovereignty of Israel has also unique value as a refuge, a haven for all those persecuted, squeezed out, stateless Jews from all over the world. According to this conception, while Israel has a special value to the Diaspora, she cannot claim superiority, or primacy or centrality. Neither is superior to the other, both are necessary and equally valuable ingredients in the life of Jewry. Both Diaspora and the Land of Israel supplement, support and nourish each other. In modern times each of them would be in precarious a position without the other. Full co-operation between them is necessary but it must be co-operation on the basis of equality. Each should draw its strength from the other but not in such a way as to weaken or undermine the other's position. When the State of Israel makes an important move on the international scene, its repercussions of the position of the Diaspora ought to be considered. Israel should conceive its immigration policy not without regard to the needs of other centres of Jewish life. Israel, for example, should abstain from drawing masses of immigrants to its shores if by doing so entire centres of Jewish life are certain to disappear. The total disappearance of any of them must be regarded as a permanent loss of an instrument in Jewish orchestration.

Whatever the future of the new centre in the State of Israel it should never seek to dominate the scene of the Diaspora, it should never look upon the Diaspora as a phenomenon to be despised, as either a second class or purely transitory manifestation of Jewish life. The relationship of Israel to the Diaspora, although of a special character, is not that of a soul to a body. It is rather in the nature of a relationship of different centres in a body. The brains, the heart or the lungs are all centres with different functions but none is the centre with a capital 'C'. The centre with a capital 'C' lies in a sphere which is far beyond the reach of any single community and which unites all Jewish communities throughout all their long historical trek.

Those are the four basic conceptions of the role of Israel and the Diaspora. While Israel subscribes to the first conception, most of the Americans are divided in their support of the remaining three conceptions, perhaps with preference for the last conception.

Israel and the American Jewry are in a sort of dialectical intercourse, each holding the other in check and each stimulating the other, presenting a unique challenge. Israel herself presents a unique mixture of the independent State and the Diaspora. The pull of the Diaspora and the force of the new State are in constant battle with each other within Israel, partly merging and inter-penetrating, and often producing an odd mixture. They are facing each other partly with resentment and hostility and partly with love and understanding, but they have to come to terms with each other, as both are inseparable and necessary ingredients in the life of Jewry. Their ideas and philosophies are different but so also are the historical positions and tasks.

4.

The Israeli-Russian Encounter

THERE ARE three distinct phases and aspects of Judaic-Russian encounter: the Jewish-Russian, the Communist-Zionist, and the Soviet-Israeli. They are closely linked and merged into each other.

The Jewish-Russian encounter started in modern times with the Jewish 'Pale' and the policy of pogroms organized by Tsarist Russia, such as in Kishiniev and Gomel (1903) and in Zhitomir (1905). The policy of pogroms backfired on the Tsarist regime. Jewish youth, held up to hate and contempt, turned into first-class revolutionaries. They fought their own battle against the Tsarist oppression, the battle for Jewish emancipation as well as the battle of the Russian people as a whole; the two merged into one.[1] Communism was thriving both on Jewish thought (Marx) and action. Lenin's second in command was Trotsky, his lieutenants were Kamienev, Zinoviev, Litvinov, Radek, Sverdlov and others. Without exaggerating the Jewish role in creating the Communist State, we can say that it was far from negligible, mainly due to the policy of pogroms.

However, if the Jews expected national and cultural emancipation from the Communist Revolution, they were soon disappointed. The hoped for emancipation was achieved only individually, i.e., by Jews as individuals, not collectively as an ethnic group. Lenin, and after him, to a greater degree, Stalin, refused to grant the Jews *de facto* the privilege enjoyed by sixty-odd other ethnic and linguistic groups officially recognized in the U.S.S.R. The principle of the Soviet rule: 'National in form and socialist in content' was not applied to the Jews. They had to content themselves with the 'content' only.

Also the Communist rulers have been disappointed with their Jewish supporters. Those were soon withdrawn from the first rank of the movement, and a number of them perished (Kamienev,

---

[1] *Bund*, formed in 1897, regarded itself as part of the international revolutionary socialist movement.

Zinoviev were executed and Trotsky murdered). By and large the Communist rulers, following Marx, saw in the Jewish mentality the typical outgrowth of the bourgeoisie and petit-bourgeoisie. The Communists saw in the posture of the Jew a strong resistance against the claims of the totalitarian and authoritarian all-embracing State. The Jew was accused of internationalism, of maintaining links with the outer world. In the final march of Communism to its ultimate frontiers the Jew was found not very congenial and rather a challenge. He was accused of an 'idealist distortion'. The anti-Jewish policy was closely linked to the struggle for power between Stalin and Trotsky.

The other result of the Tsarist policy of pogroms, especially when the new oppressive laws of May 1882 of Count Ignatiev[1] came into operation, was the swelling of Jewish emigration from Russia, primarily to the U.S.A. and to England, but also to a smaller extent to Palestine. The Jewish population in Palestine which in 1880 numbered 50,000, mainly old men of Middle Eastern origin, doubled in the next thirty-four years with immigrants coming mostly from the Russian Empire (of which much of Poland was then part). Pioneers such as Ben Gurion, Ben Zwi, Sprinzak, Ben Yehuda, Gordon, Kaplan, Trumpeldor and Jabotinsky were all Russian citizens, some of them deeply devoted to Russian culture. When they settled in Palestine, they knew no other world than Russia-Poland. They represented a Westernized version of Russian culture. The so-called Western Jew in Israel is the Jew imbued with a Westernized Russian-Polish culture. It is a very peculiar culture, in which elements of East and West are intermingled, elements of the larger 'Russian ghetto' and of the more confined Jewish ghetto intertwined with Western ideology. It is a culture which breeds passionate movements.

The immigrants brought with them two distinct ideologies and movements. One was a militant nationalism, highly idealistic, romantic, ruthlessly dedicated to the idea of Israel's independence and dominated almost in an obsessive way by the myth of a sacred nationhood which upholds and justifies everything. It was embodied on the Israeli soil in Zionist Revisionism. Trumpeldor, the Russian warrant officer who won decoration in the Russian-

[1] By the May Laws the Jews were forbidden to live in country villages and small towns up to 15,000 inhabitants.

Japanese war, jointly with the Russian journalist Jabotinsky, formed the first Jewish Legion, which fought first in Gallipoli and later on in Palestine in the First World War. The heirs of this militant nationalism were the terrorist groups of the Irgun Zwi Leumi and the Stern Gang, and now to a certain extent Herut with Begin at the helm. The Polish Jews, fed on romantic Polish literature, were often attracted to this movement. Like the Polish revolutionaries who fought against the Tsarist oppression of Poland they felt that 'greatness has been thrust upon them'; they gave their lives freely for their cause as Israeli 'freedom fighters'.

The other ideology linked with revolutionary Russian movements was the egalitarian ideology, represented by various combinations of socialism and Zionism. The two most important of these were the Poale Zion (Ben Gurion) and Hapoel Hatzair (Joseph Sprinzak), which later on (1930) achieved union in Mapai, before it split again into three or four factions. The pioneers of this movement could have been described as 'sans-culotte socialists', full of righteous indignation against the bourgeois and the rich, doctrinaire revolutionary individualists who took equality literally and applied it to their own lives by developing Kibbutzim, the Histadrut and many other socialist ventures.

The two movements, the militant nationalism and the militant socialism, were at loggerheads with each other and battled for the soul of Israel. The latter proved stronger, better organized and led, and more resourceful. It captured the Zionist world leadership in the Congress of 1933 and soon afterwards (1935) also gained control of the unofficial government in Israel, becoming since that time the master of Israel's destiny. The socialist egalitarian movement was instrumental in shaping the structure and the policy of the new State. And even after fifty or sixty years strong traces of this original Russian-Polish Westernized culture, of course in the Jewish version, are discernible in the style and vocalization of Israeli leaders.

So one could say that while the Jewish element contributed to the erection of the Communist State, the Russian element in its turn also contributed to the creation of the Jewish State.

Now we come to the Zionist-Communist encounter. Perhaps it

is not an accident that both Zionism and Socialism have a common ancestor in Moses Hess, who in his 'European Triarchy' developed the programme for international socialism, and in 'Rome and Jerusalem' the programme of Zionism, later on taken over and developed by Herzl. Hess at first collaborated with Marx and Engels, as publisher and co-editor of the *Rheinische Zeitung* and later on *Gesellschaftspiegel*. He inspired both of them with his ideas of international socialism, although eventually they turned against him. The ideas of the emancipation of the Jews and the emancipation of man in the new social order had a certain affinity, and the Jews often saw them in the same light and lumped them together. But when developed, the two ideas soon fell apart.

From the Jewish side serious attempts were made to keep socialism and Zionism in step and strong movements of Zionist socialism of various degrees and brands developed both in the Diaspora and in Israel; however, on the Communist side the possibility of harmonious co-operation between them was denied from the outset. Zionism has been regarded by the Communist leaders as reactionary bourgeois ideology, as the expression of chauvinism and nationalism, linked with the idea of national exclusiveness and racial superiority. The Soviet regime soon banned all Zionist activity and forbade any attempt at emigration to Palestine. Hebrew was proscribed in 1924 and relegated to the shelves, as the 'church Latin of the religious Jews'. Yiddish as a lingua franca of the Jewish working class has been tolerated to a degree up to the late forties, when the Yiddish newspapers, publishing house and theatres were closed down. Lately a certain revival of the Yiddish language followed a general trend towards liberalization.

Jewish nationalism in the eyes of Communist doctrine had one peculiarity, which was lacking in other ethnic groups, namely its organic link with Jewish religion. The ethnic element is impregnated and dominated by its link with Judaism as a religion and this of course made the Jewish ethnic group a reactionary formation, basically hostile to the aspirations of Communism.

In its struggle against Zionism the Soviet regime hit on an idea meant to be the Soviet answer to Zion. This was the idea of a Jewish territorial home in a purified, Communist expurgated version of Jewish-Yiddish nationhood. This idea was expressed in the establishment in 1928 of a Jewish territory in Birobidjan, where Jews could develop their own national and cultural characteristics. This territory was advanced in 1934 to an autonomous region under the banner of the 'Soviet-Jewish Statehood'. However, the Soviet Jews failed to respond to the call, the attempt proved a failure and was soon forgotten.

The Soviet attitude towards Jews is full of complexities and contradictions. It cannot be described simply as anti-Semitism; it is much more involved. The anti-Jewish attitude is directed more specifically against the Jewish bourgeoisie and has a class connotation which follows an old tradition based on Marx' pamphlet on the Jews. When the Soviet authorities underline in their publicity of economic crimes that a disproportionate number of them are Jewish (by stressing Jewish-sounding names or their family origin), they turn against the remnants of Jewish bourgeoisie or petit-bourgeoisie. Again the famous anti-Jewish pamphlets such as *Judaism without embellishments* (1963) or F. S. Mayatsky's *Contemporary Judaism and Zionism* (1964) or M. I. Shakhnovich's *The Decline of Judaic Religion* (1965), although mostly venomous in tone, are directed not so much against Jews as against Jewish religion as such, as part of a general anti-religious propaganda. The Stalin-fabricated plot of Jewish doctors to murder him (1952) was an act worthy of Tsarist pogrom policy but it was more a personal act of Stalin's schizophrenia than an act of Soviet policy. During Stalin's terror regime there was a mass slaughter of Jewish writers and artists but there was also a mass slaughter of others, and it is very difficult to compare them in relative numbers to ascertain the degree of Jewish discrimination. Anti-semitism as a policy is rejected and condemned officially and unofficially. 'All recent Soviet encyclopaedias and dictionaries have entries on anti-Semitism and denounce it as an "extreme form of racial chauvinism" rampant in the West and non-existent in the countries of the Soviet bloc; so did a volume of the Large Encyclopedia published in 1950, i.e., at the height of Stalin's anti-semitic persecutions.'[1]

The Jews as individuals occupy high positions in art, science, technology, industry and trade. To mention only a few: the present Soviet economic reforms, introducing the principle of competition in industry was proclaimed by Jews such as Professor

[1] Maurice Friedberg, 'On Reading Recent Soviet Judaica'. *Survey*, p. 171. January 1967.

Liberman and academician Leonard Kantorovitch in *Pravda*. The 'strongest metal' claimed by Russia was attributed to Professor Ruvin Garber, the famous Nobel Prize winner. The physicist, Lev Davidovich Landau, for whose life the Soviet doctors fought persistently for six months,[1] was twice awarded the Lenin Prize for Physics. In literature it is enough to mention the Nobel Prize winner, Pasternak, in films, Eisenstein, in music, Oistrakh, Ashkenazy, in journalism, Ilya Ehrenburg and David Zaslavsky. The percentage of Jewish students at the universities and academies is the highest in the country.

When Kruschev was accused of anti-Semitism he replied, 'My son-in-law and my grandson are Jewish', and so were also Stalin's, whose brother-in-law was Kaganovich. Molotov's wife described herself to Mrs Golda Meir: 'Ich bin a Yiddishe Tochter'.[2]

One cannot speak about Soviet anti-semitism at large, one can speak only about anti-Jewish manifestations in specific fields, notably religion and against certain sections of the population and more specifically about complete suppression of Jewish culture and of course Zionism and all pro-Israeli sympathy. It looks as if the Soviet Authorities highly appreciate their Jewish citizens, give them full opportunity for developing their individual talents and want to keep them and prevent them from emigration. They intend to speed up the process of their assimilation and acculturation, trying to impress their Jewish citizens that the Jewish religion is reactionary and obscurantist and not worth keeping, as it fosters petit-bourgeois mentality with parasitic and criminal tendencies, as shown in the records of economic crimes. They try to show that the Jews have no reason to be proud of Israel, as her record is imperialistic and reactionary in her exploitation of the native Arab population. So the outcome of all that is the implied hint to their Jewish citizens to throw away their Jewish identity and become thoroughly Russian in spirit, mind and soul. This has been the most consistent, the deepest and the longest attempt of acculturation of the Jewish masses, which previously had a very high consciousness of being a separate ethnical entity with a language, literature and culture of their own.

[1] Alexander Dorozynski, *The Man They Wouldn't Let Die. Lev Landau.* Secker and Warburg. London 1965.

[2] Marie Syrkin, *Golda Meir*, p. 280. Gollancz. London 1963.

How does the Jewish population react to this enormous con-centrated pressure of almost fifty years standing? The depth of assimilation and acculturation is difficult to assess as there are no statistics available. The official figures indicate that out of 500,000 Jews in Moscow only 30,000 registered as observant Jews for receiving Matzos for Passover. However, from contacts by Jewish tourists, journalists and observers and by the Israeli diplomatic and trade representatives a strong impression prevails that the will to survive and retain Jewish identity is very strong. On the basis of Israeli diplomatic experiences (for example, when Mrs Golda Meir went to a Moscow synagogue the attendance from the usual 300 persons went up to an estimated 30,000 plus) one can say that 'The Soviet had not succeeded in eradicating Jewish consciousness among its Jewish citizens'.[1] This impression is also confirmed by a very talented journalist Ilie Wiesel in his book, *The Jews of Silence* (New York 1967). All the criticism of Israel, he contends, falls on deaf ears. The Israelis are seen as 'all righteous men and heroes' and there is a messianic yearning for Israel. This gives Israel high hopes to regard the 3,000,000 strong Soviet Jewry as a huge reservoir for potential immigrants to Israel.

However, if the Russian Jews were allowed to emigrate to Israel in significant numbers, this would have a weighty impact on Israel's cultural, social and political scene, creating for her great and embarrassing problems. No one can foretell at present the degree of disenchantment of the new immigrants, who see Israel through such rosy spectacles. It is difficult also to envisage a clash between personality structures developed under Soviet Communism and those developed in Israel. The Russian Jew is an enigma probably to himself but even more so to others. He may be a complete new type of Jew, hitherto unknown in the annals of Jewish history. No one can tell how the alloy of Judaism and Communism has worked in bringing about a new man, how the intense concern of Judaism with ethical, spiritual problems reacted to the intense concern of Communism with social, economic issues. It is obvious that the Russian Jew is a new phenomenon, which can surprise both the Diaspora and Israel when the frontiers are open, as one day they certainly will be. The emergence of the Russian Jew as an active participant

[1] *Op. cit.*, p. 232.

of the Jewish fate in the Diaspora and Israel may mark a new page in the history of the Jewish people.

Now we turn to the more specific Israeli-Soviet encounter. It started in 1947 under most auspicious omens, when the Soviet Union unexpectedly joined hands with the U.S.A. against the British Government in UNO declaring their support for a Jewish State in a partitioned Palestine (U.N. Assembly Resolution on partition of Palestine of 29 November 1947). From the time when the unofficial fighting with the Arabs started on 30 November 1947 up to the very end of the War of Independence, the Soviet Union supported the Jews in Palestine both in arms and diplomacy. After protracted discussions between Moshe Shertock (Sharett) and Andrei Gromyko in New York the Soviet gave their approval to an Israeli-Czech arms deal which was crucial, perhaps even decisive, in Israel's struggle for survival. Ten thousand rifles and 450 machine guns in the first delivery, afterwards artillery guns, including 75 mm guns, Messerschmitt fighter planes and many other weapons simply saved the young, badly equipped Israeli army from collapse.[1] The Soviet Union often paralysed the hostile action of the British Government in the Security Council. When, at the end of February 1948, the British were willing, in co-operation with the U.S.A., to establish some sort of interim trusteeship in Palestine, meant primarily as a burial of the UNO Assembly Resolution on partition, the Soviet Union opposed this plan. The U.S.S.R. also supported the American proposals for imposition of sanctions against the Arab States which invaded the area allotted to the Jews, while the British delegates successfully opposed those sanctions.[2]

After the Declaration of Independence of 14 May 1948, Moscow was among the first States to recognize the State of Israel. Stalin's support for Israel was based probably not on sympathy for Israel, but was conceived primarily as an anti-British move to weaken the position of the British Empire in the Middle East.

[1] O'Ballance Edgar, *The Israeli War*, p. 44. Faber and Faber. London 1956, and Jon and David Kimche, *Both Sides of the Hill. Britain and the Palestine War*, p. 205. Secker and Warburg. London 1960.

[2] John Marlowe, *The Seat of Pilate. An Account of the Palestine Mandate*, p. 248. The Cresset Press. London 1959.

Stalin conceived the liquidation of the Palestine Mandate as the first step towards the collapse of British power in the Middle East. Simultaneously with the support for Israel, Stalin reproached the Arab States in war with Israel for concentrating their activities too much on war against Israel instead of against 'the Anglo-American Imperialism'. Maybe he was hoping to establish a Soviet bridgehead in Israel. In that he failed. But he was right in envisaging that the British power in the Middle East would in due time collapse with the liquidation of the Mandate in Palestine, as soon afterwards one British position after another in the Middle East had to be given up. Soviet diplomacy could fish very successfully in the troubled waters of the Middle East following the Arab-Israel conflict.

The Soviet support for Israel continued up to the middle of 1949. When in September 1948, Mrs Golda Meir with the first Legation of Israel appeared in Moscow, she was very warmly received and acclaimed.[1] Soon afterwards, when it was clear that Israel would fall in the orbit of the U.S.A. instead of being a Soviet bridgehead, and the Anglo-Arab line began to break, Soviet policy took the Arab side, turning more and more against Israel. From that time onwards the age-long aspirations of Russia to establish a springboard in the Middle East and to secure her flanks could have been achieved only through her co-operation and friendship with the Arab States. And so while Soviet Russia helped Israel in her struggle for independence, Israel helped Russia in establishing her leverage and ascendancy in the Middle East. However, this ascendancy was established at Israel's expense.

The results of the new Soviet policy were most clearly seen in the Sinai Campaign, when the fruits of the Israeli victory were denied to her primarily by Soviet intervention. On 5 November 1956, Marshal Bulganin, the President of the Council of the U.S.S.R. wrote to Ben Gurion, the Israeli Prime Minister, condemning Israel as 'criminally and irresponsibly playing with the fate of the world' informing him that the Soviet Ambassador would be withdrawn in the case of non-compliance. And after Israel's hesitation to withdraw her forces from Egyptian territory he sent to Israel a second warning, asking Ben Gurion 'to draw the appropriate conclusions from the lesson, which the latest

[1] Marie Syrkin, *Golda Meir*, p. 219. Gollancz. London 1963.

events indicated for Israel'; the threat of Soviet rockets being implied.

In the great emergency leading to the Six Day War, Russia's stand in favour of the Arab cause was even more determined and partisan, arming and inciting the Arabs to risk the confrontation with Israel and the West, and after the Six Day War manoeuvring against Israel in the United Nations and in the capitals of the great powers. The vilification and denigration of Israel reached heights of a distorted and at times grotesque propaganda. But this has not prevented Israel from keeping the fruits of victory in her hands. There was in 1967, no threat from Premier Kosygin, similar to that of President Bulganin in 1956, as this time there was no backing of the Russian demands for Israeli withdrawal to her pre-June frontiers by the U.S.A.

The anti-Israeli Soviet policy has some relieving features for it is more a matter of expediency than principle. It sides with the Arab States but does not identify itself with the Arab cause. It does not seek the destruction of the State of Israel. In the UNO declarations following the Six Day War Premier Kosygin repeatedly accepted Israel's Statehood and her right to exist in peace.

Six months after the end of the June War, the Warsaw three-day conference of foreign ministers of U.S.S.R. and seven other East European countries called on Israel to withdraw from occupied territories but avoided branding Israel as an 'aggressor' and conceded Israel's right to peaceful co-existence, recognizing for every Middle Eastern State, 'The right of each of them to exist in the form of an independent national state under conditions of peace and security'.

I would say that the specific situation of Israel as an embattled island in the Arab sea under Russian protection and assistance, makes it imperative for Israel to address herself to Soviet Russia with all the attention and all the resourcefulness in her power. Israel has no formal allies; it is not a member of NATO or CENTO or any other alliance. It stands alone, but in fact it is in the American-Western camp. The position and aspirations of Israel lie in joining the Third World, the world of unaligned nations, and but for Russia's hostility Israel would be eager to do so.

Russia has gained a strong foothold in the Middle East, which is almost a Russian sphere of influence. Israel must, willy nilly, pay heed to this fact. She must be able to steer in such a way as to come to terms with Russian power. Also there is always the possibility of releasing hundreds of thousands of prospective Jewish immigrants from Russia who are the last hope of a big revival of the flagging demography and economy of Israel. The future of Israel is more in Russian hands than in any other. There is no disputing the compelling need to come to terms with the Power which is more and more encroaching upon the region but it is not yet clear how this may come about.

One is tempted to speculate about the possibility of a collectivist or Communist regime in Israel. Could such a regime offer something of value to Israeli society? Perhaps in some respects it could. The Israeli society needs a greater measure of discipline, social control, and greater strength at the centre of power, greater sustained productive effort, greater austerity, greater insistence on duties rather than on rights, on what is due to society rather than on what is due to the individual. It needs less consumption and more investment. It needs greater stability of wage and price levels. It needs a greater measure of long-distance planning. All those things are usually offered by the Communist regime to those nations which cannot otherwise achieve them through self-discipline and democracy. However, those gains would be offset by wastage through the economy of command and rigid planning, through bureaucracy and fraud and of course by withdrawal of American investments. But the whole speculation on this theme is completely devoid of reality. A Communist regime in Israel would be a flagrant contradiction to the mood, temperament, character and mentality of practically the whole of the population. Democracy, the right to criticism and dissension, lie in the very bones of the Israelis. Free voting, free dissension, free discussion are sacred things and even the right to strike is regarded as one of the sacred human rights. In such a mental climate it would be fatal even to attempt a Communist regime, and even if it could be established it would fall down on the day-to-day resistance of the population.

The Communist Party in Israel, after its split in 1965 into two rival factions, one Israeli and the other supported mostly by the

Arabs, has in the last election to the Knesset won 4 seats out of 120 (about 3·4 per cent of the total votes including the Arab minority). Out of this the Jewish faction led by Mr Sneh and Mikunis won one seat (approximately 1·1 per cent of votes) against 3 seats (2·3 per cent) of the Arab faction, led by Mr Wilner. The Arab faction is more a party of national protest than of class protest, while the Jewish faction adopted a platform of Jewish patriotism and 'Reform Zionism'. The Mikunis' formula reads: 'The patriotic spirit of our party expresses itself in our identification with the fatherland and the people of Israel'.

Strangely enough the Soviet leadership favoured the Jewish faction more than the Arab faction, regarding it probably as more representative of Israeli society and attaching greater hopes to its activities. However, any hopes or fears for Jewish Communism in Israel, except in circumstances of complete social and political disintegration of the State and a mood of desperation, can hardly be entertained. Communism might have been born out of Jewish spirit as much as Christianity was, but both in their final manifestations are hardly acceptable to the Jewish mentality. One is reminded of the observation of Pascal in his *Pensées* that the Jews are 'great lovers of things foretold and great enemies of their fulfilment'.

There is a parallel between the historical enmity of Judaism and Christianity and the ensuing enmity of Jewry and Communism, although both had a common Jewish seed in the message of Jesus and Karl Marx's writings. The alliance between Jewish intellectuals and the Left which was marked at the beginning of the century, still apparent in the middle of the century, has since been curtailed and severely damaged. Considerable hostility developed between Communism and Jewry and there has been a general cooling-off of relations between Jewish intellectuals and the Left Wing movement. This has been widely demonstrated in the attitudes to the issues involved in the June War and its aftermath, when what is regarded as the Left declared itself all over the world as anti-Israel.

I believe the disenchantment of Jewish intellectuals and artists with the Left is a significant event for the life of the Diaspora and may also be not without influence on world ideological movements.

5.

The Israeli-German Encounter

THE JEWISH-GERMAN encounter, the most fateful and the most tragic in the long history of the Jews, starts in modern times with what is known as the period of Jewish Emancipation. Its herald was Moses Mendelsohn (1729–86), one of the three greatest Moses in Jewish history. His translation of the Hebrew Bible into German and the simultaneous publication of the two texts inaugurated the intensive Jewish study of both German and pure Hebrew. This was the starting point of the Haskalah (The Jewish Enlightenment), which had two bases: modern Hebrew literature and the spread of the German language as almost the second language of the Jews. German came to be regarded not only as the matrix of Yiddish but as a language very akin to Jewish in modes of expression, most propinquous to Judaic ways.

Mendelsohn's authority in Germany, his friendships with great philosphers and writers, especially with Lessing, who became an early champion of Jewish rights in his famous *Nathan Der Weise*, served as a symbol of a breakthrough, of a dawn of a new and enlightened area on both sides, of a call for opening and leaving the ghettos, both imposed and self-imposed. The Jews gained encouragement and self-confidence. Did not Lessing say that each of the three monotheistic religions may be equally true in proportion to its sincerity and its tolerance to other religions? That was for the Jews the true voice of Germany, the Germany of Kant, the herald of eternal peace, of Schiller, the herald of freedom and of Goethe, the herald of new humanism.

Germany became the spiritual home of Central and East European Jews who, after all, formed the big majority of European Jews. Germany was regarded as the key to Christian civilization and German-Jewish co-operation as the most fruitful and most natural symbiosis. Was not Yiddish itself, the vernacular of Diaspora Jews, a sort of dialect of old German? The fruitfulness of the symbiosis could be seen in Jewish figures of international fame who emerged one after another on the German-Austrian scene. In politics there was Julius Stahl and Gabriel Rieser on the right, Eduard Bernstein and Walther Rathenau in the centre, Marx and Lassalle on the left, in poetry, Heine and Ludwig Boerne, in music, Mendelsohn and Meierbeer, in theatre, Max Reinhardt and Rudolf Schildkraut, in philosophy, Hermann Cohen and Ernst Cassirer, in painting, Max Liebermann and Franz Marc, in literature, Jacob Wassermann, Leon Feuchtwanger Franz Verfel, in science, a string of Nobel Prize winners, to name only a few. The greatest scientists who left a lasting imprint on the modern age, Marx, Einstein and Freud, were all the products of this symbiosis. An American ambassador to Germany before the First World War, James Watson Gerard, publicly proclaimed that the Jews represented the only real culture in Germany.

The Jews lived with Germans longer than with any other European nation and their mutual links were also closer and more intimate. So it was not surprising that Zionism's first hopes went in the direction of Imperial Germany. Herzl's first moves were to secure Germany's protection for the future national home in Palestine. The first key figures in his quest for statesmen-protectors were Archduke of Baden and through him the Emperor Wilhelm II. Herzl wrote in the *Neue Freie Presse* and in *Die Welt* articles of eulogy towards Germany. When he addressed the Emperor Wilhelm II, requesting his intervention with Turkey, he asked for a Charter for a Jewish Land Company for Palestine and Syria 'under German protection'. 'Heil Dir in Siegerkranz' was sung by the student choir of pioneers in one of the first Jewish colonies in Mikveh Israel in Palestine, when Herzl met the Emperor on his visit.

The German Jews identified themselves completely with the German nation. Already Moses Mendelsohn was 'German by birth, Jew by descent and yet a German patriot'.[1] Jacob Wassermann, regarded as one of the greatest German writers declares in *My Road as German and Jew*: 'I am a German and Jew, one as much completely as the other. Neither is to be separated from the other.' Feuchtwanger, when already in exile, described himself as a German writer of Jewish extraction, deeply related to the German language and culture with an urgent desire to go back to Germany as soon as possible.

[1] Katie Magnus, *Jewish Portraits*. Routledge and Son. London 1925.

The East European Jews, whenever they ventured out of their ghetto, first came into contact with the German language, German books and culture. The language of instruction in the Haskalah was German. Both liberal and revolutionary, Zionists like Chaim Weizmann or Sokolov or non-Zionists, drew their first breath of European air in German atmosphere. Trotsky, Rosa Luxemberg, Radek, Parvus and hosts of others served their apprenticeship first in Berlin or Vienna. During the First World War the East European Jews were praying for victory of the two Kaisers, hoping for their political and cultural emancipation after the destruction of the Tzarist regime. Whenever the German army came into a townlet or hamlet in Eastern Europe, the commander first made use of the Jews as the interpreters for the local population. The assimilation of the Jews in Eastern Europe took place to a large degree rather to the German than to the local culture. And this itself contributed to the rise of anti-semitism among the local inhabitants, as often the Jews were accused of being agents of the German *Ostpolitik*.

This was the first phase of the Jewish-German encounter, which was on the Jewish side, if not a love affair, at least the first attachment and their first hope in the Jewish-Christian encounter. They were bewitched by the wide horizons opened up by this relationship. When the Jew emerged from his dream world in the ghetto, his first encounter was Germany and he could not help falling into the trap of Lessing's vision. That was so natural that it could not have been otherwise. He was not the only one who believed in Goethe's Germany. Nobody took seriously Heine's warning of what would happen when Germany went berserk, when 'Thor will leap up and with his giant hammer start smashing Gothic Cathedrals'. 'Then', warned Heine, 'when you hear the rumble and clatter—beware.'[1] The rumble and clatter were already heard after the First World War, when aggressive Teutomania took over. *Die Fehme,* the secret terrorist nationalistic organization murdered Jewish politicians and writers, among others Walter Rathenau and Rosa Luxemberg. That was the first lightning of the thunderstorm which broke over European Jews in the tidal wave of Hitlerism which engulfed the majority of European Jews.

The second phase of Jewish-German encounter took the Jews

[1] Heinrich Heine, *Religion and Philosophy in Germany.* Paris 1834.

by surprise. Jewish hopes were brutally squashed and the attachment turned to bitter hatred. At first the Jews could not believe
that Goethe's Germany was blotted out and a hangman's
Germany appeared in its place. They waited for the re-awakening
of Goethe's Germany from day to day, regarding Hitler's Germany only as a temporary derangement, a sort of psychopathic
seizure. When they read and heard Hitler's threat to wipe out
European Jewry, they did not take it seriously, as they did not
believe that such a thing could happen in the civilized Christian
world. And this disbelief cost them six million souls. The
immensity of the threat was so gigantic that the Jews took it
only as a flight of a perverse imagination. If today we heard
somebody rumbling his threats to exterminate the whole white
race or the whole black race or the whole human race, would
we take it seriously? Perhaps after Holocaust Number One we
should take it seriously.

The reversion of Jewish-German relationship was so sudden,
the inversion of rejected hope and attachment so intense, that
the Jews were simply stunned, which explains to a large extent
the hopeless bewilderment with which they accepted their fate.
Three versions of the new relationship have been current among
the Jews.

The first version: Hitler Germany is only one face of Germany.
The Holocaust is the work of this Germany. Goethe's Germany
still exists and will sooner or later reassert itself. This version has
been, and is still to a large extent, popular among German Jews.

The second version regarded the Holocaust as the work of
Germany as such, the whole of Germany. There exists only one
Germany and the whole of Germany took part in the Holocaust
to a degree. The guilt lies with the German nation as a whole,
it is a historical guilt, which needs historical acts of atonement.

The third version extends the guilt to Christian civilization as
a whole. For the Jews Germany was the Key to Western Christen-
dom. She represented the Christian civilization *par excellence* with
all the flowering of the Christian mind in its theological, philo-
sophical, artistic and scientific accomplishments. If this nation
could fall to such depths of anti-Jewish hatred, it means that there
is no hope for a peaceful, co-operative and fruitful Jewish-
Christian dialogue. The guilt lies, therefore, not only with the
Germans but with Christian civilization at large. The conduct of

the war by the allies, which brushed aside the threat of the annihilation of the Jewish masses and completely disregarded the possibilities of their rescue, and the ominous silence of the Vatican during the war, were additional arguments. However, the last version by and large did not survive the end of the war, especially after the emergence of the State of Israel.

The Holocaust of course brought on its tidal wave of destruction not only the inferno of the Jewish destiny, but also a new hope and a new rebirth in one of the greatest miracles of history. It fired the enthusiasm, the determination and the courage of the Jewish fighters for freedom. It inspired also world public opinion and Jewish friends all over the world to mobilize their active support, political, military and financial, for the new State in its struggle for survival. The destructive powers have made a constructive contribution to Jewish history, not for the first time.

And so we come to the third, post-Hitler phase of Jewish-German encounter.

The need for reconciliation was felt on both sides. Germany felt the need for expiation and atonement. Whether it was Hitler's Germany or Germany at large, the fact is that the crimes were committed in the name of Germany by the then legitimate German power. Germany needed an act by which she could disengage herself from the criminal past, not only by the punishment of the guilty, whenever they could be found, but also by compensation of the victims as far as possible. A general contribution to the State, which gathered the remnants of the concentration camps, a contribution to the development and security of this State, was an obvious act of penance with a clear language of its own.

Also Israel herself needed the act of reconciliation, as blind anti-German hatred could not be allowed to go on unheeded for ever. Hatred is self-destroying and self-perpetuating in a chain-reaction. The anti-German hate has been and is still so virulent in Israel, that an act of reconciliation was called for as a check and means of regaining a proper balance of mind. Besides, Germany will again emerge as a powerful state in the middle of Europe with considerable voice in international affairs. A permanent alienation of such a power could become dangerous to the future existence of Israel. Also, no-one would dispute the need and the duty of Israel to strengthen the economic and military basis of the State which was built *inter alia* to provide shelter for the remnants of the concentration camps.

In spite of the obvious need of both sides to turn over a new leaf, the legacy of the crime was loaded with such an enormous weight of guilt, shame and outrage that it was extremely difficult to reach an honourable and satisfactory agreement. On the German side the formal acceptance of guilt by the State as such was dreaded as an act of national shame and humiliation, as a sort of collective Canossa before another State. As such the act was historically unprecedented and it speaks highly for the moral stature of Dr Adenauer, the author of this act by which he meant to purge Germany from its past.

On the Israeli side the acceptance of German reparation, by the State as such, not only by victims or their relatives, but by Israel as an heir of the victims and legal representative of Jewry at large, was a highly controversial act, loaded with deep scruples and instinctive repulsion. It was vetoed by some Israeli parties. It had a semblance of blood money in Arab feuds and it could easily evoke the spectre of Jewish materialism, which cashes in even on the greatest tragedy of Jewish history. On the Israeli side there was a very strong inner struggle between emotionalism and rationalism, between the instinctive and emotional *no* and rational and logical *yes*. It was partly due to Adenauer-Ben Gurion friendship that both sides eventually overcame their scruples and obstacles and signed the reparation agreement known as Treaty of Luxemburg of 1952.

In the Treaty of Luxemburg Germany agreed to pay to Israel the sum of 3,500m. marks over twelve years on account of the costs of settlement in Israel of the refugees from Germany and Central Europe at large. In addition Germany committed herself to pay compensation to individual victims not only in Israel but in all parts of the world for forfeited or stolen property, for sufferings in concentration camps and loss of health, profession, liberty and in some cases of life. The total sum paid on this account is estimated in the region of 45,000m. marks.

The agreement as carried out in the period 1953–66 had a great effect on Israel's economy and the whole Israeli atmosphere and mentality. The reparation payment gave the Israeli economy a considerable impetus enabling her to develop her infra-structure in roads, ports, power systems, merchant navy and so on. A host of factories and workshops were erected from this money. The reparations eased the transition of Israel from an under-developed country to the third, 'take-off stage' or even to the fourth stage, 'the drive to maturity', to use Rostow's terms for stages of development.[1] The reparations which flowed into Israel averaged, over the period 1953–66, about 9·3 per cent of the foreign deficit and 9·7 per cent of Israel's gross investment.[2] This may seem a small ratio of the total resources, but taking into account the acceleration principle and the multiplier effect it had a very considerable impact, not only on the standard of living but also on the whole equipment of the economy.

However, the German restitutions had also a dysfunctional value as the transition to a new level of affluence was too quick and too unexpected. Some of the restitution payments received by relatives and victims was spent easily on good living. The unexpected sudden flow of money produced a new frame of mind, a sort of 'get rich quick' attitude. It encouraged all sorts of speculations with distortions of normal income distribution. It contributed to the strengthening of the 'revolution of rising expectations' which, even before the reparations, reached Israel in full strength.

The reparations also had another effect on the Israeli society in ethical, psychological spheres. It produced a feeling of malaise, a sense of collective guilt. The new affluence had an ominous echo, coming from the gas chambers and concentration camps. The restitution payments were often accepted for the murder of close relatives, who died in concentration camps. This was blood money in the strictest sense, tainted and unwholesome money. The feeling of malaise was widely spread and contributed to the deterioration of the moral standards.

The sense of guilt in Israeli society was produced by its schizophrenic attitude to Germany. The majority of Israeli people have not accepted the expiation of German people as a sincere act of atonement. They did not manage to cleanse themselves from the feeling of anti-German hatred, hence mass demonstrations against Germany and her legal representatives, whenever the occasion arises. On the other hand the German restitution

[1] W. W. Rostow, *The Stages of Economic Growth*, pp. 7–9. Cambridge University Press. 1960.

[2] Mr Y. Tishler and Dr F. Ginor in the *Report of the Bank of Israel*. 1966.

money was accepted. This acceptance of compensation without the ethical cleansing effect of reconciliation, without sincere effort of real reconciliation in mind and spirit produced a feeling of guilt. By not accepting the sincerity of German atonement the reparations accepted by the State of Israel became, in the minds of Israelis, a symbol of desecration of the memory of the victims of the Holocaust.

Of course it easy to preach forgiveness and to ask the present generation for forgiveness for such a monstrous act is to ask for a saintly attitude. And yet the Jewish teaching requires the act of forgiveness for those who sincerely repent, as a religious duty, and out of this teaching came the injunction of the Jew of Nazareth: 'And if he sin against thee seven times in the day and seven times turn again to thee, saying, I repent; thou shalt forgive him' (Luke 17, 3, 4). God's forgiveness is conditional upon your own forgiveness ('As we forgive them . . .'). The great Jewish psychologist and Prophet knew all about the cleansing effect of the act of forgiveness, needed for both sides to break the vicious circle, as much as the Jewish sages, the authors of the Day of Atonement. Without forgiveness the chain effect of hatred goes on without end and the crime is perpetuated in its evil effect in the minds of both sides. The sense of guilt, which the Israelis feel in connection with the Reparations Agreement can be removed only by real efforts towards Jewish-German reconciliation in mind and spirit, which will do away with the schizophrenic Israeli attitude towards a new Germany.

The Jews never condoned the idea of collective guilt and collective responsibility for any misdeeds committed by individuals, groups or governments. Such an idea, which often served as a justification to hold Jews to ransom by their sworn enemies, has been repugnant to the Jews and condemned by them. The Jews must be careful not to fall into the old traps set by their enemies, traps which endanger both their body and spirit alike.

6.

The Israeli-Afro-Asian Co-operation

AGAINST the background of the Arab boycott Israel feels strongly the need to reach out in friendship to the world around her, especially to the new Afro-Asian nations. Israel believes that already in her initial stage of development she can repay her international indebtedness by aid and assistance to other developing countries, sharing her experiences and the lessons she learned in the process of her development. Israel is the only developing country among the new states of the last two decades which has passed from an almost primitive, traditional stage to the third stage, in Rostow's terminology, 'to the take-off stage', and actually one could even say to the fourth stage, 'the drive to maturity', in which '10 to 20 per cent of the national income is steadily invested, permitting output regularly to outstrip the increase in population'.[1] No other developing country has achieved so much in such a short time. Her national income per head in 1965 averaged 1,069 dollars, which exceeded that of Italy's 884 dollars and was only about 25 per cent lower than that of France (1,379 dollars), England (1,439 dollars) and West Germany (1,449). She is rapidly approaching the level of affluence of the highly developed European countries.[2] In the last decade the rate of growth of her national income exceeded 10 per cent; her exports increased by $5\frac{1}{2}$ times (1954–63); her investment rate averaged about 30 per cent of gross national product between 1960–3 (though half of the investment funds came from abroad). Israel, which was a semi-barren country in 1948, now produces three-quarters of her own food requirements, although her population has doubled since the inception of the State.

---

[1] W. W. Rostow, *The Stages of Economic Growth*, p. 9. Cambridge 1963.
In the last decade Israel has invested annually between 25–8 per cent of its gross national product.

[2] In January 1965 over 152,000 cars were registered in Israel, i.e., one to every four families (625,000 families).

Israel is a showpiece of Western capitalism in developing countries. It is also a showpiece of anti-colonialism. She shows how much can be achieved with political independence. The achievement of Israel's twenty years of independence cannot be compared with those of the twenty previous years in drive, progress and forward movement in all respects. Israel's achievement can give heart and hope to the downhearted developing countries which see their interminable rough road ahead.

Could Israel's example be followed in investment plans for other countries? Can her institutions and schemes serve as a model to be emulated by others? There are several elements which make the Israeli situation unique. The influx of capital from abroad, which in 1964–5 was reckoned at 200 dollars per head of population, was on a unique scale, because Israel is part and parcel of world Jewry and because of other factors such as restitution claims. The Israeli population is well equipped with skills of technology and science. The ratio of scientists, technologists, engineers and doctors per head of population is very high. For instance the number of doctors in Israel has more than doubled since 1950 (in 1960, 5,944) and is the highest per capita in the world. Also the number of academically educated engineers per capita is very high. The ratio of such engineers to ordinary technicians is in Israeli industry 1:1, while in Europe 1:3 or even 1:4. During the last five years 2,140 engineers graduated from Technion. This enabled Israel to develop intensive training schemes on a vast scale which involved 161,000 adults in vocational training courses in the period 1949–63, apart from 18,000 in vocational high schools and 11,000 apprentices in special schools. There are 17 government research institutes with Weizmann Institute leading with a very high level of basic research, and their number is constantly growing. The bigger companies develop their own research units and there are a number of development companies with big research programmes in fields such as Dead Sea Works, Chemicals and Phosphates, Israel Mining Industries, water desalination scheme, nuclear research, oil, mineral and water prospecting schemes. Israel in fact takes a full part in the scientific and technological revolution of the West. Also the ethos, the ideology and mentality of the population were rather an asset to economic development. The European population of Israel was used to a relatively high standard of living and was determined to regain it in their new country. An enormous influx of immigrants, although poor in the main, was a stimulus to investment and marketing. The natural increase of the population is not excessive. There is political stability in democratic institutions, in itself unique in developing countries, showing political maturity exceptional in such young countries without political traditions to fall back upon. The smallness of the country is also an asset in development, as far as the building of infrastructure and communications are concerned. On the other hand Israel carries an excessive load of expenditure on armaments, imposed by the never-ending war with the Arab states. All the same, Israel's achievements in absolute terms are remarkable. Whether they are remarkable in relative terms, per unit of capital invested, is another story which waits for the considered judgement of dispassionate researchers in the future.

Although the conditions of Afro-Asian countries are not comparable with those of Israel, there are many common problems. Many techniques and experiences in Israel and her insight in the handicaps and snags of transition, her resourcefulness, drive, energy and organization could be utilized to good purpose by those countries. Israel can teach other developing countries not only what to do in planning their development but also what not to do. Israel can teach others from the mistakes she herself made in her development by over-ambitious and extravagant projects, by her impatience for quick and spectacular results, by her rigidity of wage structure, controlled by the integral and powerful Trade Unionism and by the mixture of capitalism and socialism which pulled Israel back and forth in opposite directions.

Israel has been very keen to impart her experiences and help to other developing countries. Since the Straits of Aquaba have been open to shipping (after the Suez Campaign of 1956), Israel has found a new outlet for her pioneering in Afro-Asian countries. The term *chalutziut* (pioneering) was used by the Israelis for the first time in connection with services offered to other countries less fortunate in their pace of development. Since 1958 1,755 Israeli experts have been engaged in development projects in countries of three continents, Asia, Africa and Latin America; simultaneously 9,186 trainees from developing countries have studied a number of subjects in Israeli courses and institutes, including farming, afforestation, rural planning, irrigation and water economy, town planning (since 1948 415 new villages have been established in Israel), co-operation, trade unionism, youth movements, teaching, defence and army training, health schemes, training of nurses and doctors and welfare officers (there is a special medical course for students from developing countries in Jerusalem). A number of conferences of international experts have met in Israel such as the Rehovot Conference on Developing Countries in 1964, the Tel-Aviv Conference on Co-operation in 1965, the Conference on Fiscal and Monetary Problems in 1966, and a Conference on Workers' Education and Training. A number of jointly owned enterprises in Afro-Asian countries are undertaken by Israeli firms, especially by the Histadrut-owned Solel Boneh for housing, road building, hospitals and factories.

The Israelis have developed highly effective technical assistance in many parts of West and Central Africa, in about 30 member States out of 38 members of the organization of African Unity formed in Addis Ababa Conference in 1962.

At the reception (5 March 1968) of the new Israel Ambassador to the U.S.A., General Rabin, President Johnson paid tribute to Israel's contribution to the development of other countries saying, 'We have admired the generosity and skill with which Israel has contributed to the development of other nations'.

In fact the response among Afro-Asians to Israeli initiatives has been very positive. The Israelis as instructors are more popular than Americans, British or French. Israel is a country of small-scale industry with 60 per cent of the industrial labour force employed in plants of less than 100 workers, while the American-European experts are used to dealing with problems on a large scale hardly relevant to the conditions of small developing countries. They also talk down from the heights of their achievements, while the Israeli's attitude is rather that of an older brother. Israeli experts have no political axe to grind and their arrival is not felt as a renewal of old colonialism under a new guise. Also their attitude to race problems is more genuinely understanding and fraternal, not as frequently in the West only made to appear as such.

What are the most interesting and original Israeli models which lend themselves for export to Afro-Asian small countries —apart from the Army organization which is an obvious model to copy?

I would say that the most important institutions such as the Kibbutz, the integral farming co-operative and the Histadrut, the integral Trade Union organization, hardly lend themselves to exportation. The Kibbutz requires a specific ideology, mentality, level of education and social ethics which are difficult to emulate at will. The Kibbutz is actually a primitive organization turned modern. It is a modern version of a primitive village community, which combines work with leisure, education and an entire way of life. It is a form not unknown in African or Asian tribal communities which are often integral co-operative ventures of combination of working and living, outwardly similar to the Kibbutz. The Kibbutz is outwardly too close to the African tribal experience to be of great use in Africa's drive towards modernization, which often requires the freeing of the individual from the tribal links and chains. Modernization in African economy means primarily individualization, not excessive integral socialization in a collective. The Kibbutz experience has significance only in its deeper values linked with ideology, mentality and ethics, and its copying in a primitive community may reproduce the paraphernalia only, not the essence and substance of the Kibbutz. Its imitation in African educational and cultural conditions might hold up the process of modernization and adjustment of African village life. Much more viable for African conditions is the model of the Moshav, the smallholders' co-operative with various degrees of integration, which could help, I think, substantially in developing African farming. Lately a Moshav experiment was started on Israel's initiative in Cameroon.

The Histadrut as the integral Trade Union Movement is hardly applicable to the new Afro-Asian countries. Such a model would be overpowering in a small country, contributing to an excessive rigidity of wages imposed by unions which often overreach their target by slowing down the process of industrialization. However, some of the Histadrut institutions such as insurance schemes of various kinds or the health schemes in Kupath Cholim could be applied with good results.

There are a number of Israeli experiments and experiences which could be worth trying out in Afro-Asian countries, such as development towns, regional planning, industrial training and adult education with Ulpanim (residential teaching centres of Hebrew and citizenship), the system of labour exchanges, irrigation schemes and water economy—to mention only a few.

The enormous diversity of technical, scientific, organizational, industrial and commercial skills makes it imperative for Israel to fulfil herself in service to others, which in the long run would serve her own well conceived self-interests and contribute to the vivifying and expanding of her own economy. She herself can learn a great deal by teaching others from her own record of achievements and failures. Only in this way can she break down the wall which the Arab blockade has constructed around her.

The political effectiveness of the Israeli policy of technical assistance has been tested in the UNO Assembly Emergency Session in 1967 dealing with the Israeli-Arab Conflict. The West and Central African countries with the exception of Congo (which was vulnerable to the threat by Algeria holding Mr Tshombe) did not join in the anti-Israel resolutions. The same applies also to most of the Latin American countries which are also provided with technical assistance by Israel. And so the policy of technical assistance bears already ample fruits for the Israelis not only in social psychological terms but also politically and economically.

7.

The Discrepancy Between Israel and the Diaspora

IN SPITE of the wild enthusiasm shown by the Diaspora during the June emergency of 1967, the discrepancy between the Diaspora and Israel is constantly growing. It is based on a dissimilarity of basic positions, and of directions of social and cultural change, and also on ideological discongruity—one could say disharmony. This process is inevitable, and would have arisen whatever course Israel had taken, but it has been aggravated by the policies of Israel.

The reasons for these cultural discrepancies are obvious. The two divergent sectors of world Jewry, the Western under the influence of Christian civilization, and the Eastern under that of Moslem civilization, have been transformed in practice into Diaspora and Israel. The Oriental Diaspora, previously found in Moslem countries, has practically disappeared, having been almost entirely transferred to Israel. Israel herself is undergoing a process of Orientalization, because of her geographical location, her constant warfare with the Arabs, and the differential fertility of the Oriental section of the population, as well as under the impact of a general archaization of culture. The general inspiration of Hebrew culture is derived from ancient times, and even the Kibbutz is the archaic turned modern. In contradistinction to this trend, the Diaspora is becoming more and more Westernized, more and more imbued with Western cultural values, in an atmosphere of freedom, tolerance and full citizenship.

Another factor is the process of the nationalization of the Israeli culture. Israeli culture becomes increasingly a national Hebrew culture, while Jewish culture in the Diaspora is becoming increasingly denationalized in a Jewish sense, fusing to an ever greater degree with the cultural trends of various countries. This discrepancy cannot be stopped, for it is a natural outcome of a nationalization of Hebrew culture which cannot be followed by the Diaspora. The nationalization of Jewish culture in the Diaspora would be out of tune with the realities of Jewish interests. The Diaspora cannot follow Israel on her road to full nationhood. Such a course, if it were possible, would cripple the Jewish culture of the Diaspora, and make it a shadow of the Israeli culture.

The nationalization of religious life in Israel produces the same gulf. Religion in Israel assumes more and more the character of what I call *religionality*, meaning religion fused with nationhood and strongly linked with the idea of the State. Of course the Diaspora cannot subscribe to this process, which is foreign to its aspirations and character, as it lacks an atmosphere of Jewish nationalism. The Diaspora cannot follow Israel on this path, even if she were willing to do so. The Diaspora's policy and ideology have always been directed against manifestations of religion in public life, while in Israel, religion is an integral part of her Statehood. The Diaspora abhors the legal definition of 'Who is a Jew' and opposes strongly any attempt by public or private institutions to establish criteria for classifying men as Jews or non-Jews. To give only one example, Anglo-Jewry was always strongly opposed to the inclusion of religion in the national census. In contradistinction, Israel has developed a rigid and highly dogmatic formula for such a definition of Jewishness.

The Diaspora moves more and more towards Reform Movements in religious practice, which in due time may develop into separate denominations, similar to the denominations of the Christian religion,[1] while Israel keeps strictly to the monolithic system of the Orthodox persuasion.

Religion in Israel assumes more and more the character of priestly religion and church organization which is foreign to the Diaspora Jewry.[2]

[1] 'Indeed, it looks as if the fragmentation of Jewish religious life in the New World is approaching the stage, when we have to think in terms of different Jewish denominations on the Christian pattern. Already today the rift between an Orthodox synagogue and a Reform temple, with its untraditional officials and form of worship, is as pronounced in the eyes of the respective protagonists as between a Catholic church and its Protestant counterpart.' Emmanuel Jacobovits, Chief Rabbi of Britain and the Commonwealth, *Journal of a Rabbi*, p. 60. W. H. Allen. London 1967.

[2] 'But in Judaism there is no church, there is only the community which takes shape through the actions of the individuals. . . .' Leo Baeck, the

The discrepancy between Israel and the Diaspora is growing also in the occupational structure of their respective populations. One could speak about an increasing incompatibility between the two occupational structures. Israel needs primarily craftsmen, workmen, farmhands, technicians, but not professionals, scientists doctors, lawyers, merchants and managers, who form the great majority of Diaspora Jews. The ever-rising educational standards of the Diaspora present a great hindrance to the immigration of Jews into Israel in greater numbers. The majority of Jewish youth in the U.S.A. are at present college educated, and have little prospect of fruitful absorption into Israel. Israeli society itself produces a surplus of professionals and scientists who are leaving Israel in considerable numbers, finding no productive outlet in the country. There is nothing new in the problem itself. It has been treated by such Jewish sociologists of the last generation as Jacob Lestschinsky,[1] B. Weinryb, Nachmann Syrkin and others, who were concerned about the one-sided, partial and narrow character of the occupational structure of the Diaspora. The pioneers of old solved this problem of incompatibility of occupational structure in their own way by rejecting intellectual and commercial pursuits, but now the time of pioneering is over. Moreover, the incompatibility is growing. In the Diaspora the 'minority character' of the occupational structure is stronger than ever due to an ever-rising trend towards higher education.

In ideological terms also the disparity between Israel and the Diaspora is growing. The Diaspora produces a definite ideology based on a concept of service to humanity as a whole and on the ideal of an ethical amelioration of the human condition. Israel is primarily attached to the ideals of Jewish nationalism and separatism, which militates against the universalistic concepts of the Diaspora. The Diaspora sponsors the movement for Human Rights. In the international conference on Human Rights in Geneva in February 1968, marking International Human Rights Year, among the ninety organizations which took part were five Jewish organizations. This shows the great interest of world Jewry in this movement. However, Israel herself cannot subscribe

---

venerated Spiritual Leader of German Jewry in the last generation, *The Essence of Judaism*, 1965 Edition, p. 272. Schocken Books. New York.

[1] 'Die Umsiedlung und Umschichtung des Juedischen Volkes.' *Weletwirtchaftliches Archiv*. July 1929.

to this movement, as the Universal Declaration of Human Rights of 1948 is not observed in Israel, which is transgressing Article 16 (1).

An even greater clash between the Diaspora and Israel can be seen in the conflict between a basic ideology linked with a minority situation, that of the Diaspora, and an ideology linked with the position of a dominant majority, as in Israel. 'Often it seems that the special task of Judaism is to express the idea of the community standing alone, the ethical principle of the minority. . . . The fact of always being in the minority intensifies and spiritualizes the ethical task. . . .'[1] The basic ideology of the Diaspora is closely linked with its situation as a permanent minority, and cannot, of course, be shared by Israeli Jewry, which is in the position of a dominant majority, discriminating against its own hostile minority.

There is also a growing discord between Israel and the Diaspora in regard to the conception of Jewish identity. The Israeli conception favours a unitary, monolithic, one could say pan-Judaic, conception based on the primacy and centrality of Israel as a focus of identity, conceived in strongly national terms. The Diaspora favours a pluralistic, diversified and composite conception, regarding Pan-Judaism as a hazardous ideology, full of perils for the survival of Jewry, which has always been dispersed and patterned in a mosaic-like structure. A pan-Judaic, unitary identity would go against the grain of all Jewish history and experience.

Jewry has always been a pluralistic entity, and any attempt to define it as a single unity and to keep it in a unitarian frame is bound to failure. If it should succeed, it would bring many dangers, of abuse and misuse, of distortion and impoverishment, to Jewish life. The creativity of Judaism and its fructifying force lies in its plurality, in the enormous variety of all its diffusive and plastic forms, which have been assumed in the past and are likely to be assumed in the future. Its fructifying force consists not in withdrawing itself into a closed system but in remaining an open system, open to outside stimuli and ready to weave itself into various strains of civilization.

Moses Hess, one of the forerunners of Zionism, wrote: 'I claim that the divine teaching of Judaism was never at any time com-

[1] Leo Baeck, *op. cit.*, pp. 272-3.

pleted and finished. It has always kept on developing, its development being based upon the harmonizing of the Jewish genius with that of life of humanity.'[1]

And the modern representative of the Jewish Reconstructionist Movement, Mordecai M. Kaplan, expressed this in a similar way: 'If Judaism is to become creative once again, it will have to assimilate the best in contemporary civilization'.[2]

Israel is concerned with world Jewish unity in action, but this does not depend on a unitary Jewish identity based on a monistic conception of Jewish culture. It depends on the deeper sources of Jewish awareness as such, awareness of common origin, of a common fate and destiny, and of common tasks, and even more on the will for Jewish survival, which has been ingrained in the Jewish mind from the beginning of time.

The growing discrepancy between Israel and the Diaspora does not affect the strong feelings of solidarity between them in times of need, and, if any of the Jewish centres is threatened from outside, the other centres respond immediately with offers of help, as can be seen by the deep concern of the Diaspora for the predicament of Russian Jewry, or by its extraordinary support for Israel in her June emergency.

There is no 'end of the Jewish people',[3] neither in Israel nor in the Diaspora, although they are both likely to develop different patterns of Jewish life. Being different is neither wrong nor unusual within the Jewish historical experience. They can march separately, more comfortably without encumberances, more effectively, and more creatively, and they can join forces if the need arises. The end of the Jewish people has been prognosticated often both by non-Jews and Jews alike, but the vitality of the 'old fossil' is now stronger than ever, and its vitality will be all the stronger, the greater its diversification, allotropy and diffusion.

[1] *Rome and Jerusalem*, p. 86. 1862.

[2] *The Greater Judaism in the Making*, p. 452. New York 1960.

[3] George Friedmann, *The End of the Jewish People?* Hutchinson. London 1967.

Part V

conclusion

1.

Challenge and Response

I F W E use Arnold Toynbee's scheme of challenge and response to describe the process of growth and decline of civilizations, we can ask whether Israel's élite has made adequate response to the challenges presented by the external and internal forces confronting their country. Of course, Israel as a State is only an infant, or at best a teenager, and she has a long way to go to reach maturity, a full inward and outward maturity and a full consciousness of her own being, of her role to play in the community of nations as well as in the community of the Jewish Tribes all over the world. Her failings, whatever they are, can be forgiven as in many ways the failings of an adolescent who tries to find her way in the world.

Now let us review the main challenges in the economic, poiitical, social and ideological spheres.

First, there is the challenge presented by climatic conditions, by physical geography, by flora and fauna, by the emptiness of the desert and the lack of an infra-structure, making Israel not only an under-developed, but rather a completely undeveloped country. At first there were no water resources, no mineral resources, no abundant plant or animal life, no industrial or technological resources. Israel has had to build up agriculture and industry as well as transport and commerce. This challenge has met with a skillful, vigorous and successful response. The foundation stones for a thriving economy have been well laid after centuries of neglect, and the desert promises to bloom again. Within one generation Israel has passed from being an undeveloped, to being an almost developed country. Her national[1]

---

[1] Israel's economy has attained a very fast rate of growth. In the period 1954–64 the Gross National Product increased by 11 per cent per annum and by 7 per cent per capita (granted an increase of population of 3·8 per cent half from immigration and half from natural increase).

income per head in 1965 averaged 1,069 dollars, which exceeded Italy's 884 dollars and was only about 25 per cent lower than the figure for Britain or France. In one or two generations' time the Negev may be turned into a great industrial complex through desalination assisted by nuclear energy. Tel-Aviv has become a major centre of commerce, and Haifa a leading Mediterranean Port, with Ashdot as its complement. Great future plans are afoot for an Eilat-Ashdot route as a substitute for or complement to the Suez Canal. Israel has built an impressive physical and economic environment for her fast-growing population.

However, the same cannot be said about social and human environment. An adequate, just and balanced social and human environment has not yet been created. The two Israels, the European and the Oriental, are still in existence and seem to move even further apart with the rise of affluence. There is little doubt that the European section is much better equipped for the race for prosperity, while the Oriental population is less able to cope with the problems of a technical and scientific civilization. Generally speaking, class and status distinctions[1] are on the ascendant, with strongly entrenched status positions, and the gulf between poverty and luxury, between the fashionable quarters and the slums, is growing fast.

The challenge which was presented by the needs of the Jewish population squeezed out from the Diaspora, has also been met with exceptional resourcefulness and effectiveness. Israel has quadrupled her Jewish population, from 550,000 to 2,300,000, in nineteen years, providing a sanctuary and home for those who were deprived of it. However, this number includes also some who have been squeezed out of Arab countries because of the hostility engendered by the existence of Israel.

The challenge of economic independence has not yet been effectively mastered. The deficit in the balance of payments still runs around 500,000,000 dollars (521m. dollars in 1965), and shows great persistence over the years, in spite of all efforts to

[1] According to the Report of Joseph Ben-Or, Assistant Director General of the Ministry of Social Welfare in Jerusalem, 1967, the lowest stratum, consisting of 13 per cent of the population, receives 4·5 per cent of the national income, while the highest stratum, consisting of 10·6 per cent of the population—26·6 per cent, and when social services are included, the lowest 5·6 per cent, and the highest 31 per cent.

overcome it. However, it shows a constant decline in terms of its proportion to the general resources of the country. The road to economic independence may be long, but Israel is taking it in her stride. And more and more debts are being incurred on a financial and commercial basis, rather than on being a charitable one. But all the same, charity, in the widest sense, still plays a large part in boosting Israel's economy, and exerts an influence which is far from healthy and normal.

Now as to the political challenge, both internal and external. The internal political challenge presents itself in the form of the need for stable and continuous democratic government. The response to this challenge can be classed, as not entirely satisfying, but adequate for the purpose. Israel had for twenty years governments led by Ben Gurion, Sharett and Eshkol, all leaders of the Mapai, which formed the nucleus of power in their coalition governments. Israel, a small, new and developing state, in the throes of a deadly conflict, is perhaps unique in being able to preserve a full working democracy and internal stability. This stability is partly due to the impact of the threat of Israel's survival, coming from her Arab neighbours. During the June War Israel was able to form a truly national government composed of all parties except the Communists. The merger in January 1968 of three previously divided Labour Parties (Mapai—the mother party, Ahdut Avoda—which seceded in 1944, and Rafi, which seceded in 1965) which gives the Israel Labour Party 54 seats out of 120 in the Knesset, is a very big step forward towards internal consolidation. This new majority party will give the Israeli Government freedom from protracted negotiations with its coalition partners, which often took up to three months before a coalition government could be formed. It will also give the Government freedom of action. There will be no need to dilute the acknowledged policy of the governing party to suit coalition partners, and thereby to sacrifice what is regarded as the common good. It will also give the party a heightened sense of responsibility for the affairs of the State.

Israel is moving towards a two- or three-party system which shows a process of considerable maturity and integration, astonishing for such a young country built up of so many diverse elements. It shows also the functional value of the deadly external threat of extermination. How lasting this new achievement is, and whether it will continue if external pressure is eased, only the future can tell.

In external political relations the response to the overriding challenge is bitterly disappointing. The Arab population in neighbouring countries form not only the external foes, but also the 'external proletariat' to use Toynbee's term. As Israel grows and develops, the economic, technical and cultural contrast between Israel and her neighbours grows deeper and more ominous. The Arab-Israeli conflict also assumes the character of a social cleavage, between 'the haves' and 'the have nots'. This challenge has been met up to now successfully only in military terms. The Six Day War solved some of the problems of Israel in terms of a marked improvement in her security and lines of communication, but it added many more problems, even more complex and grave. The conquest of these newly held territories provides Israel with enormous challenges and opportunities, but also brings the dangers of over-extending herself in commitments, unwarranted aspirations and ambitions beyond her capacities and capabilities. There is also the danger of yielding to the temptation to abuse power, and those of over-confidence and arrogance. These dangers are real enough. The translation of victory into an acceptable peace settlement will require a long, patient, consistent and persistent peace policy on the part of Israel, using all the ways and means of peace and all manner of goodwill, and resisting the temptation to an easy policy of retaliation. Chaim Weizmann, the first president of Israel, saw two requirements for achieving a peace settlement: first, to convince the Arabs that the Jews have no expansionist aims beyond the boundaries of their natural habitat:

> there exists such a fear in the heart of many Arabs and this fear must be eliminated in every way. Second—and this links up with our own internal problem; they must see from the outset that their brethren within the Jewish State are treated exactly like the Jewish citizens.[1]

No one can say that these guide lines were followed in the day to day policy of present-day Israel.

The Arab question for Israel cannot be solved on the battlefield. No victories of Jewish arms, even the most spectacular and the

[1] *Trial and Error*, p. 570. Hamish Hamilton. London 1949.

most comprehensive, no chain of victories to come, can bring Israel the peace desired. What is required of the Jews in Israel is to fall back on their spiritual resources, which have been very great in the past and which are still available to this spiritual race. The Jews must go out to win the soul of the Arabs, not by cajoling it, but by offering something of the permanent values of the inheritance that once was theirs. It is a difficult process but there is no alternative; separatism and nationalism is no answer to the position of the Jews in Israel.

Now, let us turn to the challenge presented by the Israeli 'melting pot', the task to turn the 'mixed crowd' into one nation with its own language, and one set of values, norms and standards. This challenge has been met successfully, and the response is far better than one could have expected in such a short time. The institutions of integration are firmly established, growing stronger and more efficient. However, this homogenization is perhaps too hurried, too mechanical, and too superficial without making use of all the valuable ethnical ingredients deposited in the historical experience of the various Tribes. But the pressing needs arising out of a constant national emergency must also be considered.

The performance of Israeli society in social, economic and military terms points to a high degree of success in the transformation of disparate strains into one cohesive and effective national unit. It is enough to point here to the performance of the Israeli army in three wars. A fine army is unimaginable in a corrupt or disintegrating society. One does not need to be a militarist to construe the high morale of the Army as an index of the morale and cohesiveness of the society.

The challenge of the 'melting pot' in terms of culture as contrasted to civilization and social process, presents a different aspect. I use here the term culture to mean cultural creativeness, in the same sense as Alfred Weber in his cultural sociology. Weber distinguishes social process, civilization and culture, the latter equivalent to creativeness.[1] Creativeness in Weber's conception is the synthesis of the society and the individual personality. Such a synthesis is until now still lacking in Israel; one can rather feel in Israel a clash between society and individual personality. Israel has not yet produced a fully integrated and harmonious personality structure in accordance with her own

[1] *Cultural History as Cultural Sociology.* (1935.)

requirements and style of life. For the time being the impact of Israel on the personality structure is rather disintegrative and disruptive. The masses of the population who have come from various countries, cultures and strata, find themselves in the process of remodelling, reshaping, exchange and renewal of identity, and in those conditions no harmonious and integrated personality structure can develop. Thus the synthesis between the style and ethos of society and the creative individual could not yet have been achieved. The tone, texture and depth of Israeli culture are rather flat and shallow. The creative impulses in Israeli culture are up to now weak and Israel's élite is fully aware of this situation. The pulse of cultural life in Israel beats very firmly but it is mostly of imported or imitative character. I believe that Israel's leaders will have to pay much greater attention to the strains of personality structure, which arise from the impact of Israel's ethos on the mentality of the immigrant, in order to ease the shock of transition to the new culture.

Now we come to another challenge, that provided by Israel's needs for substantial and constant immigration, more specifically from the West, what is called the Western Alija. This need has been aggravated by the demographic threat to the Jewish majority arising from the Six Day War. A small island placed in a vast Arab sea can easily be overwhelmed by a demographic avalanche, and by the general process of Orientalization. A modern State placed in such a sensitive position as the Middle East also needs a certain size of population to maintain economic viability.

The response to this need can come only from the Western Diaspora, but up to now the Israelis have been unable to produce an image of Israel, or working and living conditions in Israel, or a way of life, or an ideology which could serve as a magnet to the large Jewish masses in the West.

In spite of the great enthusiasm of the Diaspora for Israel during the June emergency, the discrepancy between Israel and the Diaspora is growing in both occupational and ideological terms. The discrepancy in occupational terms is caused by the rise in the educational standards of the Diaspora youth, who are for the most part college educated and have little place in the occupational structure of Israel. The answer to this discrepancy could perhaps come through a further intensive economic development of Israel, especially of its science based industries. It will be much more difficult to resolve the ideological discrepancy between Israel and the Diaspora, arising from divergencies in their basic situations, and in directions of social and cultural change.

It looks as if, in the long run, the response to the need for *Alija* can come only from within Israeli society itself. If the Oriental section of the Jewish population does bring down its demography to the standard of the Western section, but the other way round, Israel could go a long way to replacing the need for a Western Alija. What is called internal Alija is the most effective, the most productive, the most economic and integrative way to acquire new citizens. The will to die for the land is not enough. It must be matched by the will to live, if the Jewish population is determined to retain the reins of sovereignty in their hands. The hopes placed in a great Alija are, except for unseen circumstances, such as Jewish catastrophies or an opening of the Russian frontier, more or less illusory.

Closely akin to the last challenge is the task of harmonizating basic life interests between Israel and the Diaspora, in order to avoid a clash of double loyalties. Israel is eager to present herself as the protector and defender of the interests and rights of the Diaspora all over the world. The Diaspora is not very keen on Israel assuming this role. The Diaspora would be content if Israel would not harm its life interests by pursuing unilaterally her own policies inside and outside Israel without regard to the position of the Diaspora. There is little doubt that the Diaspora has gained a great deal from Israel, not only in ideal terms as the fulfilment of an age-long dream for the re-establishment of Zion, but also in terms of prestige and standing among the nations, especially among those who judge people by valour, strength and feats of arms. The Diaspora has also gained a haven and refuge for Jews squeezed out of other countries. But all these gains are not unequivocal, and were paid for by disabilities and liabilities.

The position of the Israeli Jews as a dominant majority, facing a hostile minority who are often treated as second-class citizens, is, from the point of view of Diaspora interests, a liability. The close links of the State with the dominant Jewish religion in Israel is a liability from the point of view of the position of the Diaspora, which has always turned against manifestations of religion in public life. The inability of Israel to honour fully the Universal

Declaration on Human Rights is a liability from the point of view of the Diaspora's traditional sponsorship of human rights.

Vast Jewish populations, which had lived for hundreds of years peacefully in Islamic countries, lost their homes primarily because of Arab-Israel hostilities.[1]

Not infrequently Jewish communities are exposed to harassment on account of political moves or the conduct of the Israeli Government. The voting of Israel in the United Nations on many international disputes is resented by governments of other countries which harbour Jewish population. Suffice to point out the effect of Israeli Government's stand over apartheid in South Africa, which has caused antagonistic action in South Africa, or the effect of Israel's voting on Algeria, or the effect of the June War on the position of Jews in Russia, Poland and other Communist countries, or on the plight of Jews imprisoned in Arab countries.

Also the immigration policy of Israel is not always identical with the interest of the Diaspora. The interest of world Jewry is to maintain its various cultural and social centres all over the world, see them prosper and develop and cultivate their own special fields. Jewish life has been enormously enriched by contacts with other cultures, and each Jewish centre has something to contribute to the wealth of Jewish experience. The interests of Israel go in the opposite direction. She wants to grow at the cost of other centres. When she warns Jews of other countries about anti-semitism, present and future, it is in the tones of an immigration agency. The anti-semitic leaders of central European countries have always had a great understanding of the Zionist cause, and Zionist propaganda for immigration has often sounded like an echo of anti-semitic propaganda. When the Israelis hear about anti-semitic outbreaks anywhere, two thoughts come into their minds, and one of them is: well, that will persuade more Jews to come to Israel.

There is no denying the fact that Israel, by her behaviour can

---

[1] In the period since the inception of the State of Israel up to 1966 the Jewish population in Islamic countries declined from about 925,000 to 235,000. Whole communities were uprooted such as in Yemen, which lost 96 per cent of its previous Jewish population, or in Egypt, whose Jewish population declined from 75,000 to 2,000 or Iraq with a decline from 120,000 to 6,000 or Morocco from 225,000 to 65,000.

provide a great deal of ammunition to be used against the interests and claims of the Diaspora. Hence her obligation and responsibility, if she regards herself as a Jewish State, caring about Jews qua Jews everywhere. In a way it may be more difficult for the Israeli Jews to combine their double loyalties (for Israel and the Diaspora) than for the Diaspora Jews (for their own country and Israel). First, because in the West the double loyalty in a pluralistic society has turned more and more into a multiple loyalty (to UNO, to the West, the Common Market in Europe, etc.), and lost a great deal of its troublesome aspect, while Israel is a unitary Nation State. Second, because in Israel the two loyalties, being nearer to each other, may also more frequently clash. The policy of the Israeli Government frequently affects the position of the Diaspora, while the policy of other countries does not in most cases concern the position of Israel.

The challenges of Israel to the Diaspora, and vice versa, have not yet found a satisfactory response, not even in a clear formulation of these very intricate and complex problems. It is actually the most important problem of modern Jewry, which needs very hard thought to present crystal clear alternatives for the future.

Now we come to another challenge, the challenge of the past. How to deal with the past, is a very big and unsolved problem in Israel. Of course, the past is the cherished heritage, the roots of Judaism and Israel, the hallowed tradition enshrined in the Book, in myths, legends and folklore, which has been the binding element of the Tribes through the ages. The location of the Tribes now back in the Land enforces the pull of the past, especially of the very ancient past of which we know but little, and most of that in legend and myths rather than actual history. The glorification of the past has a functional value for Israeli society, as an integrative factor, serving also as a justification for political claims. However, there are some inherent dangers in an excessive veneration of the past. The excessive pull of the very ancient past means the pull of the childhood of the race, and can bring about an atmosphere conducive to childhood fantasy. It may contribute to creating a dreamworld of sentimentality and unreality, and there are signs of this in many sections of the Israeli population.

Another danger of inordinate admiration for antiquity is that it may turn the Israeli society into a relic of the past. The emphasis placed on the holy past by the merchants of the sacred could turn Israel into a curiosity shop for the nations, who would be willing to pay for the privilege of being shown the antiquities and curiosities of the Antiquarian Nation.

Another danger is that of over-indulgence in commemoration practices, which are laudible in themselves, but tend to reach a compulsive level. Too much remembrance is going on all the time. Of course the Jewish religion is based on commemoration; Pesach—remember the slavery in Egypt 3,500 years ago, Sukhot —remember the wandering in the desert with your own tent, Shavuot—remember the mount Sinai Revelations, Purim—remember the Persian persecutions by Haman, Tisha Be Ab— remember the destruction of Jerusalem by the Romans, Chanukka —remember the Maccabi Uprising, and now remember also Massada and Bar Kochba uprising. And again, remember the Warsaw Ghetto Uprising, the heroes of Jerusalem, the martyrs of independence, and the anniversaries of Herzl, Weizmann, Ben Zwi, Jabotinsky and many others.

Israel has not yet come to terms with this challenge of the past, how to pay respect and homage to the past, while keeping a right distance from it, avoiding excessive lamentation and weeping and leaving some room for the living also. This commemoration mania can affect the mental health of the nation, the more so as it clashes with a growing materialistic outlook. It can easily develop into public hypocrisy or cynicism or, to use Goffman's term, into 'role-distance'. By 'role-distance' Goffman means psychological moral distance and detachment in playing a certain role with a sort of tongue-in-cheek manner, as an artifice.[1] A certain amount of cynicism is encountered among many Israelis. Bombast, verbiage and bathos are not uncommon in Israel, hence the flourish of humour. Jewish humour is well known all over the world for its excellence and sharpness, which must be due to the 'role-distance' of the Jews in many countries of the Diaspora. In Israel Jewish humour has a large field of its own, and it feeds itself on the role-distance of the Israeli citizens. This role-distance comes partly from newness, and therefore the mechanical nature of many new functions, whose performance is based on copying foreign models such as, for instance, parades, ceremonies or international etiquette. When one looks at the parades and the pomp and the people who take part in them, one can see the

[1] *Encounters*. Indianopolis Bobbs-Merril, 1961.

incongruity, the mechanicalness and the implied role-distance, which easily fall victim to the sharp Jewish tongue.

Last but not least we come to the challenge presented by the Jewish religion in the new Land. It is perhaps the most serious challenge to which a response has been up to now completely lacking. The Jewish religion in Israel has not yet adapted itself, or even tried to adapt itself, to the atmosphere and conditions of a free, independent, modern and open society in its free international interchange with other nations. It is still basically the religion of the ghetto, breathing the atmosphere of the ghetto and walled up by taboos. It is still based on an outward conformity to ritual and customs rather than on any inward awareness of a living faith. The bonds of ritual religion which were meant to enforce the cultural isolationism of the Jews have not been broken, no one has even attempted to break them. From this follows the aridity of the Jewish religion in Israel, its lack of a living faith, such as has always been the motive power behind all great achievements of history, as well as of Jewish history. The overwhelming majority of Israeli society live at present in a spiritual vacuum as far as organized religion is concerned, not only in an atmosphere deprived of faith, but in an arrogant, intellectual and anti-faith mood. Of course they are not the only people in western society who share this predicament, but the position is much more serious for the Israelis as Israel is by its nature a spiritual entity.

However, some signs of a new religious climate can be seen in the emergence of a novel and curious secular version of Judaism centred around the veneration and love of the Land which becomes a Holy Land in the literal sense. This secular version has many possibilities for further development and transformation which are difficult to forsee. It can be deflected and deformed into sheer nationalism, but it could also assume a finer flowering of the human spirit in greater universality. By and large the Israelis are caught between two most powerful mystiques which have always flourished in the Land: the mystique of violence, and the mystique of redemption. These mystiques are fiercely contending for the mastery of Israel's soul. Which mystique is going to win in the end? The mystique essential to Judaism, or the mystique relevant to the realities of forty years' war?

Index

324